Stabilizing Currency and Preserving Economic Sovereignty Using the Grondona System

Patrick Collins
Independent Researcher, Japan

IGI Global
PUBLISHER of TIMELY KNOWLEDGE

A volume in the Advances in Finance, Accounting, and Economics (AFAE) Book Series

Published in the United States of America by
IGI Global
Business Science Reference (an imprint of IGI Global)
701 E. Chocolate Avenue
Hershey PA, USA 17033
Tel: 717-533-8845
Fax: 717-533-8661
E-mail: cust@igi-global.com
Web site: http://www.igi-global.com

Library of Congress Cataloging-in-Publication Data

Names: Collins, Patrick Quentin, 1952- author.
Title: Stabilizing currency and preserving economic sovereignty using the Grondona system / by Patrick Quentin Collins.
Description: Hershey, PA : Information Science Reference, [2022] | Includes bibliographical references and index. | Summary: "This book describes how implementing Grondona's system could help individual countries to independently improve their economic stability, while creating a growing network of currencies between which the exchange-rates will become increasingly stable"-- Provided by publisher.
Identifiers: LCCN 2021040463 (print) | LCCN 2021040464 (ebook) | ISBN 9781799883029 (hardcover) | ISBN 9781799883036 (paperback) | ISBN 9781799883043 (ebook)
Subjects: LCSH: Currency question. | Foreign exchange. | Monetary policy. | Grondona, L. St. Clare.
Classification: LCC HG255 .C554 2022 (print) | LCC HG255 (ebook) | DDC 332.4/6--dc23/eng/20211007
LC record available at https://lccn.loc.gov/2021040463
LC ebook record available at https://lccn.loc.gov/2021040464

This book is published in the IGI Global book series Advances in Finance, Accounting, and Economics (AFAE) (ISSN: 2327-5677; eISSN: 2327-5685)

British Cataloguing in Publication Data
A Cataloguing in Publication record for this book is available from the British Library.

Advances in Finance, Accounting, and Economics (AFAE) Book Series

ISSN:2327-5677
EISSN:2327-5685

Editor-in-Chief: Ahmed Driouchi Al Akhawayn University, Morocco

MISSION

In our changing economic and business environment, it is important to consider the financial changes occurring internationally as well as within individual organizations and business environments. Understanding these changes as well as the factors that influence them is crucial in preparing for our financial future and ensuring economic sustainability and growth.

The **Advances in Finance, Accounting, and Economics (AFAE)** book series aims to publish comprehensive and informative titles in all areas of economics and economic theory, finance, and accounting to assist in advancing the available knowledge and providing for further research development in these dynamic fields.

COVERAGE

- Corporate Finance
- Field Research
- Economics Geography
- International Trade
- Economics of Intellectual Property Rights
- Comparative Accounting Systems
- Economics of Migration and Spatial Mobility
- Fiscal Policy
- E-Accounting
- Entrepreneurship in Accounting and Finance

The Advances in Finance, Accounting, and Economics (AFAE) Book Series (ISSN 2327-5677) is published by IGI Global, 701 E. Chocolate Avenue, Hershey, PA 17033-1240, USA, www.igi-global.com. This series is composed of titles available for purchase individually; each title is edited to be contextually exclusive from any other title within the series. For pricing and ordering information please visit http://www.igi-global.com/book-series/advances-finance-accounting-economics/73685. Postmaster: Send all address changes to above address.

Titles in this Series

For a list of additional titles in this series, please visit:
www.igi-global.com/book-series/advances-finance-accounting-economics/73685

Evaluating Trade and Economic Relations Between India and Southeast Asia
Anita Medhekar (Central Queensland University, Australia) and Harpreet Kaur (Central Queensland University, Australia)
Business Science Reference • © 2022 • 347pp • H/C (ISBN: 9781799857747) • US $195.00

Handbook of Research on Global Aspects of Sustainable Finance in Times of Crises
Ibrahim Yasar Gok (Süleyman Demirel University, Turkey & Freie Universität Berlin, Germany)
Business Science Reference • © 2022 • 442pp • H/C (ISBN: 9781799885016) • US $285.00

Handbook of Research on Developing Circular, Digital, and Green Economies in Asia
Patricia Ordóñez de Pablos (The University of Oviedo, Spain)
Business Science Reference • © 2022 • 521pp • H/C (ISBN: 9781799886785) • US $225.00

Handbook of Research on Climate Change and the Sustainable Financial Sector
Odunayo Magret Olarewaju (Durban University of Technology, South Africa) and Idris Olayiwola Ganiyu (University of KwaZulu-Natal, South Africa)
Business Science Reference • © 2021 • 573pp • H/C (ISBN: 9781799879671) • US $295.00

CSR and Management Accounting Challenges in a Time of Global Crises
Ionica Oncioiu (Titu Maiorescu University, Romania)
Business Science Reference • © 2021 • 278pp • H/C (ISBN: 9781799880691) • US $215.00

Impact of Global Issues on International Trade
Ahu Coşkun Özer (Marmara University, Turkey)
Business Science Reference • © 2021 • 291pp • H/C (ISBN: 9781799883142) • US $215.00

Handbook of Research on the Empirical Aspects of Strategic Trade Negotiations and Management
Nuno Crespo (ISCTE – Instituto Universitário de Lisboa, Portugal) and Nadia Simoes (ISCTE – Instituto Universitário de Lisboa, Portugal)
Business Science Reference • © 2021 • 446pp • H/C (ISBN: 9781799875680) • US $265.00

IGI Global
PUBLISHER of TIMELY KNOWLEDGE

701 East Chocolate Avenue, Hershey, PA 17033, USA
Tel: 717-533-8845 x100 • Fax: 717-533-8661
E-Mail: cust@igi-global.com • www.igi-global.com

Table of Contents

Preface: Historic Shift from One Monetary Era to the Next vii

Acknowledgment xix

Chapter 1
The Long-Predicted Failure of the Post-Bretton Woods "Non-System" 1

Chapter 2
Inevitable Failure of Inconvertible Paper Money 9

Chapter 3
Unsustainability of Debt-Based Money 19

Chapter 4
Fiat Money Is "Riba," Which Islam Forbids 36

Chapter 5
What Could or Should Replace Existing Monetary Arrangements? 47

Chapter 6
Inescapable Role of Real Currency Convertibility 74

Chapter 7
The Other Side of Convertibility: Commodity Price Stabilization 86

Chapter 8
The Grondona System of Conditional Currency Convertibility Based on Primary Commodities 96

Chapter 9
Illustrating the Grondona System in Operation 126

Chapter 10
Simulation of Four National CRDs' Operations 133

Chapter 11
Discussion of CRD Simulation Results 159

Chapter 12
Multi-National Implementation 171

Chapter 13
Potential for Further Evolution of CRDs 189

Chapter 14
Frequently Asked Questions 197

Chapter 15
Summary: Implementing Real Convertibility of Existing National Currencies Is a Realistic Alternative to a "Great Reset" 218

Chapter 16
Past Response to Grondona System 226

About the Author 240

Index 241

Preface: Historic Shift from One Monetary Era to the Next

ABSTRACT

2021 is the 50th anniversary of the historic end of the US dollar gold exchange standard in 1971, which was established in 1944 at Bretton Woods. Since most international trade uses US dollars, and most governments' foreign-exchange reserves are largely US dollars, this was a major event which undermined confidence in the monetary system. The price of an ounce of gold which was $35 in 1971, is around $1,800 in 2021, so the value of the US dollar has fallen by about 98% in real terms, while indebtedness, inequality and financial instability have grown to reach new heights. This has led to widespread discussion of alternatives to the US dollar-based system. Many politicians seem to be acquiescing to the idea of a single global system, but this book argues that the decentralized system devised by Leo St.Clare Grondona, whereby individual countries independently stabilize the real value of their currencies, would be far preferable for many reasons.

Historic events do not occur very often. They have major consequences and long-term implications which we remember and commemorate for decades, centuries, and even longer. Moreover, our understanding of them takes decades to clarify as more details about their causes and effects become clearer over time.

A historic event occurred 50 years ago on August 15, 1971, when President Richard Nixon ended the US government's guarantee to exchange gold (of 11/12 purity) for US dollars at $35 per ounce. Vigorous arguments were made in favour of this move at the time: the idea of a "gold standard" was widely mocked as outdated, and it was called inappropriate and illogical to set US monetary policy according to the worldwide demand for gold. It was also said to be unnecessary nowadays, since the US government's expert advisers would ensure that monetary policy was optimal.

From a competing point-of-view, President Nixon's move was said to mark the beginning of the end of the USA, by knocking away the last obstacle holding back the theft of Americans' wealth by the financiers who create the national money supply. Although a gold standard has well-understood weaknesses, it was the US federal government's formal guarantee to redeem dollars in gold, on demand, which persuaded 43 other countries' governments to agree to use dollars in settling their trade bills and international debts. In addition to other advantages, this system of gold "convertibility", which ensured that dollars were "as good as gold", had the weight of tradition, having been relied on for centuries to ensure the real value of currencies.

However, after being abandoned in 1971 – "temporarily", as was said at the time – no new agreement was put in its place. Under guaranteed gold convertibility, if the quantity of dollars being put into circulation increased too fast, so that they lost value through rising prices, the US government was punished by losing its gold to foreign governments which traded in their dollars for gold. This obliged the government to raise interest-rates (among other responses) to increase the value of holding dollars rather than gold, which earns no interest. Without the ability to convert their dollars into gold, holders of dollars became impotently dependent on American economic policy, which was no longer under similar pressure to preserve monetary discipline.

Half a century later, how has it been? In terms of gold, the change in the value of the dollar has been striking: from 1/35 ounce in 1971 it has fallen to 1/1,800 ounce as of mid-2021 – a fall of 98% in 50 years. By contrast, under the earlier sterling-led gold standard, the price of gold in 1914 at the outbreak of WW1 was the same price that had been set in 1717 by no less than Sir Isaac Newton. Under inflation, the prices of different goods and services do not all rise at the same rate, but as a rough indicator of how significant inflation has been, the price of housing in much of the USA and Europe has risen by roughly the same factor of about 50 over the past half-century. Such a loss in the value of the dollar reduces the value of people's savings around the world, making life harder and more unfair than necessary wherever people hold dollars.

In other words, events following the end of the US dollar gold standard strongly suggest that an institutional obligation to limit the inflation of the supply of dollars is not just helpful – it is essential. For a range of reasons, both visible and invisible, for the past half-century the people responsible for creating the US money supply have continually created new money faster than the growing US economy needed, thereby progressively destroying the real value of people's savings, and changing the way the economic system works.

Perhaps this might be acceptable if everyone suffered proportionally the same losses? Unfortunately they do not: the rich are far more able to protect their wealth than the poor, and so the gap between rich and poor has grown ever wider. In the USA those earning middle or lower incomes have seen no real growth in their incomes for the past 30 years. Moreover, in 2020 alone roughly $2 Trillion in wealth is said to have shifted from these middle and lower classes to the billionaire class. And in 2021 the current head of the US central bank, the "Federal Reserve System", stated that a higher rate of inflation will be tolerated in order to protect financial markets.

This same story has been repeated throughout history: as a country gets rich, its people relax the discipline that enabled its success. This is seen in many ways, but can perhaps be typified by the fact that the children of US politicians no longer join the armed forces. Why do the people with the power to create money create too much? It would be nice to believe that heads of government and the financial world are highly disciplined and morally strict. However, in reality they are under continual competitive pressure to retain power – and to achieve this the "power of the public purse" is one of the major resources. How can they resist spending too much? . . . unless there is a strict check which everyone understands and accepts, such as the check traditionally imposed by gold convertibility?

Today, in the face of extreme instability in financial markets, historically high levels of debt – of individuals, companies, and governments – and rapidly growing use of new Internet-based currencies independent of governments, there is much discussion of the need for new policies to put the world economy on more stable foundations than the greatly weakened US dollar. As we approach a historic turning-point, it is still unclear what policies will succeed the dollar-based system, and how successful they will be in reviving stable economic growth. Among other possibilities there is discussion of a "New Bretton Woods" – presumably a form of revived gold standard – and/or the use of Internet-based digital currencies, both private and public. Perhaps the most important question is: WHO is to decide the coming system? Clearly this is the role of government, and in more democratic countries this should be the result of wide and open discussion among not only government politicians and bureaucrats, but all interested parties representing different groups in society.

Unfortunately, democratic governments are under continual threat of degenerating into plutocracy – inappropriate influence on government by rich people who consider themselves qualified to decide policies from behind the scenes, without their ideas being openly debated as is done in democratic systems, however inefficiently. The would-be plutocrats who wish to change society, but do not wish to do this as others do, through political action to persuade the public, today include billionaire salesmen, speculators and financiers claiming to be philanthropists, visionaries or statesmen. Members and organisers of various "think-tanks", they are typified today by members of the self-styled "World Economic Forum" (WEF), whose views are widely quoted in the news media which they control, and who buy political influence through campaign contributions and media coverage for favoured politicians. As astute commentator Hilaire Belloc described more than 100 years ago in his booklet "The Free Press", elected politicians depend on two things: "money and limelight" (Belloc, 1911), both of which billionaires can provide them. Hence today many leading politicians openly admit that members of the WEF and other would-be plutocrats are friends, and they often meet them or their agents.

In order to "keep our eyes on the ball", we must constantly ask the age-old question: "*Cui bono*?" In whose interest? It is not difficult to see that the policies which unelected billionaires work to have implemented invariably promote their own economic interests. As examples, among other policies, the WEF has long advocated "globalization", which includes rewriting the rules of global trade to suit giant corporations, weakening anti-monopoly laws on news media and financial corporations, promoting rapidly worsening restrictions on the fundamental freedoms of speech, public assembly, choice of healthcare, religious worship, and other policies that the general public would not support if openly debated free from propaganda.

Most threatening today is these globalists' plan, in the face of threatening economic turbulence, for what they call a "Great Reset", which would include the imposition of a new world monetary regime – a "one size fits all" system for the world. Their major argument seems to be that the recent instability of financial markets is unavoidable, and so there is no better alternative than implementing a new, centrally-controlled, digital money system which would encode everyone's private information in a global database . . . though most details still remain unclear.

In order to achieve this goal, globalists can induce or aggravate monetary instability through the activities of giant banks and investment funds. This is intended to make their agenda seem preferable by making it difficult for individual countries' governments and businesses to preserve economic stability. In addition, the corporate news media which globalists control, both legacy media and Internet-based, are now engaged in massive, coordinated censorship in order to prevent discussion of alternatives to the policies they advocate, or even questioning of their dishonest version of news about innumerable daily events around the world.

However, history shows that allowing people freedom to choose their own fate, whereby different regional groups and countries follow different policies, is the culturally and economically most productive solution. Races, religions, cultures, countries and their governments have evolved over millennia as societies adapt to face ever-changing conditions. For the greatest benefit of the most people, this process should be allowed to continue, and not be hijacked by a self-selected group of unelected, self-interested billionaires. This is clear even from the simple point-of-view that, in the face of major uncertainties about the future, trying many different ideas – trial and error – is the traditional, natural way to learn what works best. Today, all countries face unprecedentedly rapid changes in the technological environment, which pose major challenges to society. There is no reason to believe that globalists know what is the best policy for all countries – and no evidence to believe that they would implement it even if they did. In contrast to genuine heroes and nation-builders of the past, their viewpoint seems to be well described by Adam Smith in his famous phrase:

"All for ourselves, and nothing for other people, seems, in every age of the world, to have been the vile maxim of the masters of mankind." (Smith, 1775)

More recently these would-be "masters of mankind" have been aptly named "feral elites", planning to profit in every way they can, at everyone else's expense, who unfortunately have the ear of many political leaders. However, they seem to be forgetting another saying from the past: "The castle isn't safe if the village isn't happy". Or perhaps they believe that the general public in the rich countries are nowadays so pacified by television and other entertainments that they cannot resist whatever plans the plutocrats make?

One policy that is urgently needed to resist the tyranny of globalists' "Great Reset" is a means whereby individual governments can independently stabilize the value of their existing currencies. The policy that needs to be implemented must also be politically "practical", in the sense that it can be adopted without needing to make major changes to other existing policies. So, for example, in this sense an all-or-none policy such as suddenly implementing a new currency would not be "practical". Hence the required policy must allow governments to improve their economic stability incrementally, and without depending on international agreements, since these would require time-consuming negotiations; introduce unrelated issues; and make the country vulnerable to the other countries breaking their commitments. But is there such a policy available?

In a word, yes. This is the Grondona system of conditional currency convertibility based on primary commodities. Deceptively simple, and so often dismissed by lazy and/or biased commentators as just another variant of the well-known idea of a "commodity standard", the Grondona system is fundamentally different. By implementing "automatic" convertibility like the gold standard, but in a way which adjusts flexibly to movements in market prices, it would avoid the innumerable problems facing all proposals that depend on international negotiations – and in addition makes it possible to accurately simulate the effects of the system's operation, as shown in this book.

Although defining and preserving the value of the monetary unit is essential in order to preserve the value of people's savings and facilitate economic growth, it has been surprisingly difficult for economists to decide how best to implement this idea. In the search for a reliable means of stabilizing the real value of whatever currency or monetary units are used, politicians and economists have spent decades trying to devise an international, or nowadays global, system. But in doing so they have been "barking up the wrong tree": the present problem is not amenable to solution by international negotiations among experts, as globalists would like everyone to believe. This is indeed one of the wider and deeper lessons of economics: some problems are better solved through the impersonal operation of "market forces" – that is, free competition under the rule of law – than by negotiations between government experts. The most famous case is of course economic growth itself, which, in many – though not all – fields, is achieved more effectively in countries with economic freedom than under government central planning.

Consequently, instead of trying to negotiate another centralized global system like Bretton Woods, based on a single dominant currency, which would inevitably involve diplomatic horse-trading, geopolitical bullying, compromises on unrelated issues, and so on, the alternative of enabling each country to stabilize the real value of its own currency independently would have many advantages. However, this is easier said than done: professional economists have been trying for more than a century to devise a system to achieve this, but none has succeeded in developing a convincing blueprint.

This book invites readers to consider that, in fact, this specific problem was definitively solved by Australian writer Leo St.Clare Grondona (1890-1982) in the 1950s – when his proposed system was widely praised in the British press, and was even debated in the British parliament, with one of many supporting reviewers going so far as to write that it "*...will define the* *beginning of an era as surely as did the introduction of the gold standard*" (Manager, 1958). Grondona did not himself propose his system as a new basis for the world monetary system. In the early days of the Bretton Woods era his goal was much more modest: to reduce the extreme volatility of industrial commodity prices over the trade cycle, which continue to be a huge weakness in the working of the world economy.

But times change, and the implementation of Grondona's simple, reliable mechanism for stabilizing the real values of currencies in terms of primary commodities would now eliminate any need for a "neo-Bretton Woods" system by which a central group of people would get a controlling grip on most or all other economies. In the present era, a decentralised structure in which each country's government independently stabilizes its own currency will clearly be far preferable for most countries than a revival of the neo-colonial structure that was acceptable for the post-WW2 era dominated by the USA.

Fortunately, assessment of the soundness or otherwise of Grondona's system is not affected by the many debates about economic policy that have come and gone among professional economists since the 1950s. Although there is an enormous literature on many topics related to the failings of the present global financial system, and also much on the topic of how to define the real value of currencies, the fundamental theoretical issues can be judged as having been resolved nearly a century ago when the two competing "giants" of 20th century economics, John Keynes and Friedrich Hayek, both wrote in favour of reducing the wide swings in market prices of industrial commodities which greatly aggravate the cyclical fluctuations in world trade, as discussed in Chapters 6 and 7 (Keynes, 1938; Hayek, 1943). Reducing the volatility of commodity prices is, of course, the very same phenomenon as stabilizing the real value of the currency in terms of those commodities, although they are usually treated as two separate topics within the field of economics. Since the views of these two competing economists encompass the dominant schools of economic thought even today, the key issue that remains is to assess whether the Grondona system would indeed be effective, as well as cost-effective, in implementing this fundamental policy on which Keynes and Hayek uniquely agreed, but for which they did not themselves produce a plan of implementation.

For those who may feel it unlikely that an "unknown" like Grondona could have succeeded where numerous eminent economists failed, it is worth noting that Grondona was not an academic but a person of wide-ranging practical experience: farmer, writer, journalist, soldier, civil servant, business consultant, military educator, administrator, public relations agent, and economic commentator. Perhaps for this reason the practicality of his proposals was recognised by such economists as Roy Harrod, who wrote laudatory prefaces for several of his books, including the last (Grondona, 1975), and was a confidant of Keynes, as discussed in Chapter 8.9 below. Although Grondona understood the potential value of currency convertibility (having lived and worked under the gold standard in his youth), he was not familiar with the mechanics of money creation in modern banking systems, and so he concentrated on the price-stabilizing aspects, rather than the reciprocal currency-stabilizing aspects of convertibility. This book focuses on the latter, since this is the central issue today: reducing the steep volatility of commodity market prices is a "bonus" that will arise with the adoption of his system.

In the following chapters we discuss the problems which the relative decline of the USA and its dollar are causing for other countries, and the inadequacy of alternatives proposed to date. While covering a wide range of topics, the discussion centres on US economic and monetary policies, since the US dollar is still used for about three quarters of world trade and currency reserves. The rest of the book introduces Grondona's system; shows simulations of its operation in several countries; and describes how implementing it could help individual countries to independently improve their economic stability. It also discusses the phenomenon that, as more countries adopt the system, they will thereby create a growing network of currencies among which the exchange-rates will become increasingly stable.

Chapter 1 describes the post-WW2 Bretton Woods system, its failure in 1971, and the destructive economic trends to which the "post-Bretton Woods non-system" of floating "*fiat*" currencies has given rise. In the face of the declining role of the US dollar and resulting international financial instability, the need for some better system to replace it has become a major topic of discussion.

Chapter 2 discusses the history of failure of paper currencies unbacked by any real assets. This suggests that the dollar-dependent part of the world economy is now on a slippery slope towards monetary chaos, and so urgent efforts are now needed to create a sound, preferably permanent, basis for a new international monetary system.

Chapter 3 discusses perhaps the most striking weakness of the US dollar-dominated monetary system, which was warned against by Thomas Jefferson in his famous advice not to let private banks control the monetary system. Ever since this was allowed to happen in 1913, the US economy has become progressively indebted and "financialized". Long hidden, but now widely understood thanks to the Internet, continuing control of the money system by private banks is neither reliable nor acceptable, and could certainly never provide stability.

Chapter 4 discusses a third viewpoint from which present monetary arrangements are unsatisfactory, that of Islamic economics, which considers debt-based *fiat* currencies to be immoral, unjust and socially destructive. In understanding this, Islamic economists have been more perceptive than mainstream western economists who mostly ignore this festering weakness at the heart of their system. They must now work together to solve this problem by creating a truly stable foundation for the world economy.

Chapter 5 considers the three main directions which are being proposed as a possible basis to succeed the present "non-system" of floating *fiat* currencies: revived gold convertibility in some form, privately-created Internet-based currencies, and central bank digital currencies, all of which seem likely to play a greater role in future monetary arrangements. New uses of the Internet and computer software are developing so rapidly that it is not possible to predict the final form of such arrangements. In addition, all three of these systems lack any clear plan to stabilize the real value of the currencies involved.

Chapter 6 discusses the age-old principle of stabilizing the value of paper currency by guaranteeing its convertibility into real commodities on demand, which was recognized by all the classical economists as a necessary condition for preserving money's real value. It also considers the idea dating from the 19th century that, instead of gold and/or silver, as were used in most such systems, convertibility should be based on a range of industrial primary commodities. However, in order to achieve this a more complex system is needed, since the market prices of industrial commodities need to be able to move over a much larger range than gold, which has few industrial uses.

Chapter 7 describes the fact that such a system is also, in itself, a system to stabilize the market prices of primary commodities. These are famously unstable, frequently swinging by -50% and +100% or more, causing difficulties for both producers and users, and thereby hindering economic growth. This objective was endorsed in principle by both Keynes and Hayek, but proposals to date to establish an international system to realize the idea have been unrealistic, and so likely to hinder rather than encourage economic growth – and so have not been adopted.

Chapter 8 introduces the Grondona system of conditional currency convertibility which was designed specifically to simply achieve the counter-cyclical stabilization of commodity prices, and describes how it was widely recognized in the 1950s as providing a definitive solution to this problem. Activated by market forces rather than government decisions, the Grondona system would enable individual countries to benefit directly from its reliable, economy-stabilizing influence, in a way impossible for any internationally negotiated scheme. Perhaps most importantly, the funds needed to acquire reserves of commodities under the Grondona system can legitimately be created *de novo*, as happened under the gold standard.

Chapter 9 describes a simulation of how the system would have operated in Japan if it had been implemented during the 1980s. In doing so it illustrates a major strength of the Grondona system, namely that, by being activated by markets, the effects of its implementation can be accurately simulated using past market data. The simulation also shows the simplicity of the system, enabling it to achieve a range of economic benefits through using market forces to partially stabilize the real value of the Japanese Yen in terms of a range of commodities.

Chapter 10 shows the results of more recent simulations made by using a computer model of the Grondona system operating in four different countries – Indonesia, Malaysia, Turkey and Pakistan. Simulations clearly show the system's counter-cyclical stockholding of the primary commodities involved, which would reduce instability in each country's commodity-using industries, while their combined effect would exert a stabilizing influence on the real value of the national currencies.

Chapter 11 discusses various details of the results of the simulations, including how the overall expansion and contraction of the money supply induced by the operation of the system would be broadly counter-cyclical for the macro-economy as a whole, helping to resist both inflationary and deflationary pressures. It also discusses remaining uncertainties about the effects of the system's operation.

Chapter 12 discusses the effects of multinational implementation of the Grondona system, whereby, even without any formal collaboration, the operation of several different countries' systems would complement each other, increasing their overall stabilizing influence on commodity prices and trade. The important synergistic benefits of a group of countries implementing the system together, which grow as the number of participating countries grows, are also discussed.

Chapter 13 discusses the potential for further evolution of the Grondona system once governments have some experience of its operation. This particularly includes the feasibility of adding gold and silver convertibility to the system, as well as other basic manufactured products.

Chapter 14 answers a number of "Frequently Asked Questions" in order to clarify a number of popular misunderstandings about the Grondona system, particularly concerning how it differs from other proposals made over the years.

Chapter 15 summarizes the book's main points. The author argues that the Grondona system offers a timely opportunity for countries which do not wish to be herded into a centralized, global money system, which would inevitably be unresponsive to their national needs, to stabilize their national currencies independently. Through its various stabilizing influences, the Grondona system could also help to protect smaller countries from monetary destabilization, whether economic or geo-political in origin.

Chapter 16 includes some of the published eulogies and strong political support which Grondona's work received in the 1950s and 1970s, and discusses the failure of a 1976 British government committee to recognise its importance.

SUMMARY

The traditional means of stabilizing the value of a paper currency has been to make it convertible on demand into a real asset, the most famous and long-used being gold. On the historic date of August 15, 1971, the guaranteed convertibility of the US dollar into gold, to which the value of 43 other currencies was linked via fixed exchange-rates, was suspended, after only 27 years. Since then the dollar has been an unbacked "fiat" currency, and its value in terms of gold has fallen by 98%, since US policy makers face no strict constraint to ensure the monetary discipline necessary to preserve the dollar's value. Although it remains the dominant currency used for international trade and central banks' reserves, the US dollar is losing its ability to provide a stable basis for the world economy, and there is now vigorous discussion about what is to take its place.

One possibility urged by those in favour of globalization, such as the members of the "World Economic Forum", is for all countries to agree to use a new global digital money system which they are preparing. However, in the current state of technology and geopolitics it would be impossible to trust that this would be implemented for the benefit of the general public, and not in order to forward the interests of globalist plutocrats.

A far better solution would be for every country to stabilize the real value of their currency independently, and thereby avoid any need for a single currency to provide backing to them – if such a system could be implemented. As it happens, a system to achieve this was published in the 1950s, devised by Australian writer Leo St.Clare Grondona, which is the subject of this book. Although not adopted by the British government, at a time when the US dollar was still “as good as gold”, Grondona’s system was widely praised in the British press. Half a century after the end of US dollar convertibility, the Grondona system’s time has now come: all that is needed is for the government of some innovative country to set the ball rolling.

REFERENCES

Belloc, H. (1911). *The Free Press*. https://www.gutenberg.org/files/18018/18018 h/18018-h.htm

Grondona, L. (1975). *Economic Stability is Attainable*. Hutchinson-Benham.

Hayek, F. (1943). A Commodity Reserve Currency. *The Economic Journal, 53*(210/211), 176-186.

Keynes, J. (1938). The Policy of Government Storage of Foodstuffs and Raw Materials. *Economic Journal (London), 48*(191), 449–460. doi:10.2307/2225437

Manager. (1958). Editorial. *The Manager, 26*(3).

Smith, A. (1775). *An Inquiry into the Nature and Causes of the Wealth of Nations*. Academic Press.

Acknowledgment

The author wishes to acknowledge the indispensable contributions of colleagues Jamil Ahmed, Assistant Professor of Economics at the University of Baluchistan, and Dato' Ahamed Kameel Mydin Meera, formerly Professor and Dean of the Institute of Islamic Banking & Finance at the International Islamic University Malaysia.

Chapter 1
The Long-Predicted Failure of the Post-Bretton Woods "Non-System"

ABSTRACT

The monetary system implemented at Bretton Woods in 1944 made the US dollar the centre of the world economic system, with 43 other countries' currencies linked to it via fixed exchange rates. However, once the US government broke its promise to redeem dollars in gold at $35 per ounce on August 15, 1971, expansion of the supply of dollars was no longer constrained, and like many currencies before it, the lack of monetary discipline led to inflation through which the value of the dollar has fallen by about 98%. The "oil shock" of the 1970s led to the introduction of the "petro-dollar" system whereby Saudi Arabia, then the largest oil producer, agreed to accept only US dollars in payment for its oil in exchange for the US government's pledge to defend it. This shored up demand for the fiat US dollar, enabling it to survive until its now approaching endgame.

INTRODUCTION

The story of the creation of the "Bretton Woods System", or at least the uncontroversial part of it, is well-known. In July 1944, as the war in Europe was nearing its end, a conference was held at Bretton Woods in New Hampshire, at which forty-four countries agreed on the design of the monetary system they

DOI: 10.4018/978-1-7998-8302-9.ch001

would use in the post-war world. Due to the economic and military dominance of the USA, they agreed to use the US dollar as the basis of the system, and to link their national currencies to the dollar with fixed exchange-rates. In turn the US government promised to keep the dollar convertible into gold at $35 per ounce: this facility was only open to governments, so it was named a "gold exchange standard". Such a "wholesale" standard was significantly different from the "retail" gold standard that operated until WW1 (and fitfully between the two world wars), whereby individuals could freely exchange currency notes for gold coins at ordinary banks. Nevertheless, as long as the US government's guarantee of dollar convertibility lasted, it preserved the real value of the dollar in terms of gold.

Fixing exchange-rates facilitated international trade and investment, and in order to help each country maintain its dollar exchange-rate within 1% of the agreed rate, the International Monetary Fund (IMF) was set up. Each currency's exchange-rate with the US dollar was stabilized primarily by the government altering interest-rates, and/or buying and selling dollars. For countries in difficulties, the IMF provided loans, conditional on the receiving government implementing policies designed to strengthen their currency's exchange-rate – typically including cutting government spending. In 2021 the IMF has more than 180 members – implying that, despite receiving plenty of criticism over the decades, most governments find the IMF's services useful.

The International Bank of Reconstruction and Development, now known as the World Bank, was also set up at the Bretton Woods conference, initially to help repair the infrastructure and property damage caused by the war, and later to aid economic development in member countries around the world.

1.1 1971, AUGUST 15 – BEGINNING OF THE END

After US President Richard Nixon closed the "gold window" on August 15th 1971, foreign governments could no longer exchange US dollars which they owned for gold at the rate of $35 per ounce, as the US government had guaranteed since 1944. The immediate reason was that the level of the US government's gold reserves had been falling as foreign countries' governments increasingly exchanged their dollars for gold, because they were losing confidence in the value of the US dollar due to the rate of inflation increasing. Under the traditional gold standard, losing gold reserves effectively obliged the government to raise interest-rates, thereby making it more attractive for businesses, people and governments to hold liquid assets as currency in bank accounts earning interest, rather than holding gold, which does not earn interest. However, in 1971 President Nixon faced the political calculation that if interest-rates rose before the next election it would reduce his chance of winning, since rising interest-rates raise the cost of loans to businesses and individuals. For this reason there is continual pressure from the business world and the general public to have lower interest-rates – but this can lead to inflation if not sufficiently resisted.

The end of the US dollar's gold convertibility ended other countries' obligation to preserve a fixed exchange-rate with the dollar. Instead of this they started to "float" against the dollar in foreign-exchange markets, which now began to grow in scale. Some economists welcomed the opportunity for exchange-rates to be decided by market forces, which they claimed would be more efficient than fixed exchange-rates, enabling countries to tailor their exchange-rate to suit their trade conditions. So, for example, Germany and Japan, which generally have trade surpluses, would see their exchange-rates rise steadily against other countries, while countries with trade deficits, like the USA and UK, would see their exchange-rates decline.

However, despite this idealistic expectation of floating exchange-rates facilitating macro-economic adjustment, in practice the continually varying exchange-rates between all the different countries' currencies became a target for speculation. As a result, within a few decades the daily turnover on foreign-exchange markets grew to a hundred times the volume of daily international trade – although foreign-exchange markets started in order to facilitate trade. The tail is now wagging the dog, and raising business costs by wasting resources, since foreign-exchange trading is a "zero-sum" activity – that is, one trader can profit only if another trader makes a loss. This contrasts sharply with economically productive activities whereby everyone profits, and wealth increases.

Those with some knowledge of economic history understood that after President Nixon ended the guaranteed convertibility of the dollar, the price of gold would rise – in other words the value of the US dollar would fall in terms of gold. Foreign governments became more reluctant to hold dollars, since the USA was now free to expand the supply of dollars, with which Americans could buy anything in the world, even as the value of the dollar fell due to inflation, without suffering any further loss of its gold reserves. This led to various economic and geopolitical developments.

As fixed exchange-rates failed and led to floating rates, which still continue today, due to the absence of any widely supported alternative, volatility of foreign-exchange markets increased. This meant that the currencies of smaller countries became vulnerable to manipulation, due to speculation on an ever greater scale by "hedge funds" using billions of dollars to drive movements in exchange-rates, as well as via a range of financial "derivatives", which are largely means of betting on market trends. This process is stuck in a vicious circle: so long as economic growth remains as weak as it has been in recent decades, investors' "search for yield" becomes more aggressive, exacerbating short-term volatility, and thereby weakening the operation of the market system in generating economic growth. The establishment of foreign-exchange futures markets, advocated by supporters of floating exchange-rates as a means of improving the efficiency of foreign-exchange markets, also added to the potential for speculation, market manipulation and volatility.

So how are nations to get back to greater stability of exchange-rates and other economic conditions? As an example of one major effort in this direction, the creation of the Euro effectively fixed exchange-rates between European member countries. However, the lack of flexibility has put massive stresses on weaker economies, such as Portugal, Ireland, Greece and Spain (sometimes referred to as PIGS). In the face of long and deep recession in the EU triggered by the 2008 financial crisis starting in Wall Street, and greatly aggravated in 2020 and 2021 by governments' unprecedented policies to "lock down" their economies, it is currently far from clear that the Euro will survive much longer. Despite this, imposing a single global currency on as many countries as possible is now a major goal of advocates of "globalization".

1.2 THE FIRST "OIL SHOCK"

In 1973 the Organisation of Petroleum Exporting Countries (OPEC) flexed its muscles for the first time, raising the price of oil from less than $4 per barrel to nearly $12 in 1974, which set off unprecedented inflation in oil importing countries (Garavini, 2019). Without the anchor of US gold convertibility enforcing monetary discipline, inflation in many countries, including much of the OECD, reached the unheard of rate of 20% per year, at which rate prices double in less than 4 years. This had innumerable socially and economically disruptive consequences, notably waves of strikes as different groups within society tried to recover their loss of income caused by rapidly rising prices. Cumulative inflation since 1971 is easily seen in house prices, which have risen in many countries by several thousand percent over 50 years: a house that cost thousands of dollars in 1971 typically costs hundreds of thousands today.

The destructive effects of inflation are legion, notably reducing the value of people's savings, thereby making economically disciplined people poorer, favouring debtors by lessening the value of debts, and making company accounts seriously misleading. Keynes famously called inflation the surest way of destroying a nation, adding that it was particularly insidious because not one person in a thousand understands its true cause. In addition to causing financial losses and problems in preparing true business accounts, over the longer term inflation also damages society by weakening the grounds of people's knowledge of their own history and the world around them. For example, as prices of houses, land and other assets rise continually it becomes impossible to compare changes in value over decades, except by using official tables of annual inflation-rates, which weakens peoples' understanding of history and their own society.

1.3 THE PETRO-DOLLAR SYSTEM

Among other geopolitical consequences, the end of gold convertibility of the US Dollar also led to the "Petro-Dollar" agreement. With the end of the Bretton Woods system, the attractiveness of the US Dollar as a "reserve currency", used by many countries for international trade and national savings, was greatly reduced. So in 1974 the US government finalised a deal with Saudi Arabia, the largest oil producer in OPEC, whereby the USA would defend it militarily, provided that it would agree to only accept US dollars from customers for its oil (Tanous & Rubinstein, 1978). This gave a strong incentive to oil-importing countries throughout the world to hold dollars, in order to buy the oil supplies which they all needed. The Petro-dollar agreement was later extended to all of OPEC's member countries. As a result, nearly half-a-century later, some $25 trillion are now held outside the USA – more than one year of US GDP.

A major objective of the US war on Iraq in 1991-2 was to preserve the Petro-dollar system by stopping Iraq from selling oil in other currencies than dollars. With the decline in the relative importance of Saudi-Arabian oil as other sources have expanded, and with the growth of China to become a major market player, the Petro-dollar agreement is losing force (Hassan, 2013). Today Iran does not accept payment in US dollars for its oil – a major reason for the US government's endless demonising of the Iranian government.

In addition to such major geopolitical implications of the end of gold convertibility of the US dollar, as soon as it was announced in 1971 knowledgeable commentators predicted that dollar creation would become undisciplined, and the US-led financial system would end with uncontrolled money-creation leading to inflation and economic instability. This prediction has taken half-a-century to come true, but the end is now in sight: in 2020 the US government presided over the creation of several Trillion dollars – more than in any other year in U.S. history – partly in order to protect major financial institutions from huge losses. This was several times larger and faster than the earlier creation of Trillions of dollars in response to the previous financial crisis centred on Wall Street in 2008-9.

It would seem reasonable in principle to assume that the financial system of the richest country in the world would be massively stable. However, far from being a solid edifice, already in 2008 the US financial system was seen to be highly unstable, with major US banks involved in huge speculations in order to shore up their profits (Shiller, 2008). Since then the US money supply has been expanded by Trillions of dollars in order to stimulate the stagnating US economy. This process accelerated in 2020 due to the unprecedented economic "lockdowns" implemented by many state governments which closed many businesses, thereby ending the prior economic "boom" and causing record levels of unemployment. As millions of newly unemployed Americans became unable to pay their rent, landlords and their banks were put in jeopardy. If banks become unable to repay their loans, they would have to close ATMs, which would immediately cause nationwide chaos. The federal government temporarily forbade eviction of people in arrears on rent or a home loan – but this was only an extraordinary, short-term measure which could not continue for long, and merely delayed a second surge in homelessness this century.

Separately, and prior to this recent crisis, there has been a huge increase in indebtedness by governments, businesses and individuals worldwide in recent decades. A parallel anomaly has been the unprecedented reduction of Japanese interest-rates to zero in 1995, from where they have still not risen significantly 25 years later. Initially criticized and even mocked by commentators in other countries, zero interest-rates have spread to Europe and the USA, reflecting the severity of the lack of new industries that are needed to re-employ those being displaced from older and declining industries. Among other influences, interest-rates reflect the demand for investment, rising during a boom when many companies are investing simultaneously, and falling when the demand for investment funds is depressed.

That is, even before the 2020 "lockdowns", weakening economic trends in the USA were already entrenched: although the US dollar is still reportedly used in some 80% of international trade by most countries of the world, there has been no growth in real US middle-class incomes for 30 years or more. This trend is due partly to the extreme inequality that the government has allowed to develop, with the zero-sum financial services industry at the top of the heap. The revelation during the 2020 "lockdowns" of how much the US economy depended on imports even of essential medicines and medical equipment from China and other low-cost countries was surprising and shocking to many people, as a sign of how far the loss of domestic manufacturing had been allowed to continue.

Another reason for the declining role of the US dollar around the world is the US government's policy of targeting the dollar-denominated bank accounts of government organisations, companies and individuals in countries with which the US government has political disagreements. In an era of unprecedented financial innovation, including rapidly evolving financial uses of the Internet (discussed further in Chapter 5 below), this has had less effect in harming the targets of this policy than in stimulating the development and adoption of non-dollar-based alternative financial systems. This has led to further weakening of the dollar's earlier role facilitating economic activity worldwide.

Interestingly, predictions that post-Bretton Woods economic arrangements based on the US dollar would inevitably fail once it was no longer backed by gold, come from three different directions, based on different viewpoints about what was the most fundamental flaw. These are discussed in turn in the following chapters.

SUMMARY

Following the end of the US dollar gold exchange standard in 1971, inflation has reduced the value of the dollar by around 98%, weakening its role as anchor for the world economy – although more than two thirds of world trade is still accounted in dollars, as are most of central banks' reserves. As inflation reached double figures in the 1970s, the USA negotiated the "petro-dollar" system whereby it guaranteed to defend Saudi Arabia in exchange for the Saudi Arabian government accepting only US dollars as payment for oil, of which it was the world's largest producer. During the 21st century to date, tens of thousands of US factories have been closed down and their work "offshored", while the financial system has gradually concentrated in the hands of a small number of giant corporations. In parallel the economy has experienced slow growth and ever-worsening instability, while inequality of income and wealth in the USA has reached record levels. The unprecedented policy of "locking down" millions of mostly smaller businesses in 2020 and 2021 has greatly aggravated these problems, leading to widespread prediction of a major recession. These problems can all be seen as results of the lack of monetary discipline arising with dependence on *fiat* money.

REFERENCES

Garavini, G. (2019). *The Rise and Fall of OPEC in the Twentieth Century*. Oxford University Press. doi:10.1093/oso/9780198832836.001.0001

Hassan, T. (2013). *The Dead Petrodollar System*. CreateSpace.

Schiller, R. (2008). *The Subprime Solution: How Today's Global Financial Crisis Happened, and What to Do about It*. Princeton University Press.

Tanous, P., & Rubinstein, P. (1978). *The Petrodollar Takeover*. Arrow Books.

ADDITIONAL READING

Flandreau, M., & Eichengreen, B. (1997). *Gold Standard in Theory and History*. Routledge.

Chapter 2
Inevitable Failure of Inconvertible Paper Money

ABSTRACT

Since the invention of paper money, it has been understood that it is difficult for its creators to resist issuing so much that it loses value. Long experience led to the single uniquely effective means of resisting this fraud: this is for the issuer to guarantee to convert their paper money, on demand, into some defined asset, such as gold, on fixed terms. With the end of the US dollar's guaranteed convertibility into gold, its value became dependent on decisions by leaders of the US government and financial system, unhindered by the need to keep it stable. Predictably, this led to unprecedented inflation of the supply of dollars, leading to ever-rising prices and continuing decline in the acceptability of dollars and US geopolitical leadership.

INTRODUCTION

"Experience shows that neither a state nor a bank ever had the unrestricted power of issuing paper money without abusing that power: in all states, therefore, the issue of paper money ought to be under some check and control; and none seems so proper for that purpose, as that of subjecting the issuers of paper money to the obligation of paying their notes, either in gold coin or in bullion." (David Ricardo, 1817)

DOI: 10.4018/978-1-7998-8302-9.ch002

Money is one of humans' great inventions. Without it, people would have to use barter in order to obtain the many different goods and services which they want to use. But barter becomes increasingly impractical as the number of goods to be bartered grows – to hundreds of millions today. The earliest things which were used as "money" were objects which humans spontaneously considered to be valuable due to their rarity and durability. Various forms of "money" evolved, as a handy asset that anybody was happy to receive in exchange for other goods – because they knew that other people would in turn be happy to accept it in exchange for their goods. After using various durable objects such as rare shells or bits of metal in various shapes, in many countries coins made of gold and silver, of known purity, became the standard form of money (Money museum, 2021).

In parallel it became one of kings' traditional roles to supply the money used in their country. For centuries this comprised coins of gold, silver and other metals. Typically the value of coins as money was greater than their value as metal – the difference being known as "*seigniorage*", the profit from coining money, which belonged to the king. Unauthorised minting of such coins, known as counterfeiting, enabled counterfeiters to steal the wealth of the general public. Sometimes called a "victimless crime", because the value was stolen from the public at large, counterfeiting was typically a capital offence, for which the punishment was execution.

However, since gold and silver are heavy and bulky, it became more convenient to use paper certificates guaranteeing that their owner had real gold money accessible in safe storage. This of course introduced the problem of fake certificates: there was no way to know for sure whether the holder of the certificate actually possessed the gold and silver which they claimed to have. This created an important job – that of being trusted to honestly hold gold and silver safely for their owners, and to issue trustworthy certificates of ownership.

Predictably, competition between gold merchants providing these services led, inevitably, to dishonesty, whereby people storing gold safely for others would lie about how much they had, and lend paper certificates, or "notes", to customers claiming more gold than they actually had. This was easy to do, because the issuers of notes – now formalised as "banks" – found that most people did not need to see their gold very often – and so they only needed to keep enough gold to cover a fraction of the notes they issued in order to be able to provide gold to customers who demanded it. Of course, if a bank's customers lost confidence and all asked for their gold at once, the bank could not pay them, and people lost money as the bank collapsed. So maintaining confidence became of central importance in those early days of banking. Unfortunately, in this way the banking industry was based on fraud from the start – in the sense that money-lenders learned how to profit from payments they received for storing customers' gold which they actually used for their own profit by lending it to other customers.

With the use of paper money, the value of seigniorage became even greater, since the nominal value of paper money is far higher than the actual cost of making the printed paper. It is both a strength and a weakness of paper money that large quantities can be made at very little cost. As a result, the people with power to print money have a strong incentive to print more and more – and indeed this has happened repeatedly throughout history. So much so that the history of paper money is an endlessly repeated story of failure, over many centuries. The political pressure on governments to expand the money supply – so as to get "something for nothing" via the "victimless crime" of inflation – is too tempting for politicians subject to elections to resist. Good governance therefore requires some rule to prevent political leaders from damaging the economy in this way.

As David Ricardo noted (at the head of this chapter), the best way to minimize this problem is to oblige issuers to provide gold or silver coins in exchange for their notes, on demand – that is, immediately anyone asks them to. Another classic statement about the importance of convertibility of paper money is that by Adam Smith:

"A paper money, consisting in bank notes, issued by people of undoubted credit, payable on demand, without any condition, and, in fact, always readily paid as soon as presented, is, in every respect, equal in value to gold and silver money, since gold and silver can at any time be had for it ..." (Smith, 1775)

There are innumerable stories of banks issuing too many notes and trying to delay having to redeem them with gold coins or bullion – before failing, and leaving their debts unpaid. Thus, in addition to the repeated lesson through centuries of bitter experience that unbacked paper money always loses its value, it also became "common sense" that requiring the issuer of paper money to guarantee its convertibility, on demand, into real assets – typically gold or silver – was effective in preventing the loss of value of paper money. This idea is extremely simple and understandable to anyone, which is an important attribute for such a fundamental aspect of the monetary system.

The best-known, historically most widely used means of implementing such real convertibility for paper money was to implement a "gold standard", whereby owners of the paper money in question could convert it on demand, at banks, into a guaranteed quantity of gold of defined purity. One among many persuasive voices who explained the advantage of such real convertibility was John Stuart Mill, 170 years ago in his book Principles of Political Economy, who stressed

"... the importance of adhering to a simple principle, intelligible to the most untaught capacity. Everybody can understand convertibility; everyone sees that what can be at any moment exchanged for five pounds, is worth five pounds." (Mill, 1845)

At that time, one pound Sterling was a little more than one 1/4 ounce of 22 carat gold (that is, 11/12 or 92% pure) – or 0.2 ounces of pure gold – so one ounce of pure gold was worth about five pounds. Such an easily understood and obviously reliable system would seem to be "natural" for any country in which it is accepted that government operates by popular consent, and it was indeed "common sense" for several centuries. A memorable illustration of this "common sense" is a scene in the famous film "Laurence of Arabia" in which some of the tribal leaders who agreed to fight as mercenaries are enraged when given a box of paper notes: "Where is the gold we were promised?" Anyone watching the scene understands immediately that producing pretty notes is cheap – but they are only worth as much as someone else will exchange them for – which can fall to zero when a regime is overthrown in wartime. But a real physical asset such as gold has inextinguishable value, for which something of real value has to be offered in exchange. Hence convertibility was long used to ensure that paper money preserved its real value.

(NB today the word "convertibility" is typically used to mean convertibility into other currencies – that is, from one paper currency into another paper currency. Although the ability to convert a paper currency easily into other currencies is an important part of its usefulness, this does not in itself protect its value in real terms.)

2.1 *"FIAT"* MONEY

What tantalises economists, politicians and others is that, *in theory, in principle*, a government could issue paper money in a responsible way so that it remained sound and preserved its nominal value. They would thereby save the considerable costs of having to obtain and store huge quantities of gold

&/or other monetary assets which, in practice, hardly ever move from the heavily guarded cellars where they are stored. Inconvertible paper money is called "*fiat*" money, ("Let it be so"): the value is given to it by a government allowing it to be used to pay taxes, not by having actual value like gold coins, nor by being reliably convertible into real goods. Such paper money, of which the real value is neither defined nor guaranteed in terms of physical goods, is dependent on government to preserve its value.

A recent succinct statement of both the strength and weakness of *fiat* currency, confirming the traditional understanding, is this by Pittaluga and Seghazza:

"fiat money ... although characterized by an elasticity of supply with respect to the level of production that is considerably higher than commodity money, can only be accepted if suitable institutional mechanisms guarantee the stability of its value." (Pittaluga & Seghezza, 2021)

They also describe clearly the international situation of the US dollar under the Bretton Woods agreement:

"In the international context, an international money exists when the conditions of a political exchange exist between a leading country, which bears the costs of producing trust in the fiat money (and the international monetarysystem based on it), in exchange for exploiting the seigniorage right, and follower countries, which attribute little weight to the relative gains made by the leading country's exploitation of the seigniorage right and, at the same time, derive significant benefit from the existence of an international money, and the growth in trade and output associated with it." (Pittaluga & Seghezza, 2021)

There are plenty of cases in history where *fiat* currency has been used successfully – for a while. Perhaps most notably, before combining to become the USA, the local governments of the early north American colonies issued "colonial scrip", as pioneered by polymath Benjamin Franklin, who ran the Pennsylvania mint. He learned by trial and error that, if new money was issued into the economy at the right pace, this generated new employment for many people, leading to vigorous economic growth. It was due to complaints from the financiers in the City of London that they were losing profits by allowing the colonists to print their own money, instead of borrowing gold from them, that the British government insisted that they stop issuing their own money, and instead go into debt to London, thereby enriching the British financial establishment. This led to economic stagnation and unemployment in the colonies, which ultimately led the fledgling states to declare independence and face war with the superpower of the day, rather than to give up their freedom to create their own money.

Based on the various states' earlier successful experience, the new US federal government later printed unbacked paper "Continentals" in order to organize the states to fight the war of independence against Britain. During the war, the British navy reputedly sent a specially equipped ship to the US east coast to counterfeit Continentals in order to reduce their value through inflation, in order to hinder the rebellious colonists' activities. However, despite inflation that accelerated through the war, Continentals retained enough of their value to enable the US government to prevail.

Realistically, however, except under such temporary or exceptional conditions, paper money – which nowadays has been largely replaced by data in computers – cannot be a reliable long-term store of wealth. Unfortunately, trusting that governments will continually behave responsibly in this matter is hopelessly unrealistic about the effects of strong political pressures. This is easy to understand by imagining the situation in which a political leader must decide whether to print more money – or admit that their government is unable to pay its debts and sack huge numbers of public employees.

Even Keynes, who is famous for his criticism of gold as a "barbarous relic", agreed that:

"... in certain quite possible circumstances, the obligation of convertibility might really prove to be a safeguard against inflation brought about by political pressure contrary to the judgement of the Federal Reserve Board." (Keynes, 1923).

Simply reading this comment today is a useful reminder of how far political discourse has changed over the past century. The era of the "classical" gold standard had ended with the start of World War 1 in 1914, and so the 20th century experiment with inconvertible paper money was still in its early days in 1923. Moreover, it was widely expected that Sterling would return to the gold standard, which it did in 1931, although only temporarily. It is worth remembering that the Sterling price of gold in 1914 had been set by Isaac Newton in 1717, who was given the sinecure of being the nominal head of the Bank of England as a reward for his world-famous physics research. Apart from a period of inconvertibility during the Napoleonic wars when the value of sterling in terms of gold fell by 25% before reviving, the Sterling price of gold set by Newton lasted nearly two centuries, during which Britain rose to world leadership. That experience of generations of stability under the gold standard led to a general assumption of monetary stability. This contrasts sharply with today's volatile economy, when currencies rise and fall in response to daily news, while feral "hedge funds" continually scour the world for profitable speculative opportunities through using billions of dollars to exploit this volatility.

As a policy adviser, Keynes would have been keen to keep in favour with the powers that be. Nevertheless, his respect for "the judgement of the Federal Reserve Board" is very different from the waves of criticism that the "Fed" receives today – not least for its share of responsibility for the extraordinary volatility and instability of the foundations of the US financial system. Permitting the growth of economic "bubbles" – of which the eventual bursting leads to huge economic disruption and unemployment, while the "Fed" saves what are called "too big to fail" banks – is itself a massive distortion in the economy.

Added to this is the enormous problem of corruption by giant financial companies. This concerns not only political contributions, which now reach hundreds of millions of dollars in a presidential campaign, but also even money laundering on a massive scale. A recent example was the release in 2020 of thousands of Suspicious Activity Reports (SARs) under the U.S. Financial Crimes Enforcement Network (FinCEN) which exposed several trillions of dollars of money laundering by the major banks, including JPMorgan Chase, HSBC, Standard Chartered, Deutsche Bank, and Bank of New York Mellon (ICIJ, 2020; Martens & Martens, 2019). As a further example, JPMorgan Chase paid a fine of nearly $1 billion in 2020 after being convicted of having illegally manipulated the gold and silver markets for years – and probably for decades.

The corresponding political pressures have grown to such large scale in the present-day world that, having been unbacked by gold or any other commodity since 1971, issue of the US dollar is now accelerating dangerously: 20% of all the dollars in existence were reputedly created in 2020. Massive expansion in the US money supply through 2020 and 2021, which is inevitably leading to a corresponding rise in prices – thereby stealing from everyone's savings – shows that the US dollar is no longer fit for the purpose of being the basis of the world trade system. Writing only ten years after the creation of the Federal Reserve System, Keynes may possibly have been unaware that it was privately owned, like the Bank of England. If so, he would not have been sufficiently alarmed about the ever-worse problems that this would cause over the longer term.

Another major change over the past half-century is that the establishment of the field of "Public Choice Economics" has clarified that much of government decision-making can be best understood as the result of politicians and bureaucrats working to further their own interests. This has led to clearer understanding of the limits of government's capabilities. So for example, unfortunately, there is no way to ensure that economic or monetary policy makers and advisers are the most knowledgeable and honest experts available. Economic and monetary policy are decided under great pressures from innumerable vested interests, seen and unseen. So even if those responsible for preparing policy had the right information and chose the best policy, there is no guarantee that government would implement it – due to the further range of electoral, political and geopolitical influences, as well as vested interests that operate on presidents, prime ministers and other policy-makers.

It is one of the strengths of market forces, in situations where they operate efficiently, that they entirely avoid these damaging influences. It is because of this that guaranteeing real convertibility of a currency – that is, guaranteeing the ability to "automatically" convert it into real goods – as a policy that extends the role of market forces and reduces the scope of vested interests, has been uniquely successful in preserving the value of the currency over the long-term, and has thereby exerted a powerful stabilizing influence on the foundations of the economic system where it operated.

The present, opaque and complex monetary system managed by mainly American "experts" who control how fast everyone's savings are to lose value, as well as choosing which "too big to fail" banks are to be saved at taxpayers' expense, is clearly not a confidence-inspiring system. Nor is it a sustainable basis for a new system to underpin economic activity worldwide. What is needed is a system on which people in every country can depend, through the 21st century and beyond. This needs to include ending the decline in the value of money by enabling the public to hold government accountable for it, as does not happen under today's monetary systems. The potential for stabilising the real value of currencies by reviving real convertibility is discussed further in Chapters 6 and 7, but another fundamental flaw of the present monetary system is discussed next.

SUMMARY

The invention of money, which occurred in different places around the world at different times, facilitated economic progress. Later, paper money came to be widely used as it was found to be more convenient than coins made from precious metals, particularly for large transactions. However, the use of *fiat* paper money (and *a fortiori* digital money today) creates severe temptation to print too much, which over the centuries has repeatedly been found to be irresistible. That is, those who get to use the new money profit from it, but the value to the users comes out of the pockets of everyone else, who lose wealth diffusely as prices rise and the value of their savings falls. This process typically ends when people lose any trust in the value of the currency, and it becomes worthless. Today, as governments in the rich countries are expanding their money supplies at unprecedented speed, we are once again approaching the end-game of the present cycle.

REFERENCES

ICIJ. (2020). *Global banks defy U.S. crackdowns by serving oligarchs, criminals and terrorists.* https://www.icij.org/investigations/fincen-files/global-banks-defy-u-s-crackdowns-by-serving-oligarchs-criminals-and-terrorists/

Keynes, J. (1923). *A Tract on Monetary Reform.* Macmillan.

Martens, P., & Martens, R. (2020). *3-Count Felon, JPMorgan Chase, Caught Laundering More Dirty Money.* https://wallstreetonparade.com/2020/09/3-count-felon-jpmorgan-chase-caught-laundering-more-dirty-money/

Mill, J. (1848). *Principles of Political Economy.* https://archive.org/details/principlesofpoli01milluoft?ref=ol&view=theater

Money Museum. (2021). https://www.money.org/money-museum/history-of-money

Pittaluga, G., & Seghezza, E. (2021). Money and the International Monetary System: Origins and Evolution. In *Building Trust in the International Monetary System.* Springer. https://ideas.repec.org/h/spr/frochp/978-3-030-78491-1_2.html

Ricardo, D. (1816). Proposals for an Economical and Secure Currency, with Observations on the Profits of the Bank of England, as they Regard the Public and the Proprietors of Bank Stock. Academic Press.

Smith, A. (1775). *An Inquiry into the Nature and Causes of the Wealth of Nations*. Academic Press.

Chapter 3
Unsustainability of Debt-Based Money

ABSTRACT

In addition to the problems caused by money being fiat, most modern money is moreover created not by governments but by privately-owned banking systems as debt to themselves. This is not only grossly contrary to all traditions of natural justice, it is also unconstitutional. This problem has been understood and publicised by many politicians and writers over centuries, but it is still not widely known due to the financial and political power of the perpetrators. Since it is also the main cause of the continuing increase in inequality in all the rich countries, the "great reset" being advocated by those in charge of the present system is clearly not fit to become the new basis of the economic system.

INTRODUCTION

"If the American people ever allow private banks to control the issue of their currency, first by inflation, then by deflation, the banks and corporations that will grow up around them will deprive the people of all property until their children wake up homeless on the continent their fathers conquered." – Attributed to Thomas Jefferson, 3rd U.S. President, immortalized at Mount Rushmore

DOI: 10.4018/978-1-7998-8302-9.ch003

As discussed in chapters 1 and 2, most money nowadays is *fiat*, and is not sufficiently robust against inflationary political pressures to provide a solid basis for the world economy. However, there is another important reason why the current system is coming to the end of its usefulness, due to a fundamental flaw in the money systems used in most countries today, which has been introduced by stealth over the last few centuries. In the history of paper money discussed above, a major role was played by banks, which are the descendants of the "money-lenders" of an earlier era. As well understood nowadays, though not at the time, a major feature of money-lenders' business was systematic fraud, nowadays euphemized as "fractional reserve banking", which enables banks to literally create money – formerly the exclusive preserve of governments. This has grown and spread to the extent that nowadays nearly all money is created not by governments for the benefit of the public, as was done through most of history, but by banks as interest-bearing debts to themselves.

3.1 MONEY CREATION BY PRIVATE BANKS

Part of traditional money-lenders' business was to store customers' gold and provide them with signed notes stating how much gold they possessed, which were more convenient for making business payments than carrying physical gold. They also lent their gold to other customers, by lending them similar notes to use for payments, charging them a rate of interest. In doing this, gold merchants learned that they could use the same gold to back several times as much in paper notes as they actually possessed in gold – thereby earning several times more in interest payments – provided that they could always repay any customer who wanted to take their gold back. At a time when well-run farms and other businesses could grow their output by 2-3% per year, bankers could earn about 10 times this on their capital, perhaps 30% per year. This led to the unjust and socially destructive enrichment of financiers over productive industries which has continued over the centuries to the present day.

This theft of the wealth of the population was not widely understood by its victims – nor by anyone else. A famous phrase describing this process of stealing a tiny amount from everyone is "Death by a thousand cuts": each little cut is insufficiently important for people to take steps to counteract, but if allowed to continue they cumulatively become fatal to the successful functioning of the economy, whereby those who work productively should become rich, not those who dishonestly manipulate the money supply. This would be equivalent to a situation in a large company in which the accountants write fraudulent accounts that make the accounting department ever richer, while all other employees' salaries decline.

An early example of the popular discontent caused by the injustice of unbridled money-lending fraud was the preparation in 1215 of the historic British treaty known as "Magna Carta". Although the historic document, which the local rulers in Britain forced then King John to sign, covered many issues, two of its clauses were to the effect that a debt to a money-lender must not continue to burden a debtor's widow or their children after the debtor's death.

Today, the profit that a bank earns by creating a "bank deposit" when it authorises a new loan to a customer is similar to earlier money-lenders' practice of lending several times more paper money than they had gold, which enabled them to enrich themselves at the expense of the communities and markets within which they operated. Nowadays this practice by banks is dignified with the name "fractional reserve banking", which enables banks to receive the profits from creating money "out of thin air".

As a result of the growth and spread of this system, most of the money used in most countries today is created by the banking system as debt to the banks. This system is very different from the creation of debt-free money in the past by the king or government in order to pay for activities necessary for the public good, most fundamentally national defence and justice. It hardly needs to be explained that permitting a small group of private citizens – that is non-governmental bankers – to create and use debt-based money as they wish is contrary to all concepts of justice, honest government or democracy.

1. It is unfair and indeed unconstitutional – the limitless profits of seigniorage should only ever go to the people, as represented by their government.
2. It is undemocratic and non-transparent, and has been kept largely secret through the ages, so that most people never understand it – including students of economics, who are not taught it in most universities!
3. It puts control of the direction of major investment trends in the economy into unseen, self-interested hands.
4. It represents an ever-growing, hidden influence over government, especially encouraging activities that increase debts, from which the financial sector profits.

These facts about the monetary system may be considered "controversial", because they are not widely known – including by most students of economics.

However, they are not in doubt, as they have been confirmed by a long line of knowledgeable people, some of whom are listed below, starting with President Thomas Jefferson, who was far from the first to expose the problem, but is surely one of the most credible. In order to solve the problem of establishing a sound monetary system, we have to face facts, however disturbing and perhaps surprising these may be.

If bankers' actions are coordinated – and they are nowadays by central banks' rules – they have unlimited power to extract the wealth of a society " . . first by inflation then by deflation . . " exactly as Jefferson states. That is, by coordinating in lowering interest-rates, bankers have encouraged people and businesses to take out loans for various purposes, thereby stimulating economic activity. Then by coordinating in raising interest-rates, bankers threw cold water on the economy and forced many people and companies into serious difficulties or even bankruptcy, when their assets were sold at low prices due to the recession – at which point the valuable assets were bought up by bankers and their associates – who were the only people who still had ready access to money.

Surely such a fundamental flaw in the economic system, publicly explained centuries ago by one of the greatest American presidents, should be taught to all American children? And to all economics students? Yet it is not taught at all in "mainstream" economics. This makes the subject of "economics" very different from other subjects like mathematics or chemistry or biology: the vast majority of economics teachers remain silent about the central economic problem in the world, namely the private control of the money system! As examples, despite their universally acknowledged stature, both Keynes and Hayek chose to join their colleagues in keeping silent about this central problem. And their agreed solution to what they both recognized as the most desirable means of stabilizing world economic activities, namely stabilizing the real value of money in terms of primary commodities, remains unimplemented. Still today, this central problem of privately issued, debt-based money, as well as Keynes' and Hayek's agreed solution, are not taught in even 1 in 100 university economics departments. This ignoring of such a fundamental subject would be like not teaching students of physics about the laws of gravity! Yet such is the field of academic economics.

As an early phase of this deception, the "Bank of England" was privately owned from when it was established in 1694 until it was "nationalised" in 1946. Likewise, the US "Federal Reserve System" has been privately owned from its establishment in 1913. Most of the world's central banks are privately owned today, as is the "central banks' central bank", the Bank for International

Settlements, which has worldwide "diplomatic immunity", putting it above the laws of all countries.

In addition to the problems listed above, debt-based money systems are inherently unsustainable, since they lead to ever-increasing levels of debt throughout society. Once these become unrepayable the system collapses, impoverishing a large proportion of the population who trusted their government. The zero and even negative interest-rates that central banks have introduced in recent years are part of different countries' efforts to stave off this final monetary catastrophe.

Behind the scenes financiers also compete, leading to the growth of giant banks and other financial corporations, and gradual monopolization. As President Jefferson also wrote, in the sentence before the above quotation:

"I believe that banking institutions are more dangerous to our liberties than standing armies." (Jefferson, 1824).

As a consequence of bankers' policies, the share of private wealth owned by the top 1% of the US population has risen from around 20% in 1990 to around 30% in 2021 (Federal Reserve, 2021). Another study of inequality in the USA, China and Europe shows the share of national wealth of the richest 1% of the population rising from some 25% in 1985 to some 33% in 2016, while the share of the bottom 75% remained near 10% (Zucman, 2019). The extreme level which this trend is now reaching is in line with Jefferson's warning.

Understanding of the injustice and unsustainability of debt-based money remained very limited for centuries, but has spread world-wide in recent years. In particular, it has received a huge boost from the greatly improved access to a wealth of information enabled by the development of the Internet. Unfortunately, this is now being reversed by the rapidly spreading censorship imposed by the monopolistic American Internet service providers such as Amazon, Google, Facebook, Youtube (owned by Google), Twitter, Apple and others. It is very much to be hoped that this shockingly un-American and unconstitutional behaviour will be reversed soon by governments enforcing the traditional anti-monopoly laws which, it is widely understood, are absolutely indispensable for democracy and capitalism to operate successfully.

The control of money creation by private banking systems is clearly unconstitutional, whether explicitly so, as in the case of the USA, or only implicitly in other countries, since it is fundamental "natural justice" that the profits earned by issuing the national currency should accrue only to governments, not as profits to private financial corporations. It is nevertheless allowed to continue in most countries due to the financial and other influences which the perpetrators have over lawmakers: there is no other plausible explanation for the centuries-long continuation of such massive theft.

3.2 PROBLEM OF DEBT-BASED MONEY LONG-UNDERSTOOD BUT NOT WIDELY KNOWN

It is a notable feature of the present day that such a deep-rooted problem should be so little known by the general public, although it has long been understood and openly described by numerous eminent people. Many of these people have made major efforts to correct this problem, but sadly, to date, all of them have been unsuccessful. In order to help readers unfamiliar with the subject, the following is a list of some of the more prominent people who have tried to warn the public and advise how to solve the problems it causes.

3.2.1 Thomas Jefferson (1743 – 1826)

Widely recognized as one of America's greatest presidents, and immortalized on Mount Rushmore, Thomas Jefferson encapsulated the problem that is destroying the USA today in the single, simple sentence that heads this chapter. In addition to banks' inflation-deflation trick, Jefferson also understood that the problem is not a static one, but continually aggravates, since the perpetrators of the fraud must work continually to prevent their exposure. This requires them to take control of the news media in order to prevent widespread understanding of their fraud, and to influence governments to keep the general public "poor and busy", among other actions.

It is very striking that, precisely as Jefferson warned 200 years ago, Americans today are facing a massive wave of homelessness – the second already this century – due to repossessions caused by millions of tenants' inability to pay their rent or mortgages, caused by many state governments' unprecedented policies to "lockdown" millions of small and medium-sized businesses. It will be some years before reliable histories of this period are published, but it is already clear that large corporations have been greatly enriched by these extraordinarily destructive government actions.

3.2.2 William Cobbett (1763 – 1835)

Writer and member of parliament, Cobbett was an indefatigable campaigner for monetary and electoral reform. Although he did not fully understand the details of the central bank fraud, he explained that while successful farmers could achieve annual growth of between 2% and 3%, holders of government debt managed by the Bank of England received an interest-rate of 8% without doing anything. And as he traveled throughout the country Cobbett could see this injustice making city-dwelling financiers progressively richer than farmers, enabling them to buy up land and make previously independent land-owners into tenant-farmers (Cobbett, 1817).

Cobbett also exposed the massive "land grab" that had occurred much earlier in Britain, in his history of the Reformation:

"It was not a reformation but a devastation, of England, which was, at the time when this event took place, the happiest country, perhaps, that the world had ever seen; and, it is my chief business to show that this devastation impoverished and degraded the main body of the people." (Cobbett, 1824)

Despite his immense energy, popularity, prolific writings and other achievements, Cobbett was unable to achieve the overhaul of the Bank of England that he understood was needed in order to correct the fundamental injustice corrupting Britain's political economy.

3.2.3 David Ricardo (1772 – 1823)

One of the earliest European economists, Ricardo wrote books which remain classics in their subject even today, as well as being a successful investor and member of the British parliament. Ricardo was aware of the fraud being perpetrated by the privately owned Bank of England, and prepared a plan for the establishment of a nationally owned central bank, published under the self-explanatory title: "Proposals for an Economical and Secure Currency, with Observations on the Profits of the Bank of England, as they Regard the Public and the Proprietors of Bank Stock" (Ricardo, 1816). However, Ricardo suffered a mysterious disease of the ear which led to his sudden, premature death.

3.2.4 Hilaire Belloc (1870 – 1953)

Best known as a writer of English children's books, Belloc was in fact an important writer of non-fiction books. However, these were often critical of the warmongering British establishment, and so his writings did not achieve the fame which they deserved. As an interesting reminder of how long the British news media have been controlled from behind the scenes, his short 1911 booklet "The Free Press" contains eye-opening examples of the extent of deliberate, warmongering disinformation spread by the mainstream media in the UK even 100 years ago (Belloc, 1911). Belloc demonstrated his awareness of the problem of debt-based money in his book "The Servile State" (Belloc, 1912), and also wrote about the social benefits of widespread land-ownership in "An Essay on the Restoration of Property" (Belloc, 1946).

3.2.5 Eustace Mullins (1923 – 2010) and Ezra Pound (1885 – 1972)

Widely considered the USA's greatest literary genius, Ezra Pound mentored three writers who received the Nobel prize for literature: William Butler Yeats, James Joyce and T.S. Eliot. Pound spent much of his life in Italy, of whose culture and history he was a great adept. Controversially, he supported Mussolini, whose policy he saw as defending European culture against the external threat from the Soviet Union (which Britain and the USA supported during WW2). For this he was imprisoned in a US mental hospital for 12 years after the end of the war, during which time he employed the young Eustace Mullins to research the history of the US Federal Reserve System (commonly known as the "Fed"), the privately owned controller of the US money supply since its secretive founding in 1913. In "Secrets of the Federal Reserve" Mullins exposed its history for the first time in book form (Mullins, 1952). Most importantly he explained that, although the "Fed" operates as the US central bank, making loans to the federal government and overseeing the financial system, it was privately owned since its establishment. This of course has major implications for understanding its actions, which remain opaque, as it has never been audited, despite long-standing efforts to do so by members of the US Congress.

Since the Fed's owners are a number of large commercial banks, both American and European, its objective is to earn profits for them, which it does by increasing indebtedness in the USA – of individuals, companies and the federal government – and at which it has been successful, achieving record levels of debt year by year, as discussed in many books and articles. The enormous damage that this has caused to the American economy and society has been described by many writers, including experienced American economic policy maker and commentator Paul Craig Roberts (Roberts, 2019).

3.2.6 James Buchanan (1919 – 2013)

Professor Buchanan founded the field of Public Choice Economics, for which he won the Nobel prize in 1986. Buchanan's description of how he learned the ideas that led to Public Choice Economics is entertaining and educational. As a young economics researcher he studied at an Italian university, where he was surprised to hear his teachers and colleagues talking openly about the Italian government and politicians as criminals and gangsters. In the USA he was used to politicians being spoken of as sincere professionals working for the good of the general public. But his Italian counterparts assumed that they were merely self-interested people who, instead of working in the business world, used the government system to enrich themselves. Buchanan realized that this assumption, though seemingly extreme, is no different from the assumption made in western economics that people working in business are "homo economicus" – that is, individually self-interested and trying to earn as much profit as possible. In truth this assumption is too simple to describe people's actual motivations, but making the assumption that companies are trying to maximize profits is quite effective for understanding their actions. Likewise, assuming that politicians' main objective is the self-interested goal to win elections, while bureaucrats work to have a good career by following rules and obeying their influential superiors, treats them no differently from the usual assumption about people working in business, and is effective in helping to understand why governments act as they do, including frequently working against the interests of their citizens.

Concerning government debt, Buchanan explained that Keynes was right in saying – what was more-or-less heresy in his day – that increasing government spending unmatched by taxation in order to mitigate serious recession could be economically justified, but he was wrong to say that this should be funded by government borrowing from the banking system. The national government has the authority – indeed the duty – to supply currency as required to enable economic growth to improve citizens' living standards (Buchanan & Wagner, 1977). It does not have the constitutional authority to cede this right to bankers, as the US federal government did in 1913. As a strictly independent academic, Buchanan did not participate in political campaigns, except for one – the non-partisan campaign for a constitutional amendment to prevent the federal government from borrowing.

3.2.7 American Monetary Institute (AMI)

The AMI was founded by Stephen Zarlenga (1941 – 2017) and colleagues in 1996. Zarlenga's book "The Lost Science of Money" includes much of the "hidden history" of money in the USA – that is, important facts that are not generally taught in economics courses (Zarlenga, 2002). For example, he explains the true cause of the US war of independence from Britain, which was not about the taxation of tea imports, as widely taught in schools, but about the colonists' right to print their own currency. As described above, the state governments printing paper money enraged the "money power" in the City of London, who demanded that the British government force the American colonists to borrow gold from them on which to base their money supply under the supervision of the privately owned "Bank of England". In fighting against American independence the British government was acting as "enforcer" for the City of London, the financial centre of Britain, which even today is legally independent of the British government.

Zarlenga also exposed Adam Smith, who has long been lauded as the "Father of Economics" on the strength of his book "An Inquiry into the Nature and Causes of the Wealth of Nations" (Smith, 1775). Although Smith's book contains many memorable explanations, it makes no mention of the centrally important fact that the Bank of England was privately owned from its foundation in 1694. Zarlenga surmises that this historic omission was a condition of his book being made a best-seller, and Smith receiving other singular favours during his career.

The AMI continues today to campaign for the privately owned Federal Reserve system to be replaced by a national central bank. However, it is difficult to envisage a path to achieving this: the US Congress has been unable to even get the Fed audited, after more than a century of its operation, and having even passed a Bill to that effect!

3.2.8 Professor Richard Werner

In recent decades Professor Werner has become deservedly famous for opening up discussion of the problem of the banking system and debt-based money. Having worked both in the financial world, and as professor of finance and/or economics at several different universities in Japan, Germany, Britain and China, Werner has definitively exposed many aspects of the problem. Perhaps most notably he has proved empirically that banks create money, and allocate credit within the economy – contrary to what professors of economics teach at most universities (Werner, 2015). He has thereby reinstated the credit creation theory of banking, which was widely recognized more than a century ago, but was inexplicably replaced in university teaching by the erroneous explanation that banks merely lend money deposited with them by savers to borrowers.

Werner lays the responsibility for the ever-increasing centralization of financial systems on central banks, which in many countries are nowadays independent of government oversight, and continue to obfuscate the truth about money and banks in order to preserve their inordinate power. Germany is well served by some 1,500 local banks – tens of times as many as most other European countries – many of which are operated without shareholders as non-profit organisations. However, the European central bank continues to press for the concentration of banking in fewer and fewer hands. Werner recommends decentralization and creation of community banks as the best policy to resist central banks' ever-more oppressive and anti-social policies (Werner, 2020). A series of Werner's lectures and interviews on the Internet contain unique explanations of the truth about banking systems in different countries, and about policy proposals for solving this problem, available at professorwerner.org

3.2.9 Public Banking Institute (PBI)

Founded in 2011 by Ellen Brown and colleagues, the PBI is leading a historic movement to establish publicly-owned banks, initially in the USA, following the model of the uniquely successful state-owned Bank of North Dakota, as well as in other countries, where a variety of types of public bank have achieved historic success over decades and more.

An attorney by profession, Brown started to investigate the financial system because of dysfunctional anomalies that she learned about in the monopolistic American health service. As she wrote in the introduction to her 2007 book

"Web of Debt: the Shocking Truth about Our Money System, and How We Can Break Free", the Internet has made it much easier to learn the truth about the privately owned "Fed" and the problem of debt-based money. Americans urgently need to learn how they have failed to heed Thomas Jefferson's historic warning – with exactly the consequences that Jefferson predicted.

Brown followed this book by bringing to public attention the existence of the Bank of North Dakota (BND), and the simple rules which have ensured its unique success in protecting North Dakotans from the worst of Wall Street's frauds. All revenues of the North Dakota state government are deposited in the BND, and are not allowed to be lent or invested outside the state. The BND does not compete with other banks, but partners with them in loans for five purposes: home loans, farming, small businesses, education and local infrastructure. By providing up to 50% of a bank loan at a lower interest-rate than private banks charge, BND ensures a "win-win" outcome: the customer pays less interest; the partner bank faces less risk since the borrower has a lower burden; and the state government benefits from the stimulus to the economy.

Brown has written two more books, "From Austerity to Prosperity: the Public Bank Solution" (Brown, 2013) and "Banking on the People: Democratizing Money in the Digital Age" (Brown, 2019), as well as hundreds of articles on related topics at ellenbrown.com. The campaign for public banks which Brown stimulated has grown rapidly nationwide, and is approaching success in a dozen states. By gradually redirecting credit to purposes beneficial for the general public, rather than for the client corporations of the giant banks, new public banks could progressively reduce private banks' control of the US economy and government at the root. Moreover, with the potential for networking and synergy enabled by Internet-based services, this movement seems to be a very promising approach to finally ending the debt-based money scandal.

3.2.10 Bill Still

Still produced the best-selling educational video "The Money Masters" in 1996, which is freely available on the Internet, since when it has reportedly been seen by a hundred million people worldwide – making Still one of the great educators in history. It explains the monetary fraud perpetrated on the American people by the creation of the privately owned Federal Reserve System in 1913, in a way easily understood by anyone, with no need for specialised knowledge of economics. Still was an invited speaker at the 3rd RIFCON (discussed in Chapter 4) where there was a fascinating exchange between Still and other advocates of debt-free paper money, and supporters of gold, including Sheik Imran Hosein. Still's Youtube channel is a regular source of related news items and commentary – though nowadays progressively censored by Youtube, which is trying to keep the truth from the general public for as long as possible.

3.2.11 Victoria Grant

Finally, as a valuable illustration of how anyone can understand the problem of debt-based money, 12 year-old Victoria Grant explained it in a 2012 video in just 7 minutes (Grant, 2012). The accusation is unanswerable, and the crimes involved are indefensible. Politicians, economists and journalists can only ignore the challenge posed by this 12 year-old child! Many people unfamiliar with the subject find it hard to face the fact that the news media which they have long depended on are complicit in covering up this fundamental scandal by continuing to ignore it. This is easier to understand when one recognises that the corporate-controlled media are nowadays highly concentrated, and owned or controlled by just a handful of giant conglomerate corporations connected to the banks that benefit from the problem of debt-based money.

Although the explanation of this problem is so simple that even a 12 year-old child can understand it, many people still find it difficult to face the full implications. The shocking truth is that the governments of most if not all of the supposedly democratic countries are beholden behind the scenes to bankers who, in their pursuit of ever greater wealth and power, are warmongers, among other problems, with no concern whatever for the general public. Quite the opposite, bankers are clearly determined to keep the general public in the rich countries "poor and busy" – and now even "locked down" as well, for as long as possible – so that they do not have the time or resources to challenge the bankers' unconstitutional and undemocratic power by demonstrating, or organising strikes and other means of protest.

3.3 NEED TO END POLITICAL CONTROL BY BANKING SYSTEMS

Before the above information became widely accessible worldwide on the Internet, it was very difficult to learn how banks had usurped governments' traditional monetary role and responsibility, and about the unconstitutionality of giving the power of money creation to the western banking system. The facts have never been taught in most university economics departments, and are indeed generally obscured, as described by Professor Werner above. Nevertheless, for more than two centuries, many of those who came to understand this problem have written about it, as shown above. Many more names could be added to the above list, such as historian Lord Acton (1834 – 1902) who famously summarised the problem: "The issue which has swept down the centuries, and which will have to be fought sooner or later, is the people versus the banks", or Henry Ford (1863 - 1947) for his famous explanation that a government that can borrow from banks by signing loan notes can create the same money itself, which would cut the cost of most US public construction projects by half or more. Nobel prize-winning chemist Frederick Soddy (1877 - 1956) wrote several books exposing the problems of the money system; Major Douglas (1879 - 1952) was the first to explain the system of social credit needed to fairly share the wealth resulting from the accumulated industrial knowhow created by past generations of engineers but nowadays appropriated by the financial elites; veteran US congressman Ron Paul managed to persuade his colleagues to pass a law to audit the "Fed" – only to see it fail to be implemented; Pakistan Supreme Court Judge Taqi Usmani, wrote a historic judgement explaining why the entire debt-based western banking system is inherently "Riba", that is immoral, so that Moslems should avoid it, (Usmani, 2001); Japan-based American businessman Bill Totten succinctly explained the fraudulent and unconstitutional control of the monetary system by bankers and proposed a route to reform (Totten, 2010); Stephen Goodson (1948 – 2018) monetary reformer and director of the South African central bank wrote the illuminating "A History of Central Banking & the Enslavement of Mankind" (Goodson, 2014); ex-governor of the Bank of England Mervyn King confirmed that nearly all new money entering circulation in Britain does indeed start as debt to the banking system – not as a free benefit to the government and the people, as it should – as described in detail by Bank of England researchers (MacLeay et al, 2014); the "New Chartist Movement" in Britain is pushing for the adoption of "Magna Carta

2020", which includes the right to debt-free money (Magna Carta, 2020); and others.

The above list of exposes of the dishonesty of the debt-based money system controlled by the central banks – and the silence of the media companies which the perpetrators control – is conclusive: this is the main cause of nearly all of the troubles afflicting the world economy today. No system that preserves either debt-based money or private control of the money system is fit for the purpose of constituting a basis for the world economy in the 21st century and beyond. Consequently, practical policies are urgently needed to enable countries to reduce their vulnerability to the damaging influence of the privately controlled, world-wide, debt-based money system which, more than any other problem, is the underlying cause of continuing poverty, wars, economic instability and financial crises in the world economy.

SUMMARY

The discussion in this chapter has covered the well understood but not widely known problem that most money today is created by privately owned banks as debt to themselves. Clearly contrary to natural justice and to every country's constitution, whether explicit or implicit, the undemocratic influence of hidden manipulators of the financial system over governments has been progressively worsening since before the establishment of the privately-owned "Bank of England" in 1694. A list of some of the significant commentators on this problem, from the third American president to the Bank of England today, is given as evidence of the severity of this problem. Some readers may be surprised to learn that this history is not taught at all in most university economics departments. But it is also barely ever mentioned in the entire western news media, which shows the power of the monetary controllers and the weakness of the press in supposedly holding governments to account, in order to protect the rights of the general public, as is traditionally said to be the role of the "fourth estate". Once understood, it becomes clear that major changes are needed in the monetary system if the world economy is to prosper in coming decades and centuries.

REFERENCES

Belloc, H. (1911). *The Free Press*. https://www.gutenberg.org/files/18018/18018-h/18018-h.htm

Belloc, H. (1912). *The Servile State*. https://openlibrary.org/books/OL7030720M/The_servile_state

Belloc, H. (1936). *An Essay on the Restoration of Property*. https://openlibrary.org/works/OL2132065W/The_restoration_of_property

Brown, E. (2007). *Web of Debt: the Shocking Truth about Our Money System, and How We Can Break Free*. Third Millennium Press.

Brown, E. (2013). *From Austerity to Prosperity: The Public Bank Solution*. Third Millennium Press.

Brown, E. (2019). *Banking on the People: Democratizing Money in the Digital Age*. Third Millennium Press.

Brown, E. (2021). https://ellenbrown.com

Buchanan, J. (1993). *Property as a Guarantor of Liberty. Collected Works. 18*. Liberty Fund.

Buchanan, J. & Wagner, R. (1977). *Democracy in Deficit*. Academic Press.

Cobbett, W. (1817). *Paper Against Gold, Containing the History and Mystery of the Bank of England, the Funds, the Debt, the Sinking Fund, the Bank Stoppage, the Lowering and the Raising of the Value of Paper-Money; and Showing that Taxation, Pauperism, Poverty, Misery and Crimes Have All Increased and Ever Must Increase, With a Funding System*. https://archive.org/details/paperagainstgold15cobbrich/page/n3/mode/2up

Cobbett, W. (1824). *A History of the Protestant Reformation in England and Ireland*. https://archive.org/details/cu31924029245524/page/n9/mode/2up?ref=ol&view=theater

Federal Reserve System. (2021). https://www.federalreserve.gov/releases/z1/dataviz/dfa/distribute/table

Goodson, S. (2014). *A History of Central Banking & the Enslavement of Mankind*. Black House Publishing.

Grant, V. (2012). https://www.youtube.com/watch?v=Bx5Sc3vWefE

Magna Carta. (2020). www.universal-community-trust.org/mc2020

Martens, P. Martens, R. (2019). https://wallstreetonparade.com/2019/11/these-are-the-banks-that-own-the-new-york-fed-and-its-money-button

McLeay, M., Radia, A., & Thomas, R. (2014). Money Creation in the Modern Economy. *Bank of England Quarterly Bulletin*. https://www.bankofengland.co.uk/-/media/boe/files/quarterly-bulletin/2014/money-creation-in-the-modern-economy.pdf

Mullins, E. (1952). *Secrets of the Federal Reserve*. Bridger House.

Ricardo, D. (1816). Proposals for an Economical and Secure Currency, with Observations on the Profits of the Bank of England, as they Regard the Public and the Proprietors of Bank Stock. Academic Press.

Ricardo, D. (1817). Principles of Political Economy. Academic Press.

Roberts, P. (2019). *The American economy RIP*. https://www.paulcraigroberts.org/2019/10/21/the-american-economy-rip

Smith, A. (1775). *An Inquiry into the Nature and Causes of the Wealth of Nations*. Academic Press.

Still, B. (2021). https://www.themoneymasters.com

Totten, B. (2010). *The Truth about Anglo-Saxon Capitalism*. Toyo Keizai. (in Japanese)

Usmani, T. (2001). *Text of the Historic Judgement on Riba 23 December 1999*. Percetakan Zafar Sdn Bhd.

Werner, R. (2015). A Lost Century in Economics: Three Theories of Banking and the Conclusive Evidence. *International Review of Financial Analysis, 46*, 361–379. doi:10.1016/j.irfa.2015.08.014

Werner, R. (2020). *Shifting from Central Planning to a Decentralised Economy: Do We Need Central Banks?* https://professorwerner.org/shifting-from-central-planning-to-a-decentralised-economy

Werner, R. (2021). https://professorwerner.org

Zarlenga, S. (2002). *The Lost Science of Money*. American Monetary Institute.

Zucman, G. (2019). *Global Wealth Inequality. Annual Review of Economics*. Bureau of Economic Research. doi:10.3386/w25462

Chapter 4
Fiat Money Is "Riba," Which Islam Forbids

ABSTRACT

This chapter describes another fundamental criticism of the Western economic system – that from Islamic economics. This is included not because the author is advocating for Islamic economics, but because Islamic economists generally have a clearer understanding of the fundamental dishonesty of the Western monetary system than mainstream Western economists, who almost entirely ignore this glaring flaw at the heart of the Western economic system. Having forbidden interest-bearing loans, like Islam, for its first 1600 years, Christianity relaxed its rules, and thereby lowered its guard against the "money power," which is now running rampant in what was once "Christendom." Recent collaboration between Islamic economists and "dissident" Western economists is very promising.

INTRODUCTION

"[We are now in the] final stage of a fraudulent monetary system designed to impose complete financial slavery upon mankind." Sheik Imran Hosein (Hosein, 2007)

Although the criticisms discussed in the two previous chapters are sufficient to explain why the current US dollar-based economic system is losing its international influence and popularity, there is yet another direction from

DOI: 10.4018/978-1-7998-8302-9.ch004

which unrelenting criticism of the half-century of inconvertible, debt-based, paper dollars (and paper euros, pounds, yen and other *fiat* currencies) has come. This is from the Islamic world, comprising a fifth of the world population, which forbids all activities which are judged to be "Riba" – that is, a dishonest use of money – and considers unbacked paper money to be inherently fraudulent, and so "Riba". As the Christian church also did for more than 1,600 years, Islam still today prohibits the charging of interest on loans, compound interest, and related financial devices, which are considered to exploit most people's ignorance of financial risks, and are hence "Riba".

This topic is discussed here not in order to introduce religious issues, but because, as an unfortunate matter of fact, the great majority of the work of "western" economists simply ignores the dishonesty of the debt-based monetary system controlled by privately-owned banks, which is the underlying cause of most economic problems such as poverty, unemployment and worsening inequality, as discussed in Chapter 3. By contrast, Islamic economists openly recognize this fundamental problem, and though their body of work is much smaller than that of the "mainstream" economics profession, their objective is to cure it. The small number of "dissident" western economists have the same aim, although they take a different approach, primarily to return the power of money creation to governments as the representatives of their citizens, without aiming to eliminate the practice of lending at interest.

Refusing to participate in activities that involve interest-bearing debts restricts Islamic finance to a subset of all investment activities, but is not otherwise incompatible with "western" economics or capitalism. Many western financial companies nowadays offer "Shariah-compliant" financial services, which have grown to several percent of the world market. In particular it is not incompatible with mainstream western finance, which might also be called "post-Christian" finance, having evolved in the western countries which achieved scientific and technological leadership under Christendom. Moreover, in recent decades, the "financialization" of the western economic system has given ever greater political and economic influence to banks and other financial companies, which also use financial derivatives to profit from less financially sophisticated customers, including various levels of government and consumer services. This would not be allowed if western anti-monopoly laws and regulations to protect investors were honestly applied and infringements prosecuted, but this is generally no longer the case today (Martens & Martens, 2021).

4.1 USURY FORBIDDEN IN ISLAMIC ECONOMICS

It is no more than common sense that being able to borrow money is extremely valuable in enabling people to improve their lives by, for example, buying a house or starting a new business, and hence facilitating economic growth. Islamic economics supports this, but insists that the lender must share in the borrower's risk. That is, Islam considers it to be unjust that a business failure that may occur through no fault of the entrepreneur (such as due to an earthquake, or having their business "locked down" by government), should ruin the hard-working borrower, while the lender can still demand that their loan be repaid in full.

Although this history may be unfamiliar to people living in OECD countries today, it should be remembered that Christianity too forbade "usury" – that is, lending at interest – until the 17th century, when the meaning of the word was revised to mean charging an excessively high rate of interest. As an example of this, in Shakespeare's plays written in the early 17th century, Christians are still forbidden to lend money at interest.

The reason for this ban in both Christianity and Islam was because, thousands of years ago, it was found that permitting interest-bearing loans inevitably led to ever-growing numbers of people falling into "debt slavery" to money-lenders, from which they could not escape. This source of extreme injustice caused irreparable damage to society as a whole. In those days loans were typically at interest-rates as high as 40% per year, at which rate the original loan doubled in just two years – and continued to compound at the same rate! At such a high rate of interest, a small amount of bad luck could trap a person into having to work for the rest of their life with no hope of getting free from debt. Consequently, religious and political leaders understood that permitting money-lenders to take advantage in this way of unsuspecting people – most of whom were both illiterate and innumerate – was dangerously destructive of humane society, and so it was defined as a sin in both Christian and Islamic countries: morally wrong under any circumstances.

However, the use of money, and services enabling people to borrow money for various purposes, is very helpful for economic growth. So the problem of debt-slavery led to various policies being used to prevent this social disaster. One such remedy reportedly used in ancient Egypt and elsewhere was to declare a debt "Jubilee" every 7 years, whereby all debts were cancelled, releasing all debtors from their control by creditors. The policy adopted by both Christianity and Islam of forbidding "usury", the charging of interest on loans, was an alternative way to reduce the risk of people falling into unrepayable debt.

However, as the centuries passed and economic growth accelerated, creating more opportunities for profitable investment, Christianity bent to the pressures of economic competition and watered down its hitherto outright ban on interest-bearing loans, permitting them on condition that the rate of interest was not excessively high, or "usurious". By contrast, Islamic scholars maintained their fundamental rule that, in order to preserve long-term social justice, a lender must always participate in the borrower's risk, and should not be able to profit even when the borrower's project fails through no fault of their own.

Islam is capitalistic, in that it strongly endorses the value of entrepreneurship, enabling those who work hard and productively to become rich and contribute to society. However, like Christianity in its heyday, it considered that banning interest-bearing loans was the best way to avoid the major social problems caused by permitting an ever-widening gap between rich and poor, and between financiers and everyone else – as is seen to an ever more extreme extent in the rich countries in recent decades.

The gradual concentration of an ever greater share of the wealth of most OECD countries in the hands of a tiny group of billionaires has contributed greatly to the creation of a growing underclass of increasingly disaffected people in many of the rich countries today, including growing numbers of poor and homeless. US history has been described as a ceaseless battle between democracy and plutocracy – even ex-President Jimmy Carter has stated his opinion that the USA is no longer a democracy, but has become a plutocracy, in which the government is very largely controlled by rich people behind the scenes. Certainly the USA's lax campaign finance laws enable companies and rich individuals to make very large contributions to politicians, for which they expect a return.

Islam's condemnation of all financial practices that are "Riba" includes the system of "fractional reserve banking", whereby money is created from nothing by private banks as interest-bearing loans to be repaid to themselves, which is a major source of the long-term trend to impoverish the general public, while further enriching the already very rich.

Under Islamic economics, in order that investors should share in the risks of the investments in which they are participating, all investment must take the form of "equity", whereby the investor shares in the project's risk, and cannot profit if the project fails. Although this may not sound very different from western banking, in practice it is much more difficult for banks, for whom loans at interest are relatively easy to evaluate and manage. Evaluating credit-worthiness for personal loans is nowadays even largely automated via credit-scoring computer algorithms. By contrast, assessing the risk of a business venture is more complex and time-consuming, requiring expert opinion, and is still very uncertain. As a result of this difficulty, many supposedly Islamic financial institutions in fact operate like western institutions, using different terminology but basically charging interest. Supporters of Islamic economics are trying to develop a monetary system that avoids all such flaws.

4.2 "USURY" LESS DAMAGING TODAY THAN IN THE PAST

Today Christian churches still criticise the use of "usury", in principle – but the word has come to mean charging excessively high interest-rates, like "loan sharks". It is only fair to recognise that the danger of debts driving people into slavery is much less today, at least in the richer countries, for three reasons.

4.2.1 Low Interest-Rates

Loans at interest today are far more tolerable than they were many centuries ago, when an interest-rate of 40% per year was unexceptional. By contrast, modern interest-rates are only about one tenth of this – and in recent years they have fallen even lower – close to zero – in many countries, reducing the rate at which compound interest grows, and thereby making loan repayments far less burdensome and dangerous than in the past.

4.2.2 Bankruptcy Laws

The invention and implementation of the legal concept of "bankruptcy", including both corporate bankruptcy and personal bankruptcy, enable a person or company to escape from unpayable debts, albeit at the cost of being reduced to bare poverty through losing almost all their possessions. However, bankrupts are then free to rebuild their lives – and many do so successfully. As a result of the introduction of bankruptcy laws, even "predatory" lenders have to assess the ability of their debtors to repay their loans more accurately – and to suffer losses if they drive their debtors into bankruptcy.

4.2.3 Welfare Systems

In all rich countries today, there is some form of social welfare "safety net" to protect the poor from becoming actually destitute. While these policies vary between countries and from time to time, in the rich countries today there is no "debt slavery" as occurred in the past – except illegally – and hence this risk is no longer an unanswerable reason to forbid all interest-bearing loans.

4.3 ISLAMIC ECONOMIC REVIVAL

There has been a revival of Islamic economics in recent years, due in part to support from greatly enriched oil-producing Islamic countries, and in part due to the development of computer systems that make the more complex calculations needed for Islamic financial services easier. As Islamic financial resources grow in scale to become a significant part of the world financial system, there are still major unresolved controversies, especially concerning financial "derivatives". However the basic stance is not controversial: western finance is "Riba" because it involves interest-bearing debts, but above all because the entire monetary system has been changed in recent centuries to depend on privately-issued, debt-based, *fiat* money. Clear-eyed Islamic scholars describe this radical and unconstitutional change of the monetary system in blunt terms that "mainstream" western economists are, sadly, incapable of.

In 1999, Pakistan Supreme Court Judge Taqi Usmani published his authoritative judgement that the western financial system in its entirety is "Riba", since the great majority of the money on which it is based enters the economy as interest-bearing debts to bankers who have unconstitutionally usurped the power to issue money from governments. Moreover the money created is neither an inherently valuable asset such as gold or silver, nor a legitimate means for government to pay for public services, as occurred in the past, but outright theft from the citizenry on a massive scale (Usmani, 2001).

Professor Akameel Meera has written extensively about the privately-controlled, western, debt-based monetary system being the most important source of "Riba" in the world today, and has led research into practical efforts to resist it, notably including reviving gold convertibility of currency (Meera ed., 2013). Among other achievements, Meera and colleagues developed the IGENS system (Interest-free, Gold-based, Electronic Netting System) as a practical, modern means of obtaining the benefits of gold convertibility without needing government to formally implement a rigid gold standard.

Islamic scholar Imran Hosein has written clear descriptions of the fraudulent nature of the "western" monetary system, and how it inevitably leads to an ever-widening gap between rich and poor (Hosein, 2007). He also explains the protection against this result that the use of gold and silver as money can provide, as taught in Islam since its origination.

The world economy is nowadays threatened by the collapse of the unstable "Riba" financial system led by Wall Street, and more and more researchers are adding to the body of Islamic economic analysis in order to prepare alternatives to existing monetary policies. In parallel, the number of western "economic dissidents", that is, informed critics of "mainstream" economics, has grown in recent years, leading to unique collaboration with Islamic economists.

4.4 INTER-CULTURAL COLLABORATION AGAINST DEBT-BASED MONEY

As a result of the developments described in this and preceding chapters, a fascinating movement over recent years has been the rapprochement between Islamic economists and the growing body of "alternative" western economists who recognise the dishonesty of the debt-based money system and its innumerable apologists in the academic community. The astonishing fragility of the financial system underlying the US economy – supposedly the greatest economy in the world – was revealed by the 2008 crash originating in Wall Street. That it was predicted by dissident western economists, such as in (Pettifor, 2006), but not by the thousands of university professors of economics, and commentators in the mainstream news media, is a huge feather in their cap. It is also *prima facie* evidence that current economic difficulties are not a mystery too complex for human understanding, but are the result of fundamental flaws in the monetary system that are well understood, and could be remedied if the vested interests which benefit from them did not prevent this.

The most basic idea of science is that supporters of a particular theory make predictions, and are judged by whether these turn out to be true or false. The legions of professional economists working in universities and the financial world were shown to be wrong, and the three criticisms discussed above were shown to be correct: the debt-based *fiat* dollar, of which the supply is dependent on unelected bankers rather than on governments or market forces, is not sufficiently stable or honest to provide a reliable, permanent basis for world economic growth over the coming decades and longer. As a result of a century of over-issue, the real value of the US dollar has fallen more than 98% since the creation of the privately owned Federal Reserve System in 1913, greatly enriching the "insiders" who control the system, and this decline is currently accelerating. A more stable, more reliable alternative, immune to manipulation by the powerful financial operators who control the current unjust western system, is urgently needed to enable peaceful economic growth to continue to improve the lives of the whole world population.

4.4.1 The First Three RIFCONs

From 2010 to 2012, a unique conference took place annually in Kuala Lumpur: the "Riba-Free Conference" (RIFCON), which combined leading scholars and practitioners of Islamic economics and "dissident" western economists who understand that the greatest source of "Riba" is debt-based money, which is the underlying cause of most economic problems in the world today. The three RIFCONs comprised presentations and panel-discussions by a range of scholars and practitioners from both Islamic economics and critics of mainstream western economics. These included long-term Prime Minister of Malaysia Tun Dr Mahathir Mohamed, Professor Umar Ibrahim Vadillo, pioneer of the Islamic Gold Dinar movement, Mr. Parvez Nasim, creator of a Riba-free home-financing model and chairman of Islamic co-operative housing companies in Canada, author Professor Ahmed Akameel Meera, and Maulana Imran Hosein, leading interpreter of Islamic political economy. Representatives of the "dissident west" included Ellen Brown, Founder and President of the Public Banking Institute, Bill Still, creator of "The Money Masters" and other videos which expose the dishonesty of the western debt-based money system, Dr Rodney Shakespeare, head of the UK Christian Council for Monetary Justice and visiting professor of Binary Economics at Trisakti University in Jakarta, Hugo Salinas Price, billionaire advocate of gold and silver currency, and others. RIFCONs 2 and 3 also included presentations by the author and Jamil Ahmed, presenting the Grondona system and explaining its potential contribution to solving the world's major monetary and economic problem.

Unfortunately, due to the organisers' uncompromisingly honest viewpoint, the RIFCONs did not receive sponsorship from most Islamic financial institutions, which to differing degrees still provide services that are "Riba". Consequently the continuation of the series was postponed after the first three RIFCONs. In view of the major problems facing the world economy, including particularly countries that wish to implement genuine Islamic economic policies, it is very desirable that new sponsors enable the RIFCONs to be resumed, so as to support further dialogue between the complementary viewpoints from around the world presented at the first three RIFCONs. There is still much to be learned about new opportunities and means of correcting the glaring faults of the post-Bretton Woods "non-system", which for a fifth of the world population is also "Riba".

4.5 SUMMARY OF FLAWS OF US DOLLAR-BASED SYSTEM

A country's money system is the foundation of its economy, and of its potential for economic growth, which is the source of improvements in the people's standard of living. The US dollar-based monetary system, which is currently still the basis of most international trade, has been weakening since 1971 when its real underpinning was removed, and it is now dependent on the privately owned Federal Reserve System continually creating trillions of *fiat* dollars in order to enable giant financial companies to pay their debts. This continually reduces the value of the US dollar through inflation, thereby stealing the savings of people throughout the world who use dollars as a store of value.

Although it was not clear to most economists at the time, once gold convertibility of the US dollar ended in 1971, the Bretton Woods system was no longer sustainable, specifically because the dollar no longer had an "anchor" to preserve its real value. Consequently, the dollar's value in real terms was vulnerable to continual reduction as there was no longer any check on the ability of the government and financial world to increase the supply of dollars in a manner that is entirely opaque to most of the population. It thus became only a matter of time before the system's unstable condition became economically destructive, not least because the wealthy are much better able to preserve their wealth from inflation than the general public, as more and more Americans are finally becoming aware.

In addition to its increasing instability, the US financial system's popularity is also falling, due to the US government's growing habit of bullying other countries by applying sanctions to them when their governments fail to obey "orders" from Washington. This includes the American "order" to Germany and Russia to stop building the "Nordstream 2" pipeline to supply gas from Russia to Europe, its "freezing" of US dollar bank accounts of foreign companies, governments and their staff so that their owners cannot use them, and threats to shut other countries out of the "SWIFT" system for secure international inter-bank payments. These "neo-imperialist" actions understandably make governments of other countries less and less keen to depend on a US-controlled monetary system in future.

So what is the next phase in humans' search for a sound foundation for our economic systems? What is needed is an honest, transparent, stable and sustainable system. That is, one that will preserve the real value of widely used monetary units over more than a few decades – and will not end in injustice, chaos and wars yet again. Ideally, a monetary unit should be clearly defined and permanently reliable, like physical units such as the kilogram, metre and Watt. People who have experienced nothing but the inflation and economic instability of recent decades throughout their lives may think this is unobtainable, but it is actually straightforward to improve on the present situation. However, in order to be internationally acceptable as well as sustainable, any system must avoid the criticisms outlined in this and earlier chapters. In Chapter 5 we look at the main alternatives that are being widely discussed, but which all turn out to be lacking when considered in detail.

SUMMARY

Islamic economists criticize the western economic system for its deceiving the general public about the nature of its money, which is unbacked "*fiat*" currency created as interest-bearing debt by the privately-controlled banking system, thereby giving enormous political power to unelected financiers. Although most of the world economy does not follow the Islamic rule forbidding interest-bearing loans, the Islamic viewpoint concerning the problems of the western economic world is more accurate than that of "western" economists, for whom the subject is literally taboo. These problems are the inevitable result of governments dishonestly permitting the privately-owned banking system to create new debt-based money, contrary both to their constitutions and to natural justice. In order to provide a permanent, stable basis for the world economy, a system is needed which answers the criticisms of the existing system discussed in the past three chapters.

REFERENCES

Hosein, I. (2007). *The Gold Dinar and Silver Dirham: Islam and the Future of Money*. Masjid Jami'ah.

Martens, P. & Martens, R. (2021). wallstreetonparade.com

Meera, K. (Ed.). (2013). *Real Money: Money and Payment Systems from an Islamic Perspective*. IIUM Press Malaysia.

Pettifor, A. (2006). *Real World Economic Outlook. The Legacy of Globalization: Debt and Deflation*. New Economics Foundation.

Usmani, T. (2001). *Text of the Historic Judgement on Riba 23 December 1999*. Percetakan Zafar Sdn Bhd.

ADDITIONAL READING

Meera, K. (2004). *The Theft of Nations: Returning to Gold*. Suban Jaya: Pelanduk Publications Sdn Bhd.

Chapter 5
What Could or Should Replace Existing Monetary Arrangements?

ABSTRACT

In this chapter, three main approaches to creating a new, more stable monetary system, which is under wide discussion today, are considered in turn. First, the feasibility of reviving the use of gold as backing for currencies is a never-ending controversy, kept very much alive by those who argue that "In a crisis, there is nothing else." Second, the rapidly growing use of the internet for decentralised finance or "DeFi" services is offering the public a growing range of new, reliable, low-cost financial services. Among these is the use of "crypto-currencies," which are growing rapidly but which still suffer severe instability and uncertainty. Third, the world's central banks are developing their own internet-based currencies, known as central bank digital currencies (CBDC). However, these are unlike private crypto-currencies since their use would give government control over all transactions – a degree of power which would risk enabling tyranny.

INTRODUCTION

In the previous chapters we have seen that the world monetary system is facing a turning-point as the US dollar loses its earlier dominant role, and so decisions must be made about how it is to operate in future. Most international

DOI: 10.4018/978-1-7998-8302-9.ch005

trade is still accounted in *fiat* US dollars, with which every independent country has a floating exchange-rate. As a consequence, the relative values of all currencies are subject to volatility in foreign-exchange markets – as well as to manipulation by large players such as major financial corporations, and including the USA and other countries' governments. As the economic dominance of the USA declines, and more countries find the use of the US dollar less satisfactory, alternatives to the current system are being widely investigated and implemented. A major aspect of much discussion about alternative monetary systems is the degree to which different proposals should be centralized or decentralized.

5.1 CENTRALIZATION OR DECENTRALIZATION

This dichotomy is indeed one of the major issues discussed in comparing different possible monetary systems, as well as more generally in comparing different forms of government, and particularly different forms of democracy. Broadly speaking, individual freedom is generally best served by decentralizing political power to the maximum extent practical (although the meaning of the word "practical" in such discussions is itself the subject of debate). As a rule, as larger and larger political systems become centralized, from town to county or state, to nation to supranational organisations, the overall system becomes less and less responsive to people at lower levels, while the possibility of meaningful democratic control, transparency, or redress for wrongs that occur becomes weaker and more diluted.

Since the Bretton Woods system was established, the growth of world trade, which has contributed greatly to economic growth, has been aided by international treaties. However, as international corporations have grown larger and larger relative to the size of national governments, nowadays having annual revenues of even $100 Billion or more, their lobbying and provision of expertise and personnel have led to their dominating the process of formulating trade and other policies. In parallel, the reporting of these activities in the news media, which are also owned by large multinational corporations, becomes more and more biased towards supporting these powerful vested interests.

In the years following the end of WW2, increasing international political cooperation in various fora also led to a trend towards "internationalization" of policy making, based on the argument that many problems were beyond the powers of governments of individual countries to solve. This led to government staff developing expertise in working within international organizations, and the gradual subordination of national governments to international organizations. This trend of internationalization has recently been superceded by the idea of "globalization", implying the development of international cooperation in various fields to "one size fits all" policies for the whole world. These are now continually advocated by the news media and large "global" corporations, which coordinate in advocating globalization as a means to facilitate their operations, regardless of different countries' preferences.

However, another decades-long trend that has grown in parallel with internationalization / globalization is the trend towards an ever-widening gap between rich and poor in most countries. The "Occupy Wall Street" movement, which started in New York City in late 2011, maintained a permanent demonstration for several weeks, arguing for greater recognition of the rights of the 99% of the population being impoverished by the richest 1% – until it was violently suppressed by the New York police! The trend towards worsening inequality and lessening freedom of speech has continued since then. This has given rise to the phenomenon of wealthy cosmopolitan elites continually defaming those resisting globalization as petty, narrow-minded nationalists, similar to the disdain with which "city slickers" traditionally cheat "country bumpkins", who are unsophisticated in financial matters, and so easily defrauded.

The argument that "nationalism", "regionalism" and other alternatives to globalization are out-dated, since no single country or region is able to decide policies for itself in the modern world, and so it is now time to implement a single new global system, faces the problems of lack of evidence and counter-examples. As mentioned in Chapter 1, membership of the EU, and more particularly the use of the Euro instead of their national currencies, has been very costly for smaller EU member countries, which cannot create Euros, as they were previously able to issue their own national currency. This has understandably added to popular distrust of the unelected elites working for international organizations, who typically receive large, tax-free salaries, generous inflation-linked pensions, and many other privileges.

The strength of this anti-globalist sentiment, and the growing division between the general public and the "global elites", is visible from the majority vote of the British people to leave the EU – while a majority of British politicians, who could look forward to sinecures within the EU system, supported continuing membership! The wide popularity of President Trump's "anti-globalist" economic and social policies is further evidence that globalist policies are being introduced in spite of public resistance, rather than as a result of the public being convinced that they would be beneficial and timely. Democratically elected governments should clearly not permit globalization to be imposed on their countries by unelected bureaucrats, powerful corporations and billionaires in either their own or foreign countries against the majority wishes of their people.

The planning for a single centralized "Great Reset" of human society as a whole by the self-selected, rich globalist members of the "World Economic Forum" (WEF) is an example of this. Among the many flaws in this idea, it would of course be contrary to the fundamental reason for the unique success of "western" societies, and of many others – namely that people are most productive if they are free to choose their own path through life – both individually, and collectively in companies, and via popularly elected leaders who represent them politically – not to have these decided for them by unelected "technocrats" from their own or from other countries.

Since the WEF is not a governmental body, it is not clear what is the objective of their advice: in spite of the "philanthropic" public image that the WEF projects, there is no reason to doubt that their plans are self-interested. That is, their work is intended to enrich themselves at the expense of the general public. As such, the WEF should have no influence over political leaders. Unfortunately it is clear that they have access to many leading politicians – including prime ministers and presidents, in the OECD and elsewhere. Why these few megalomaniacs have such access, and how this could possibly be good for the billions of citizens for whom these political leaders supposedly work, are unclear.

Among other effects, the WEF's activities have led to the preparation of counter-proposals for alternatives to their plans for a "Great Reset", such as that known as the "Greater Reset" project, which is specifically designed to benefit the general public, independent businesses and farmers (Greater reset, 2021). By contrast, the giant multi-national corporations which support the WEF's schemes, praise them in the monopolistic news media which they control, and ignore all other possibilities.

On the matter of monetary reform, it is clearly important that the full range of possibilities are openly and widely discussed before countries commit to any new system. In view of the increasingly pressing need for change, a range of ideas need to be considered, which differ in various ways, including different degrees of centralization or decentralization. In the following, the three main possibilities for new currency systems are discussed. This is not a comprehensive survey of systems that could follow the end of the "post-Bretton Woods" era, and does not aim to choose between alternatives being planned or under discussion. It is intended to be sufficient to understand three major approaches in outline, and to clarify the specific function which is lacking in all of them, namely a reliable and widely acceptable means of stabilizing and clarifying the real value of different currencies.

5.2 A REVIVED GOLD STANDARD

Gold's historic role as the most widely valued financial asset has continued for thousands of years already. Under the "gold standards" used in many countries for several decades or even centuries, gold coins were used directly as money. Under the "classical" western gold standard which ended in 1914, gold coins were used as cash to pay wages and to buy goods in shops, while paper bank-notes could be freely exchanged for gold coins on demand. Later, under the Bretton Woods "gold exchange standard", gold coins were no longer used as cash, but gold bullion was used for settling inter-governmental debts at the fixed rate of $35 per ounce of gold, until 1971. This gave the governments of other countries confidence to maintain a fixed exchange-rate with the US dollar: without this assurance they would have baulked at the idea of allowing the USA to buy anything in their countries with dollars which they could merely print at will. Since the end of dollar convertibility in 1971 gold has continued to be an important, though unofficial, financial asset, and its value continues to rise in proportion to the loss in value of paper currencies, due to their ever-inflating supply, though subject to major fluctuations over periods of years.

A major reason why the monetary role of gold continues, despite governments formally ignoring it, is because gold and other precious metals, unlike all paper-based financial assets, including paper currency notes, do not depend on someone else honouring a contract. That is, unlike paper notes or securities, or digital financial assets, the possession of physical gold, and its use as a monetary asset, does not depend on someone else accepting printed pieces of paper (or related digital data) as valuable. Gold's value arises simply from the fact that many people want to possess it, because they believe – correctly, as it happens, for the past few thousand years – that many other people also value it. The reasons for this are well-known: the supply of gold is very limited, and cannot be expanded rapidly; it does not deteriorate (nor even discolor, like silver); and it can be easily divided into small units. Over the recent decades of US dollars being inconvertible, Russia, China and other countries have been accumulating thousands of tons of gold as financial reserves, at around $50 million per ton at time of writing. This is in preference to holding US dollars or other US securities such as government bonds, of which the value depends on the US federal government – which is not true of gold – and could fall to zero in a crisis if the US government decided not to honour them.

As an important fact about changes now underway, including that gold seems likely to play a greater role in future international monetary arrangements, the Bank for International Settlements (BIS), known as the "central bank's central bank", made a historic move in March 2019 by upgrading gold to become a "Tier one asset" in central banks' balance sheets. Until this new rule, the only "Tier one assets" were US dollars. Since then, member central banks are allowed to value their reserves of gold at their market price, making gold a more valuable asset for the banks to hold, and thereby leading more central banks to buy more gold reserves.

It is important to recognise that, even if the use of gold as a major monetary asset is revived, its practical use will be largely performed via certificates or contract notes, either on paper or nowadays more commonly digitally, confirming that the bearer possesses the amount of gold in question. This of course raises all the traditional questions of whether and how these certificates can be trusted. In this context, it is worth remembering that even the "classical" gold standard overseen by the Bank of England in its heyday in the 19th century, was said to be "like a swan": its operation appeared to be effortless, but in practice its managers were continually "paddling hard" to keep the system functioning. This involved wide geopolitical negotiations – notably borrowing and lending gold between central banks of the gold-standard countries in order to reduce their vulnerability to speculative attacks – which was needed in order to keep the system stable since each country's note issue was only partially backed by gold – typically about 40%. This was generally sufficient to enable any central bank to supply gold for its notes whenever demanded – the major discipline being that, as its gold reserves fell, it would raise interest-rates to make holding its currency more attractive.

However, present-day proposals to revive an international gold standard face a number of serious problems. If all money was to be represented by stocks of gold held in bank reserves, the amount of gold required would be many times the total amount available at current prices. The total amount of gold in the world is less than 200,000 tons, that is about 7 billion ounces. The US "M2" money supply alone is about $30 Trillion as of mid-2021, while world GDP is several times this. Hence even a fractional reserve system would need a gold price of about $10,000 per ounce, which would require gold to be revalued by a factor of five times or more in order to provide partial cover for just a few major currencies. Even if feasible, this alone would cause major shifts in the economic system due to the very uneven ownership of gold, making its implementation unattractive to many countries.

In addition, any fractional reserve system would be vulnerable to speculative attack, not least by geopolitical competitors, who would have essentially unlimited "*fiat*" funds at their disposal. This would be similar to the way in which the gold market today is distorted by the futures market in "paper gold" contracts, of which the turnover is one hundred times more than the "spot" or cash market for "physical gold". Consequently, a realistic attempt to implement a modern gold standard would be very different from the ideal of each country independently making their currency convertible into gold, but would require detailed international agreements between many countries. This removes it from serious consideration as an ideally "practical" policy such as any sovereign national government could implement independently in terms of their own existing currency.

Another major argument against reviving gold convertibility can be appreciated by considering the complementary viewpoint: adopting a policy to stabilize the real value of money in terms of gold can equally be described as "adjusting interest-rates and other aspects of monetary policy so as to stabilize the market price of gold". Since the market price of gold is very volatile on occasions, and generally not in synchrony with market prices of industrial commodities, it is likely that this would, on occasions, entail volatile and seriously non-optimal monetary policy, which would in turn revive the traditional complaints which have ended the gold standard repeatedly in the past.

From the point of view of economic growth, although the gold standard was good for those with savings, including the very wealthy who strongly supported "sound money" policies, it had an undesirable bias towards deflation. Although falling prices are good for consumers, they make life hard for businesses, which must continually cut costs, and so also require wages to be cut periodically, which is very unpopular with employees. This deflationary bias is easily understood: when a country's gold reserves were falling, after doing what it could to borrow gold from other central banks, the central bank was obliged to raise interest-rates in order to make its currency more attractive relative to holding gold, which made business more difficult and slowed economic growth. But when a country's gold reserves were rising, the central bank was not obliged to reduce interest-rates progressively, and was likely to let its gold reserves grow, with a bias towards caution. As a result, the stability achieved by the gold standard came at a high price, by keeping economic growth at a pace below what was possible.

There are nevertheless many supporters of a return to some form of gold standard, on the grounds that, despite its flaws, it would be "better than nothing" in restraining governments from devaluing their national currencies in their efforts to retain power. The dismal decline in the real value of the US dollar since 1971 is striking evidence that, despite astonishing progress in innumerable fields of technology, there has been no progress in implementing effective rules to ensure transparency and discipline in government – notably in the country that currently provides the currency that underpins the world economic system.

Another issue that shows the need for caution is that, among holders of gold, there are apparently unknown holders of some 30,000 tons, representing about 30% of the total quantity of gold involved in trade, which is about half the total known quantity of 200,000 tons. This makes the market price of gold vulnerable to unpredictable shocks and/or manipulation, which could be disruptive for countries committed to maintaining convertibility.

In addition to this unending debate, Islamic economics explicitly aims to eventually remonetize gold and silver, which were the traditional forms of "honest money" at the time of Islam's birth, and long before. In order to make progress in this direction, a range of steps have been proposed to gradually increase the use of gold as a financial asset. One of these partial systems is that which former Prime Minister of Malaysia, Mahathir Mohamed has repeatedly advocated, namely the development of an international gold-backed currency for settling trade imbalances within Asia. A more detailed version of this proposal is to use payments in gold to settle net trade flows between countries which agree with the long-term objective of increasing the role of gold in the monetary system (Meera ed, 2013). For these proposals to succeed, several countries would need to implement this system together.

Ultimately, perhaps the strongest argument for reviving the monetary role of gold is that, in a crisis, "There is nothing else", as discussed at length in (Rickards, 2016). No other monetary asset has preserved its value for thousands of years, and no other method has been able to restrain governments from debasing their currency for decades and even centuries. Moreover, if and when a currency fails through hyper-inflation, so that no one will accept it in payment, the only asset that a government may possess which may be accepted as payment for imports may well be gold. Consequently, whether formally used as backing for currencies or not, gold will surely continue to be widely held by both individuals and governments as a "last resort".

5.3 PRIVATE DIGITAL CURRENCIES

One of the major economic and social phenomena of the present era is surely the continuing rapid evolution of Internet-based services, which continue to have major impacts on innumerable activities around the world. A recent, particularly important innovation is the "distributed ledger" system known as "Blockchain", which achieves unprecedented security of information by creating multiple copies of it, and storing it at multiple different addresses in the overall network. This ensures that information such as a transaction and its history cannot be intercepted, distorted or controlled by any unauthorized person. Based on this, a growing range of Blockchain-based "DeFi" (Decentralized Finance) services are creating innumerable new business opportunities, due to their being essentially unhackable. This innovation enables previously impossible services such as "intelligent contracts" in which a contract document is irreversibly linked to other unalterable documents ensuring and controlling its implementation, such as property deeds and their entire legal history. The ability to use ever-improving "Artificial Intelligence" (AI) systems, which rapidly scan far more data than humans can, in such services is another major innovation. In addition to making such new services available, DeFi reduces the cost and time needed for many different types of transactions by eliminating the need for "middlemen" such as bankers, lawyers and accountants, either for expertise or for security, including through maintaining a chain of custody, which can be done automatically by Blockchain systems.

Perhaps the most famous use of Blockchain to date is the creation of new, Blockchain-based currencies – widely known as "crypto-currencies" – not controlled by any government, but issued by private companies. The first and most famous of such digital currencies is "Bitcoin", of which the total value exceeds $1 Trillion at time of writing. Although this and other crypto-currencies still face important "teething troubles", including serious volatility in their value, they are already transforming the financial world by providing a wide range of new services, which are expected to continue to grow and spread worldwide.

One important reason for the rapid growth of crypto-currencies and other internet-based services is the "network effect", a phenomenon made particularly visible by the use of the internet. The more people who use any network-based service, such as a telephone, the more useful it is for new users, so its use grows exponentially – more rapidly as more users join the network. Additional reasons for the popularity of crypto-currencies include the potential for high speed, anonymity, lower costs than bank charges, independence from any one country, apparent potential for tax evasion, and others. The spread of privately produced and managed crypto-currencies raises fundamental questions about governments' monetary role, and the need for their services. For example, a group of companies which supply goods and services to each other could use crypto-currencies to pay each other, and only the net positions remaining need appear in their accounts, thereby reducing their tax liability.

It is traditionally accepted that a legitimate government has the authority to use force to collect taxes to pay for the services which it provides, most fundamentally defence and justice. Many other popular activities such as basic education, health and welfare services are nowadays also provided by governments in richer countries. However, large budgets are also used for purposes that enrich vested interests which provide large contributions to political campaigns, such as delaying the enforcement of regulations such as anti-monopoly laws, and waging unnecessary wars that enrich weapons makers and banks. This behaviour reduces government's legitimacy and popular support, and encourages the use of crypto-currencies.

In order to collect taxes, governments specify how they may be paid, thereby defining what is to be used as money. At different times in different countries, governments have accepted payments of wheat, rice, hemp or other products as taxes. These were widely replaced by coins made of gold or silver, and later by paper money produced by the government. The range of assets on which taxes are levied has increased in different countries to include property of different sorts, salaries, capital assets, profits, sales, contracts, gifts, inherited wealth and others. If a government collects taxes on financial transactions, then transactions performed in crypto-currencies which are invisible to government cannot be taxed.

All governments nowadays depend to a large extent on taxes: so for this and other reasons, in discussions of new monetary systems, crypto-currencies play a large role. Among many other innovations, much effort is focused on how to make them secure, while others are working hard to hack them. At a time of rapid technological evolution, it is impossible to predict what will be happening even a few years ahead. Even major companies which supply data services over the Internet can come and go within a few years or less, as business models based on software are easily copied, and millions of customers can migrate between Internet platforms offering similar services within a day.

For example, Facebook, Google, Amazon, Youtube, Apple, Twitter and other monopolistic American Internet service companies are imposing unprecedented censorship nowadays on a wide range of historical, political, medical and scientific subjects – including erasing hundreds of millions of users' comments, and tens of thousands of websites and contributions, including even by eminent people such as lawyers, doctors, scientists, and even the President of the USA. In response, new, uncensored news and data-sharing services dedicated to the traditional American values of freedom of speech and freedom of information are rapidly being set up, and attracting tens of millions of new users.

A problem still faced by many crypto-currencies is lack of transparency, which is an important obstacle to potentially large users such as companies putting their trust in the service. This includes the problem of the Bitcoin "whales", that is, the founders and early investors who apparently own large quantities now worth tens of $ Billions, who remain anonymous but who could cause distortions or volatility in Bitcoin's value or operation.

The revolution being brought to many industries by Blockchain-based services is discussed in detail in (Tapscott & Tapscott, 2018). Among many other topics they discuss numerous ways in which the present financial system dominated by banks uses their monopolistic power to extract payments of hundreds of billions of dollars per year for their services, which are now increasingly able to be performed far more quickly, reliably and cheaply via Blockchain services, with no need for intermediation by banks or other financial companies. However, Tapscott & Tapscott do not discuss the fundamental problem of the privately controlled banking system's unconstitutional creation of debt-based money described in Chapter 3, of which the owners are presumably also working hard to avoid losing their centuries-old sinecures of money creation and financial intermediation.

First published in 2016, they also do not discuss Internet-based censorship, which has grown into a fundamental issue in this field at time of writing in 2021. There has been a massive amount written over centuries about how freedom of speech is the ultimate bedrock of civilization, being essential in order for science, engineering, the justice system, business, government, education and other essential social functions to operate honestly and successfully. Consequently, the censorship now implemented by global Internet services, of which the monopolistic roles have been permitted by the US government, is a very serious threat to achieving a reasonable resolution to the problem of what monetary system will replace the present.

Can the Internet be reformed to preserve freedom of speech? Or is the "money power" which is responsible for the current extraordinary and historically unprecedented level of censorship going to be able to enforce global control over enough of the population to keep them trapped in a world of censored news, censored history and monopolised financial services which are highly profitable for its controllers? The "gale of creative destruction" being unleashed by the invention of the Internet and Blockchain services ensures that we cannot today predict the outcome of the present rapidly evolving situation.

Moreover, we may be on the brink of even more fundamental changes. For example, Peneder discusses the rethinking within the economics profession that is being driven by the development of Internet-based digital currencies. He emphasizes the continuity between earlier economic theories of money and the phenomena being realized with crypto-currencies (Peneder, 2021). For example, a century ago Schumpeter had already described the monetary system as being like a single current account in which money was simply the unit used to measure each person's credits and debits: consequently there was no need in principle for physically valuable assets to be used for the monetary unit, as gold was at that time. Peneder argues that the development of digital currencies is no different in principle, but the Internet now makes Schumpeter's vision an actual possibility. We might add that this depends on implementing a secure and fair system that is also socially acceptable – not one that is imposed from above by unknown and unaccountable people.

However, any such system still depends critically on the trust that participants have in the value of the monetary unit. For this reason, the use of different monetary data systems, whether paper, digital or Blockchain-based does not get away from this problem. Without a solution to this problem of how the value of the monetary unit is to be clarified and preserved, there will be periodic loss of confidence in the system which leads to crises and major moves in exchange-rates. The traditional system of real currency convertibility can help to prevent this problem.

Late in his life, Hayek gave his support to the idea of permitting free competition between unregulated private currencies, in the belief that this would lead to more reliable currencies becoming more popular (Hayek, 1976). To a certain extent, the present creation and spread of thousands of new crypto-currencies can be seen as an experiment to this effect. It remains to be seen to what extent such competition will be self-correcting: the clearly apparent tendency for popular Internet-based services to grow into monopolies gives reason for doubt, in view of their managers' success in evading anti-monopoly laws through heavy spending on lobbying politicians. On the other hand, as a promising example of an unpredicted innovation which could have wider application, popular internet-based auction sites like Yahoo and Ebay include a feature whereby users rank each other in their performance of transactions, thereby creating a very reliable, cumulative indicator of each other's reliability as a counter-party.

An important unknown is what further improvements will be made in newer crypto-currencies. Due to advances in computer software, today's new coins have a far greater range of uses than Bitcoin; their transactions are much faster, and they use far less energy. However, as the leader in the race to grow to large scale, Bitcoin has already reached a total value of $1 trillion, and is far better known than any other coins. So it may be that the slow and inefficient Bitcoin may continue to dominate the world of crypto-currencies, as the deliberately inefficient "qwerty" keyword continues its near monopoly, despite all the technological advances available in the 21st century.

5.3.1 Growing Potential of Local Currencies and Public Banks

The invention of the Internet, Blockchain technology and crypto-currencies also create the potential to greatly increase the role of local currencies and public banks, both of which have existed for centuries, with varying degrees of success in different countries. There is an immense literature on the subjects of local or alternative currencies and various forms of public banks, which there is not space to survey here. However, it is clear that the new technologies of the Internet and Blockchain greatly increase the potential contribution of such services to creating a better monetary system in the future.

Although various forms of local currency system have been developed over the centuries, most have remained small-scale, and many have been short-lived, but some have operated for decades. Some have grown large enough to have been treated as a threat by central banks, but most have been ignored by governments as they remained small-scale. However, there would seem to be great potential for collaboration between local currencies via the Internet, with Blockchain providing security of transactions, and even more promisingly enabling collaboration with Public Banks. Consequently, although the potential for evolution of local currencies into crypto-currencies linked to public banks remains unpredictable, as one possibility among many other

"DeFi" services, they seem likely to play a significant role in the future of financial services in various forms.

5.3.2 Risks Facing Crypto-Currencies

A major constraint on the growth of crypto-currencies is that, in parallel with their rapid growth and evolution, they face a number of unique and important risks, of which there is no sign of an early end.

Risk 1: Price Volatility

Most crypto-currencies experience serious volatility in their value, typified by the very public rapid rises and falls of +/- 50% or more in the price of Bitcoin within a few days. Since most crypto-currencies have no guaranteed real value, there is currently great potential for their prices to rise excessively in a "bubble" – that is, to reach a high value due to excessive optimism based on unrealistic expectations about their future growth and success. There is today a wide range of opinions among economic and financial commentators about how much of a bubble crypto-currencies are presently experiencing, and how severe a correction may be likely.

Reasons for optimism about Bitcoin include that it is apparently unique in that the quantity that can be produced is permanently limited, so that increasing demand can only be accommodated by its price rising. It also has first-comer's advantage: by far the most famous of the 10,000 crypto-currencies said to be already in use, it has a powerful marketing advantage. However, the valuation of more than $1 Trillion is divorced from the fact that the amount actually used in transactions is a small fraction of this: the majority is held by people in expectation that it will increase in value. This is the hallmark of a "bubble", going back to the "tulip bubble" in 18th century Holland: most people who bought tulips at high prices had no use for them once the price crashed.

The fact that the maximum quantity of Bitcoin is strictly limited avoids one of the problems of *fiat* currencies, but it also means that Bitcoin itself could not entirely replace an existing currency. This is because, in order to facilitate economic growth, it is far more convenient to use a currency of which the supply can be expanded appropriately – that is, as the market requires – than one of the which the supply cannot expand, which would require continual price deflation in order to accommodate continuing economic growth, which would lead in turn to reductions in wages.

On the other hand, a reason for caution about the future value of Bitcoin is the wave of competition from new cryptocurrencies that can be expected to continue to grow even beyond the 10,000 already in use. In addition to the "attacker's advantage" well-known in business strategy, the fact that Bitcoin is very inefficient in that its transactions use a lot of energy, is an important vulnerability. Moreover, having no guaranteed real value, Bitcoin is not "electronic gold", unlike some other crypto-currencies such as the "stablecoins" of which the real value is specifically defined and maintained in terms of different precious metals.

Risk 2: Security

For financial services, privacy and security from theft or interference are essential. As still new services on the still evolving Internet, it is unclear how truly secure and private crypto-currencies are or can be. It is known that they are being targeted by government decryption services, since governments are understandably concerned that the growing use of crypto-currencies will facilitate tax evasion, which is already a major cost to the great majority of the population, who are law-abiding taxpayers. However, the seriously unstable situation into which the US-led world economy is falling is a strong motivation for many people to try to protect their wealth from inflation, confiscation, or use in ways that they may consider unjust, immoral or unconstitutional.

Truly secure crypto-currencies could be a promising type of asset, although as of today it is not clear that they are possible. This is because currently there is a continuing "arms race" between developers of ever more useful and secure crypto-currencies, and ever more powerful surveillance systems designed to spy on them. Will privacy be able to win the "arms race? For example, another security problem is the use of "backdoors" deliberately built into computer software in order to enable secret access to data without users being able to detect any intrusion. Hence, crypto-currencies must be judged as being still too new to be able to entirely trust.

Another threat is the extreme censorship that is now openly imposed by large-scale Internet service companies, in spite of being contrary to the fundamental human right of Freedom of Speech. Since Freedom of Speech has been critical to the success of the European societies which led the industrial revolution, and yet its suppression is now being allowed and even encouraged by governments, it is currently impossible to be confident that truly trustworthy and transparent crypto-currency systems can be developed and operated, at least in the foreseeable future.

Risk 3: Regulation and Taxation

Another serious risk is that government intervention, at either national or international level, will greatly reduce the demand for and usefulness of crypto-currencies. Indeed, regulation is already being prepared for cryptocurrencies, such as by the US Financial Crimes Enforcement Network (FinCEN), which is the part of the US Treasury Department responsible for policing money laundering and other financial crimes. FinCEN already collects information on US citizens' foreign bank accounts, and on bank deposits or withdrawals of $10,000 or more in cash, and it is preparing new laws to oblige crypto-currency wallet companies to keep detailed records of all transactions greater than $3,000, including where the funds come from and where they are sent. Once such regulations are implemented, many crypto-currencies may lose some of their popularity, though they will still reduce the cost of many transactions, and hence the need for intermediation services such as banking.

Another related threat is outright bans if crypto-currencies are seen to compete with government-issued money. The Turkish government has banned the use of crypto-currency payments, on the grounds that their volatility makes them too risky for most investors, and that their anonymous nature creates opportunities for illegal activity. At time of writing in mid-2021, China, India, Algeria, Morocco, Saudi Arabia and other countries have also banned the use of crypto-currencies. Against this, some advocates argue that it will not actually be possible to ban their use, as long as citizens have access to the Internet. Consequently it will be interesting to see whether these countries' bans can be made effective, and how many more countries join them.

As a lesser step than actually banning the use of crypto-currencies, there are proposals such as to make it compulsory for every computer or smartphone to contain software that sends information to the government about every crypto-currency transaction. With ever-growing numbers of smartphones using software including GPS that tracks their users, this may be implemented in some countries. Another form of government intervention that might be used is taxation, which could be levied on all crypto-currency transactions, or transactions above a certain size, or particular categories of transaction. It remains to be seen how efficient this could be, or how successfully crypto-currency transactions might be able to evade such taxes.

A related trend is that companies in many countries have already implemented different types of digital money, which are distinct from crypto-currencies. For example, in Kenya approximately half the population use the "M-PESA" digital payments system implemented via mobile phones, which started in 2007. This can be used even by people without a bank account, and from the point-of-view of convenience and security, M-PESA is considered to be better than cash. In Thailand, Malaysia and Singapore, transactions in similar forms of e-money have reached the scale of Billions of dollars per year, which is about 1% of the scale of the national currency, representing steps towards a "cashless society". This would make government control of all economic activity easier, as discussed further in section 5.4 below, since all such "e-transactions" are recorded and stored in databases.

In summary, by comparison with other regulated financial markets, crypto-currencies are still in their early days, and under rapid evolution, and so are relatively under-regulated. But in order to be successful, they need standards and insurance in order to ensure their safety for use by trusting members of the general public. Currently there are also complex inter-dependencies between different crypto-currencies and related services, which pose systemic risks. These risks could in principle be prevented through regulation along the same lines as other financial markets are regulated in order to make them transparent, so that users can assess risks accurately. Although there have been some failures of crypto-exchanges, there have been no major scandals to date. Consequently there may be no need for "heavy-handed" regulation, in part due to the capability of the Internet to create its own measures of reliability. However, the absence of transparency in the operation of any crypto-currency is an invitation to fraud, which regulations will presumably be introduced to prevent, but will meanwhile create uncertainty until they are implemented.

Risk 4: Electricity Supply Interruption

It must also be remembered that all crypto-currencies depend on the Internet. Ultimately, ownership of a crypto-currency is represented by numbers in a computer network. A very large number of unique numbers are being used in this way to represent value, which is accepted by those who use the same software and so agree to the rules by which value is assigned to the numbers. Since computer networks are powered by electricity, the system whereby crypto-currencies have financial value depends on continuing electricity supply which exposes them to several unique risks from disruption of electricity generation and distribution systems, which apparently cannot be reduced to zero.

Of course, all banking and other financial services also nowadays depend on electricity supply, and so share this risk. However, in a disaster situation, the widest network with the most users will probably continue to operate the longest. Hence a national currency would presumably be more likely to survive than crypto-currencies with much smaller networks of users.

Electro-Magnetic Pulse (EMP)

One way of using a nuclear weapon is to explode it outside the Earth's atmosphere, and thereby create a violent electro-magnetic pulse (EMP) in the ionosphere. This would induce huge surges in voltage from one end to the other of all conducting wires in a wide area of the Earth's surface below the explosion, such as electricity supply cables, wiring networks in buildings and electrical machines, and electronic equipment such as computers and smartphones, unless they are specifically shielded to survive such stresses. This voltage surge could be violent enough to actually melt wiring in all these systems, thereby ending electricity supply and use until all electrical equipment had been replaced. An EMP in itself would be much less immediately destructive than a nuclear war, but it would be devastating for daily life in richer countries that depend critically on electricity, leading to years of chaos and poverty. It is hard to imagine crypto-currencies, perhaps held on "digital wallets" or smartphones protected from the EMP, continuing to be honoured as valuable by people trying to survive and rebuild society through manual labour.

Another "Carrington Event"

In 1859, on September 1, amateur astronomer Richard Carrington recorded huge fluctuations in the Earth's magnetic field near London which were caused by an unusually large solar flare and ejection of plasma from the surface of the Sun, nowadays known as a Coronal Mass Ejection (CME). The effects on Earth are similar to those of an EMP. CMEs much smaller than the Carrington Event occur every few years, and have a range of measurable influences on Earth, including altering and lowering satellite orbits by stirring up the outer layers of the Earth's atmosphere. The Carrington event was an exceptionally powerful CME, estimated to have released energy equal to a billion hydrogen bombs, and it caused fires in several telegraph stations which experienced huge voltage surges along their wires.

The probability of another "Carrington Event" occurring in the near future is unknown, but some researchers believe that it may repeat approximately every 150 years, in which case the next one is already overdue, and that even larger such events are possible. If another one does occur, then much of the world's electricity supply and utilization system – which did not exist in 1859 – could be very severely damaged. If the event lasts just a few hours, it might destroy the electricity system over perhaps half the surface of the Earth, leaving the other half largely intact. This would have massive geopolitical implications, but is impossible to predict in detail with today's science and technology.

Breakdown of the Electricity Supply System

Large-scale electricity supply networks are designed to be highly reliable, but they nevertheless remain subject to breakdowns for various reasons.

1. Poor energy policy-making. For example, the plans by governments in many rich countries to replace highly reliable electricity generation systems based on burning coal, oil and uranium with generation systems with highly unstable output, notably wind and solar energy, is putting major stresses on electricity supply systems, and makes them vulnerable to unusual weather conditions. It is not clear how far these policies will continue, but currently electricity supply reliability is continuing to worsen in many countries.
2. Mismanagement. Periodically poor management causes such unsatisfactory conditions as delayed maintenance and repair activities of important infrastructure, such as due to local government being short of funds. Because of this, prolonged electricity outages, at least on a local basis, occur from time to time in many countries.
3. Sabotage. Many electricity supply networks depend on cables carried by unprotected pylons over hundreds of kilometres, and many power stations have notable weak points, including Internet connectivity, through which they may be easy to disable, at least temporarily.
4. Political turmoil. Military forces have developed weapons such as large conducting nets to be dropped on high-voltage switch-yards that cause immediate breakdowns and fires through electrical shorting between

different pieces of equipment. Serious political disturbances could lead to power supplies being disrupted in this and other ways.

None of the above risks can be ruled out, and any of them could disable a crypto-currency system, either for an unpredictable period of time, or even permanently. This alone would seem to ensure that crypto-currencies – at least as they currently exist – will be no more than part of the solution to the monetary question. Nevertheless, despite these risks, "DeFi" using the Internet to simplify and automate many financial services will surely continue to make them cheaper and more convenient, cutting out large numbers of "middlemen". The potential for further innovation, as both hardware and software continue to develop rapidly, also offers the possibility of achieving greater transparency of company and government activities, wider use of "crowd-funding", and other improvements in financial services, with far less role for banks and other monopolistic intermediaries. Indeed, in combination with AI systems, which are now said to be on the verge of making millions of white collar workers such as accountants, lawyers and bankers redundant, "DeFi" is surely the start of a revolution in financial activities, even if it does not itself supply the stable currency unit needed to underly the economic system as a whole. This would need one or more crypto-currencies to grow to a scale of trillions of US dollars, due to their becoming very widely accepted due to their superior usefulness, which would presumably require their value to be stabilized in real terms, as discussed further in Chapter 14.10 below.

5.4 CENTRAL BANK DIGITAL CURRENCIES (CBDCS)

One aspect of the coming changes in the monetary system, which is inevitably receiving attention, is how central banks will respond to the radical changes being driven by the new technology of Blockchain and "DeFi". In their role as overseers of their national monetary systems, central banks have a responsibility to maintain the value of the national currency, which the entire population use for saving as well as for transactions, and which might be threatened if the use of privately issued crypto-currencies continues to grow exponentially. One of governments' roles is to collect taxes with which to pay for its services. If a large proportion of peoples' transactions became "invisible" through the use of private crypto-currencies, this would become impossible, and unfair on those who continued to pay taxes.

One response by central banks and governments, which see privately-controlled crypto-currencies as a potential threat, is to collaborate with security services in using their expertise in decryption in order to make crypto transactions public, and thereby taxable. Another response is to make the use of crypto-currencies illegal, as several countries are already attempting to do. However, a major issue facing such a policy is that as the technology – both the software and the hardware – continue to evolve rapidly, it may not be possible for governments to impose their will at all efficiently. There is a long history of citizens of countries in which inflation makes the national currency unreliable preferring to use another country's currency in the "informal economy". So it is far from clear that governments whose currencies are considered unreliable will actually be able to prevent widespread use of private crypto-currencies, if they are found to be more reliable.

Another response is for central banks to develop their own "Central Bank Digital Currencies" (CBDC), an option which has been under research and preparation for several years already. CBDCs are often discussed as though they are just another group of crypto-currencies, but this is a mistake – being governmental they are fundamentally different, and have a different purpose. Most monetary transactions in richer countries today already take place inside computer systems operated by banks and other financial institutions, which are designed to be secure from spying or interference by third parties. Consequently, central banks' digital money transactions are not themselves new. However, the change being planned with CBDCs is to replace all transactions currently performed with cash – ie paper notes, coins or private bank accounts – with electronic transactions overseen by the central bank. This introduces the problem that the centralised collection of all users' financial data would literally end the fundamental human right to privacy. Hence CBDCs would face a major hurdle in trying to receive public acceptance.

A digital currency controlled by the government or central bank that replaced existing money would give central banks and/or governments massive quantities of information about everyone using the CBDC. Using such information to prevent tax evasion, money laundering and other crimes are legitimate purposes, but the introduction of a CBDC system solely for this purpose would be like "using a sledgehammer to crack a nut". That is, it is well known that "power corrupts", and so putting such unprecedented power in anyone's hands, whether government or private organisations, would invite tyranny.

Moreover, it is precisely the protection of privacy and freedom that led to the extraordinary historical success of the countries that led the industrial revolution. Ending these fundamental human values would be catastrophic for civilized society: giving government organisations access to vastly more information about individual members of the general public than they have ever had before would be contrary to centuries of tradition, and would almost ensure the takeover of government by people with authoritarian intentions – literal megalomaniacs.

In addition, the present-day operation of massive databases of personal information, including financial and medical data, which are frequently subject to leaks and theft of data, gives no confidence that this level of information would be handled safely and honestly at all times, including over the long-term. Indeed, quite the opposite: there are continuing scandals in every country about misuse of private data, involving both incompetence and dishonesty, and unclear boundaries between government and corporate data. These are proof that the technology and management of massive databases are still far from being sufficiently advanced to be given such heavy responsibility as safely and transparently defending the privacy of centralized data about all citizens. Consequently, only after much more progress in creating reliable, transparent, privacy-protecting, unhackable data storage could such a system be acceptable – if this is even possible. It seems possible that further evolution of Blockchain-based or Blockchain-type systems could guarantee the transparency of data management that is needed for such systems to have public acceptance. However, it is unclear whether, even if this was technically possible, it could be politically feasible, since it would be opposed by those who would benefit from greater government powers of surveillance.

That is, the existence of such ever-growing masses of data would give those with access to it unprecedented power to influence and control the lives of members of the general public. For example, a person could be stopped from accessing money in their bank accounts or via credit cards at any time if perhaps they were heard to criticize the government. Or they could be prevented from traveling beyond, say, 2 km from their home, or using public transport or other services. The software needed to implement such systems has already been developed by software companies in several countries, and used to track users in real time. Such a system would surely be unacceptable, and indeed unconstitutional in most civilized countries – that is, countries in which all government staff, including even those at the highest levels, work under the same rule of law as they impose on citizens, and protect Freedom of Speech and other fundamental human rights.

Preparation of CBDCs also faces the problem of rapid technological change: a nationwide or even worldwide system would involve massive investment in the technological systems needed to implement and support it (even if the innovation was largely in software rather than hardware), which would inevitably take several years to implement, and which would also include recruiting and training large numbers of specialized staff. Consequently, there is a high probability that any system designed today would be obsolete before it was fully implemented in a few years – that is, inefficient, ineffective and easy to evade or hack using newer software, which will include AI software operating on high-speed computers.

Perhaps most fundamentally, it is hard to see how a CBDC would help to solve the problem that a country's existing currency faces – government's inability to resist pressure to inflate the money supply, or to prevent major changes in the exchange-rate – except by controlling peoples' use of their own money. Systems designed to achieve this have long been under discussion, such as the concept of "demurrage" – that is, the imposition of negative interest-rates on bank accounts in order to oblige people to spend their savings – when this is judged to be desirable by monetary policy-makers. Such systems would essentially be tyrannical, and if implemented for an extended period of time would also destroy the potential for economic growth which arises through innovation, stimulated and enabled by wide economic and social freedom. As a result of such considerations, the optimal role for CBDCs is under vigorous discussion and research. For example, in discussing these and other problems, Bordo emphasises that the evolution of money from physical coins, through paper notes to digital information is essentially inevitable, due to the rapid technological developments that are occurring (Bordo, 2021). Consequently Blockchain-based Internet services are surely the inevitable next phase of money, which will speed up all financial transactions, including especially international transactions, as well as improving reliability and security.

Bordo suggests that the future monetary system will probably be realized as a "public-private partnership" (PPP), with the central bank and private banks playing complementary roles. This already occurs with the US Federal Reserve System being owned by a group of private banks, which provides services to the federal government – notably managing the national currency and ensuring the stability of the financial system.

However, the invention of Blockchain technology has created more new possibilities, including the redistribution of different monetary roles to private and public digital currencies, possibly even including separating the traditional functions of money – measure of value, store of value, and medium of exchange, as discussed in (Peneder, 2021).

Another problem facing those planning a CBDC is the need to avoid destabilizing the existing financial system when major changes are initiated. For reasons intrinsic to the problems of *fiat* and debt-based monetary systems discussed in Chapters 2 and 3 above, the giant financial companies which dominate western economic systems today are unstable, carrying massive amounts of debt and derivative liabilities, on which a single default could trigger "cross-defaults" by other banks, and spread contagion to their risk-sharing counter-parties. The threat of such a default was what led to the US Federal Reserve System creating several trillion *fiat* dollars in 2008-9 in order to save the US financial system by protecting several large financial institutions from losses. During the crisis, loss of mutual confidence among large financial institutions effectively froze their activities, leading to the threat that ATMs might stop working. This would immediately cause chaos nation-wide, and so the need to avoid it makes politicians very pliant.

One of the most advanced CBDC systems developed to date is the DCEP (Digital Currency Electronic Payment) developed by the Chinese central bank: after several years of preparation, it started public trials of its prototype in several large cities in 2020, and expanded them in 2021. Held in a specialized digital wallet which users download to their smartphone, DCEPs can be used for transactions by transmitting 2D barcodes between payer and receiver. It remains to be seen how well this system operates and is accepted. A major source of controversy is that it could be combined with the Digital Social Credit Score system already in use in China, which would bring with it the threat of tyrannical control of the lives of the general public, directly contrary to the political traditions of the western countries. Consequently, the results of the trial run in China may be of considerable interest.

The specific issue of defining and stabilizing the real value of a currency, whether created by government or by a private company, is separate from the discussion of the various new roles that Blockchain-based currencies may play, whether private or public. Although it is not possible to say in advance how far stabilizing a currency's real value will resolve other issues, improved stability in the real value of various currencies will surely be very helpful in reducing the urgency to adopt a fundamentally new system. In view of the damaging and stressful experience of smaller EU countries using the Euro, it seems likely that there would be strong resistance in many other countries to having their currency managed by a supra-national or global body such as the IMF or BIS – or *a fortiori* by affiliates of the WEF. Instead, enabling the continuation of existing economic and political systems in which many separate countries continue to manage their own national currencies is surely a desirable goal, if a system more resistant to destabilization and injustice than the present one could be established.

In view of the widely accepted need for regulation in other financial markets, it will surely also be widely considered necessary for crypto-currencies and other Internet-based money to be regulated, as their role in the economy grows. Preparing and implementing such regulations is likely to be one of the roles of central banks, for which CBDCs will be one tool. There are many other interesting and important issues under discussion about the changes under way in monetary systems due to the Blockchain and other major technological changes: however, they do not need to be discussed further here.

5.5 REMAINING PROBLEM FACING PROPOSED NEW MONETARY SYSTEMS

In summary, future developments in the potential uses of digital money and governments' responses are unavoidably very uncertain at a time of such rapid technological change, but it seems likely that a range of Blockchain-based currencies, both private and governmental, or further developments of these, are likely to play a major role in future monetary arrangements, as also is gold.

An important limitation on the future role of cryptocurrencies as they exist today is their relation to existing currencies, via which they are purchased. That is, their value is defined as prices in terms of existing currencies, which vary continually with movements in foreign-exchange markets. If pessimistic commentators' fears are realized and some of the major currencies suffer hyper-inflation, successful crypto-currencies' prices will increase proportionately. But when currencies' values finally reach zero, as unbacked paper currencies have experienced repeatedly in the past, how will crypto-currencies be valued? As long as they continue to depend on existing currencies in this way, crypto-currencies cannot outlive them and so surely cannot replace them for all their functions.

Rapid developments in digital money systems are under way at so many levels, in so any countries, and with so many uncertainties remaining, that it is hard even for professionals to keep abreast of all new possibilities as they become public. Another important issue underlying all such discussion is the question of globalization versus decentralization. It is generally understood that political decisions should be made as much as possible by the people most affected by the decisions, and so political power should be devolved and decentralized as far as possible. This is the opposite of obeying pressure from above – that is, from political and financial elites – to implement "global" rules and regulations, which are convenient for those who wish to control society, but unattractive for its victims.

However, in the present book our concern is with a single question that applies to all three of the above possibilities, whether operating at local, regional, national, international or global level. Whichever of the above systems is used, or even all three together, in order for a monetary system to be useful, stable and sustainable it is necessary to define and maintain the value of the monetary unit used in real terms. Moreover, this must be done in a way that is not dependent on existing currencies, nor on continuous access to public electricity supply systems, nor even on the continuing operation of the Internet. How this can be achieved is the subject of the following chapters.

SUMMARY

This chapter has discussed the promise and the limitations of the three main approaches to creating a new currency which could help to stabilize the world economy, as the ability of the US dollar to do this continues to decline. First, revival of gold convertibility of some currencies may be implemented in some form. Second, the use of crypto-currencies based on Blockchain technology is a major innovation that is spreading rapidly due to the security, speed and low cost of the services it enables, although their value remains vulnerable to severe instability arising from several sources. Third, central banks are expected to introduce their own, Blockchain-based digital currencies with a range of functions intended to improve their ability to preserve monetary stability. (As both the hardware and software of the Internet continue to evolve rapidly, there is also the possibility of further major innovations arising.)

Considering how far one or more of these three possibilities could replace the various roles of the US dollar today quickly reveals that none of the three above approaches is satisfactory in itself: something more is required. This is because the single most important value in financial services, and *a fortiori* in a monetary system, is dependability, such as will allow investors to commit to a project that may take as long as fifty years to repay its investors, with a reasonable return to repay their risk-taking. A well-managed *fiat* currency can provide such confidence for a while: but in the event of a crisis, or even just a gradual decline in public discipline, such as is seen in most if not all rich countries, it is too easy for policy-makers to argue that just a little more inflation would be less harmful than permitting a recession which might become severe. In other words, a truly permanent foundation for a sound monetary system which could last for centuries requires something more, some policy that cannot be discarded without the general public becoming aware and sufficiently scandalized to prevent it, and which also cannot be gradually worn down by "a thousand cuts", as *fiat* money systems seem unable to resist. The answer to this fundamental requirement is discussed in the following chapters.

REFERENCES

Bordo, M. D. (2021). *Central Bank Digital Currency in Historical Perspective: Another Crossroad in Monetary History (No. w29171)*. National Bureau of Economic Research.

Greater Reset. (2021). https://thegreaterreset.org

Hayek, F. (1976). *Denationalisation of Money*. Institute of Economic Affairs. https://iea.org.uk/publications/research/denationalisation-of-money

Meera, K. (Ed.). (2013). *Real Money: Money and Payment Systems from an Islamic Perspective*. IIUM Press Malaysia.

Peneder, M. (2021). Digitization and the Evolution of Money as a Social Technology of Account. *Journal of Evolutionary Economics*. https://link.springer.com/article/10.1007%2Fs00191-021-00729-4

Rickards, J. (2016). *The New Case for Gold*. Portfolio Penguin.

Tapscott, D., & Tapscott, A. (2018). *Blockchain Revolution: How the Technology Behind Bitcoin and other Cryptocurrencies is Changing the World*. Portfolio Penguin.

Woods, J. (2021). Benjamin Graham on Buffer Stocks. *Journal of the History of Economic Thought*. osf.io/preprints/socarxiv

Chapter 6
Inescapable Role of Real Currency Convertibility

ABSTRACT

The invention of paper money created a major new problem: how to ensure its value. Historically, the most reliable means of preserving and stabilizing the value of paper currency has been for those issuing paper money to guarantee to convert their notes, on demand, into real assets, at a specified rate of exchange. The most common asset used for this has been gold, which has been effective in preserving the value of currency over a century or more, but this has not prevented serious economic fluctuations. Consequently, for more than a century, economists have argued that it would be more effective to make currency convertible on demand into a range of commodities. Unfortunately, efforts to devise a means of achieving this have not succeeded to date.

INTRODUCTION

"An effective monetary constitution (which exists nowhere in the world) that would guarantee stability in the value of the monetary unit would, indeed, work miracles ... Monetary stability would also work to ensure that the macro-economy function so as to prevent massive institutional failures akin to those experienced during the 1930s." James Buchanan, founder of Public Choice Economics, and recipient of 1986 "Nobel" economics prize (Buchanan, 1993)

DOI: 10.4018/978-1-7998-8302-9.ch006

In the previous chapter, three different approaches for replacing the role of the US dollar were discussed. From the point-of-view of users, whether individuals, companies, government organisations or others, the single most valuable feature of a currency is that its real value should be reliably stable – just as the definition of physical and engineering units such as second, litre or volt do not vary. Although it is easy to agree with this, it is not so easy to define "stable" in this context. This is because the prices of the innumerable goods and services available in a modern economy change continually, and so the value of a currency measured in terms of any one of them also varies continually. Nowadays governments and economic services continually collect data on a small number of representative goods and services and calculate an index number to show the average value of their currency. The rates of inflation or deflation that are announced periodically are calculated from movements in these price indices. Due to political pressure to make optimistic announcements, there is continual controversy over the relative accuracy and honesty of these calculations and alternative measures. Governments generally try to keep the rate of inflation, that is the rate of decline in the real value of their currency to a low figure such as less than 2%, as measured by these indices. However, even at 2% per year inflation, savings lose more than half their value over a working life of 40 years: something better is needed to provide a new, firmer foundation for the world economic system.

6.1 CURRENCY CONVERTIBILITY

Among the proposals for what is to replace the US dollar, Internet-based "crypto-currencies" are expected to play a major role, despite the problem that a breakdown of either the Internet or of the electricity supply system would make them unusable – possibly forever. This risk makes crypto-currencies at their present state of development truly a "unique" category of assets.

So far, the value of crypto-currencies is generally stated in terms of existing currencies. This is logical, since potential users need to purchase them, and to know how much they need to use in order to make a payment in an existing currency. But this means that cryptos are still dependent on existing *fiat* currencies. A major threat today is the danger of accelerating inflation, as measured by price indices, resulting from the huge expansion in the money supplies of OECD countries that has been made in 2020 and 2021. History shows that there is now a serious threat of "hyper-inflation" occurring, whereby existing currencies may lose much or all of their value. In this case, how will the value of crypto-currencies be defined? That is, we can imagine the prices of different cryptos rising faster and faster as inflation accelerates, thereby preserving the value of people's savings better than holding cash. But when the use of hyper-inflated *fiat* currencies literally ends – as has happened many times throughout history – what will the value of cryptos be? Or, put another way, how should their values be defined in order to preserve their value over the long-term, independent of the fate of existing *fiat* currencies, which they are supposed by their supporters to replace – even if they continue to be vulnerable to electric power outages? The rapid rise in price of many cryptos has been a major reason for their rapid adoption. However, although a rise in price is attractive to holders, this encourages hoarding. A rise in price of a crypto may be compatible with its use for making short-term payments, but it is not ideal for business: long-term investment is encouraged by stable and predictable currency values.

Crypto-currencies' inventers will no doubt adopt various strategies to try to preserve their value for customers. But if we look to history again, there is already a clear answer. Despite many and various theoretical proposals, there is only one may in which the value of paper currencies has been preserved over longer than a few decades, leading to unanimity among many eminent economists on how to achieve this. The only reliable way to preserve the real value of paper money or digital money – which have no inherent value – is to define the value of the monetary unit in real terms, that is as a specified quantity of a specified commodity, and to ensure this by establishing institutions that stand ready to convert currency notes, coins or other tokens, on demand, into the specified quantity of that commodity. This may become the way in which the real value of cryptos, which have no inherent value, will be preserved: this will presumably be found out in due course.

As discussed in earlier chapters, the best-known, historically most widely used way of implementing such "real convertibility" for paper money, was to implement a gold standard, whereby owners of the paper money in question could convert it on demand at banks into a guaranteed quantity of gold of defined purity. Such an easily understood and obviously reliable system would seem to be the "natural" system for any country in which it is accepted that government is based on popular consent – and this system was indeed "common sense" for several centuries in Europe and America. As quoted in Chapter 2, even Keynes, though famously critical of the gold standard, was obliged to agree that it was effective against inflation.

Nowadays, generally speaking, central banks and governments control the money supply so as to keep an index of representative prices within a specified range, nominally to resist both inflation and deflation, although this system is subject to manipulation. However, nearly two centuries ago Mill discussed this possibility in relation to gold as an alternative to real convertibility, but explained why it was unavoidably less reliable:

"Regulation by the price of bullion is a more complex idea, and does not recommend itself through the same familiar associations. There would be nothing like the same confidence, by the public generally, in an inconvertible currency so regulated, as in a convertible one: and the most instructed person might reasonably doubt whether such a rule would be as likely to be inflexibly adhered to. The grounds of the rule not being so well understood by the public, opinion would probably not enforce it with as much rigidity, and, in any circumstances of difficulty, would be likely to turn against it; while to the government itself a suspension of convertibility would appear a much stronger and more extreme measure, than a relaxation of what might possibly be considered a somewhat artificial rule. There is therefore a great preponderance of reasons in favour of a convertible, in preference to even the best regulated inconvertible currency. The temptation to over-issue, in certain financial emergencies, is so strong, that nothing is admissible which can tend in however slight a degree, to weaken the barriers that restrain it." (Mill, 1848)

This reason which Mill gives for greatly preferring direct gold convertibility, rather than operating monetary policy in order to control the market price of gold, seems just as relevant today. The sight of governments in 2020 and 2021 creating literally Trillions of *fiat* US dollars, euros, yen and pounds is a shocking example of how strong "... *the temptation to over-issue, in certain financial emergencies* ..." can be. This creation of new money leads in turn to a reduction in the value of the existing money supply – thereby devaluing everyone's savings proportionately, and so causing untold difficulties for large numbers of innocent, hard-working people.

This criticism of inconvertible currency of which the value is preserved by government experts deciding monetary policy behind closed doors, applies *a fortiori* to any digital system controlled by unseen people. The great majority of the general public would not have the time to get to understand it, even if the information was available, due to the continuing rapid evolution of digital currencies and other internet-based financial innovations, and so they certainly could not trust it to retain its real value under the economic and political pressures of a financial crisis.

6.2 WHOLESALE CONVERTIBILITY

Writers such as Mill who have explained the unique effectiveness of convertibility in preserving the value of the currency have generally considered convertibility operating at the retail level – that is, individuals being able to obtain gold (or silver) coins on demand over the counter. However, it is important that convertibility does not need to operate at the retail level: individuals do not need to be paid in gold coins – as was quite ordinary up until the start of WW1 in 1914 – in order to preserve the value of currency in terms of gold. This was proven by the initial success of the Bretton Woods "gold exchange standard", under which only governments had the right to receive gold in exchange for US dollars, but which thereby preserved confidence in the dollar's value, though operating in large quantities – tons rather than ounces.

Such a system of wholesale convertibility could in principle be extended to include non-governmental holders of currency of more than a certain quantity, such as one kilogram of gold (worth about $50,000 at time of writing), and remain effective. Customers who are large enough to use such wholesale convertibility services would be able to check the purity of gold they received, thereby exerting meaningful pressure on governments not to dilute the gold content of ingots, as they have done repeatedly throughout history. By contrast, most individuals have no immediate way to evaluate the gold they receive. Hence, under wholesale convertibility, as under retail convertibility, a government refusing to provide gold in exchange for currency would be a public sign of the failure of monetary discipline which the government would be keen to avoid.

Due to most people's unfamiliarity with the concepts of digital or crypto-currencies, the simplicity of real convertibility would be a welcome feature, giving confidence where direct judgement of reliability would be difficult or impossible. Its use could also facilitate both government and private currencies operating simultaneously by clarifying the relation between their units, as occurred under a gold standard.

6.3 COMMODITY CONVERTIBILITY

In many writings it is assumed that real currency convertibility means gold convertibility. However, the meaning of convertibility is much wider, and includes convertibility into other commodities than gold. Indeed, even during the heyday of the gold standard during the latter half of the 19th century, it was recognised that, while the gold standard did put strong constraints on devaluation of the currency, it did not prevent serious economic fluctuations, including wide swings in prices of major commodities. These aggravated fluctuations in trade between commodity exporting countries and commodity importing countries, whereby when commodity prices fell, producers' lower incomes would in turn reduce their demand for manufactured goods and thereby slow economic growth in user countries, which would further reduce demand for imports of commodities, in a vicious circle.

Consequently, proposals were made to implement convertibility into a range of commodities other than gold, such as copper, wheat, cotton and others, in order to stabilize their prices as well as the price of gold, and this idea has been supported by a continuing line of economists since then. These include Stanley Jevons (Jevons, 1877) and Alfred Marshall (Marshall, 1887) in the 19th century; Irving Fisher (Fisher,1913; Fisher 1928); Benjamin Graham (Graham, 1937; Graham, 1944); Frank Graham (Graham, 1942); John Keynes (Keynes, 1938) and Friedrich Hayek (Hayek, 1943) in the early and mid-twentieth century; Albert Hart and Jan Tinbergen (Hart et al., 1964); Nikolas Kaldor (Kaldor, 1976, Kaldor, 1983); and Jon Luke (Luke 1975) in the late 20th century. In the 21st century Bernard Lietaer (Lietaer, 2004), Leanne Ussher (Ussher 2012, Ussher 2016), John Woods (Woods, 2021) and others continue to work on the plans for commodity-based convertibility developed by Graham and Kaldor, as discussed further in Chapter 8.9 below.

Woods describes how Benjamin Graham, who is still famous for his pioneering research on investing (Graham & Dodd, 1934), considered his work recommending government counter-cyclical commodity stockholding as a contribution to economic policy to stabilise the trade cycle and the value of money (Graham, 1937) to be of much greater importance (Woods, 2021). He devoted much effort to promoting the policy, and discussed with Keynes details of how it might best be implemented (Woods, 2021).

It is of particular interest that, among the list of supporters, the two "giants" of 20th century western economics, universally known simply by their surnames Keynes and Hayek, both advocated the idea developed by

Graham. John Keynes (1883 – 1946) and Friedrich Hayek (1899 – 1992) had overlapping careers as leading academic economists based in England, championing fiercely opposing views about how economic systems work, and so about the policies that governments should follow in order to encourage economic growth. Their decades-long rivalry has been called "the clash that defined modern economics" by Wapshott in his book devoted to describing their rivalry (Wapshott, 2012). Strangely, however, Wapshott does not even mention the fact that, far from being entirely opposed in their thinking, both Keynes and Hayek wrote strongly in favour of the macro-economic stabilizing benefits of a system of currency convertibility based on primary commodities, due to the counter-cyclical stabilizing influence which it would exert on the world economy. That is, they both publicly agreed that a system which made money convertible into a range of primary commodities at specified prices would exert a stabilising influence on world trade. Their strikingly similar views are epitomised in the following short excerpts from their writings on the subject:

"At present a falling off in effective demand in the industrial consuming countries causes a price collapse ... But if ... "Commodity Controls" are in a position to take up at stable prices the slack caused by the initial falling off in consuming demand ... the vicious cycle may be inhibited at the start; and, again, by releasing stocks when consumption recovers ... prevent the inflation of raw material prices." (Keynes, 1938)

"With this system in operation an increase in the demand for liquid assets would lead to the accumulation of stocks of raw materials of the most general usefulness . . . and as the hoarded currency was again returned to circulation and demand for commodities increased, these stocks would be released to satisfy the new demand." (Hayek, 1943)

These two short excerpts concern the stabilising influence of a system of real convertibility on international trade between producers of raw materials and producers of manufactured goods, and do not explicitly discuss the other inherent aspect of the operation of such a system, namely that it would help to stabilize the real value of the currency in which it operated.

It is worth expanding on this convergence of economic thinking. Keynes and Hayek were the leaders of what continue to be the two poles of "western" academic theorising about how economic activity works, and how governments and markets respectively can best contribute to economic growth. Briefly,

Keynes favoured a major role for government in guiding the economy, while Hayek was against it, on the grounds that it would inevitably lead to excessive government interference, ending in tyranny. During the 1950s, Keynes seemed to have (posthumously) won their decades of jousting, as policies giving governments greater discretion based on his approach were adopted in post-war USA and UK, and then in most countries. But Hayek outlived Keynes by several decades and so lived to see the predicted failure of "Keynesianism", as the western world suffered "stagflation" during the 1970s – simultaneous inflation and stagnation, with high unemployment at the same time as 20% inflation.

Keynes is widely considered to have been naive about political economy, which is closer to a raw battle over power than a sincere effort to devise economic policies that benefit the general public. As a result, the "Keynesian" policies implemented in his name, by ending traditional monetary discipline that essentially forbade government budget deficits, led to ever-growing government debt and accelerating inflation. However, Hayek's insistence on stopping inflation can in turn be seen to have failed, as it has led to outright deflation. The rich countries have already suffered decades of unprecedented zero interest-rates, claimed to be needed to break out of deflation by stimulating investment, and are now facing negative interest-rates – despite there being no evidence that this will revive economic growth, while upending even the most basic ideas of how borrowing and investment work! As a result, not a few commentators are now adamant that the world is heading towards another recessionary disaster, much worse than 2008, and possibly worse than the 1930s.

And yet, despite such radically opposed views on economic policy, Keynes & Hayek agreed, in detail, about what it is hardly an exaggeration to call the central issue of economic theory: what is money? How can the value of money be preserved in order to enable it to play its extraordinarily valuable role in society as well as possible? It is the failure to answer this question definitively that led to the end of the Bretton Woods system after less than 30 years, and the extremely costly problems that the world faces today.

Unfortunately, neither of these two "giants" of economics devised an acceptable way to implement the idea, so that, despite this strong endorsement at literally the highest level of the mainstream "western" economics profession, the policy which they both recommended has not attracted the level of attention that might be expected, given their endorsements. *A fortiori,* such a system has never been implemented.

Why did they not collaborate on this key issue? And why did their biographer Wapshott not even mention the fact of their fundamental agreement on this central issue in his otherwise detailed work "Keynes Hayek" (Wapshott, 2012). And how did it come about that, although this problem was solved definitively – and recognized as such – even being the subject of a debate in the British parliament in 1958, when it was described as "epoch-making", " a modern equivalent of the gold standard " and other superlatives – it has still not been implemented, nor even seriously investigated?

6.4 DIFFICULTY OF IMPLEMENTATION

Although the idea to make money convertible into a range of primary commodities has received such strong support among the most eminent of economists, its implementation is truly "easier said than done". A very important difference between these commodities and gold is that, whereas the industrial use of gold is very limited, primary commodities are used in huge quantities throughout the world, and their prices are famously volatile, frequently falling by more than 50% or rising by more than 100% in response to changing conditions of supply and demand, due to such varied factors as weather, technology, changing trade patterns, political events or other influences. This makes the process of guaranteeing convertibility between commodities and money considerably more challenging than implementing gold convertibility, of which the price was kept within a range of just 0.2% under the gold standard. Since it would not be desirable, even if it was possible, to restrict prices of industrial commodities to such a narrow range of less than 1%, it is generally agreed that whatever rules are used to implement convertibility must accommodate continuing wide movements in commodities' market prices.

Trying to use commodities with such widely moving prices as the basis of currency convertibility may seem, *prima facie*, self-contradictory. However, since reducing, but not preventing, the wide swings in primary commodity prices could have a beneficial stabilising effect on world trade and economic growth, both Keynes and Hayek strongly supported the principle. Notably, neither wrote in favour of reviving a gold standard, which would itself have no direct stabilising influence on world commodity trade and markets, although as discussed above, it has famously been uniquely effective as a bulwark against inflation – albeit at the cost of imposing an actually deflationary influence. However, neither Keynes nor Hayek gave sufficient priority to this subject to reach a successful outcome. One reason for this was their assumption that an effective system could be implemented only through international agreement. In truth, only by relaxing this assumption can a solution be achieved. However, before discussing the solution, one more major issue must be clarified.

SUMMARY

There is a long history of recognition of the simplicity and efficacy of currency convertibility in preserving the value of the currency unit, which is the first and most fundamental responsibility of monetary policy-makers. That is, the method of guaranteeing convertibility is known to be entirely effective in preventing the devaluation of the monetary unit for which governments experience so much pressure, and has been extolled as such for centuries, if not for millennia. Consequently, missing from all three of the approaches to replacing the role of the US dollar discussed in Chapter 5 is the idea of making any new currency reliably convertible into real commodities. Advocates of reviving a gold standard are of course aware of this, and strongly supportive, but they do not have a complete solution to all the problems which the implementation of such a system would face today. However, nearly 150 years ago, western economists started to discuss a potentially better solution than gold convertibility. If a practical means of implementing it could be designed, it would be greatly preferable to guarantee the convertibility of currency into a range of primary commodities rather than only gold, since these are much more widely used throughout the economy. This idea has received wide support from a long line of economists from the 19th century until today, including from both Keynes and Hayek, the "giants" of 20th century western economics. Nevertheless, despite this strong support, this idea has not been implemented to date.

REFERENCES

Buchanan, J. (1993). *Property as a Guarantor of Liberty. Collected Works. 18*. Liberty Fund.

Fisher, I. (1913). Compensated Dollar. *The Quarterly Journal of Economics, 27*(February), 213–235. doi:10.2307/1881902

Fisher, I. (1928). The Money Illusion. Adelphi.

Graham, B. (1937). *Storage and Stability*. McGraw-Hill.

Graham, B. (1944). *World Commodities and World Currency*. McGraw Hill.

Graham, B. & Dodd, D. (1934). *Security Analysis*. Academic Press.

Graham, F. D. (1942). *Social Goals and Economic Institutions*. Princeton University Press.

Hart, A., Kaldor, N., & Tinbergen, J. (1964). The Case for an International Commodity Reserve Currency. *United Nations Conference on Trade and Development.*

Hayek, F. (1943). A Commodity Reserve Currency. *The Economic Journal, 53*(210/211), 176-186.

Jevons, S. (1877). Money and the Mechanism of Exchange. Appleton.

Kaldor, N. (1976). Inflation and Recession in the World Economy. *Economic Journal, 86*(344).

Kaldor, N. (1983, July). The Role of Commodity Prices in Economic Recovery. *Lloyds Bank Review.*

Keynes, J. (1938). The Policy of Government Storage of Foodstuffs and Raw Materials. *Economic Journal (London)*, *48*(191), 449–460. doi:10.2307/2225437

Lietaer, B. (2004). *The Terra TRC White Paper*. https://www.scribd.com/document/31636027/The-Terra-TRC-White-Paper-2004

Luke, J. (1975). Inflation-free pricing rules for a Generalized Commodity Reserve Currency. *Journal of Political Economy*, *83*(4), 786. doi:10.1086/260355

Marshall, A. (1887, Mar.). Remedies for Fluctuations of General Prices. Contemporary Review.

Mill, J. (1848). *Principles of Political Economy*. https://archive.org/details/principlesofpoli01milluoft?ref=ol&view=theater

Ussher, L. (2012). *Combining International Monetary Reform with Commodity Buffer Stocks: Keynes, Graham and Kaldor*. Economics Department, City University of New York. http://www.global-systems-science.org/wp-content/uploads/2012/11/ussher_Bancor_19Dec12.pdf

Ussher, L. (2016). International Monetary Policy with Commodity Buffer Stocks. *European Journal of Economics and Economic Policies: Intervention*, *13*(1), 10–25. doi:10.4337/ejeep.2016.01.02

Wapshott, N. (2012). *Keynes Hayek: The Clash that Defined Modern Economics*. Norton.

Woods, J. E. (2021). Benjamin Graham on Buffer Stocks. *Journal of the History of Economic Thought*.

Chapter 7
The Other Side of Convertibility:
Commodity Price Stabilization

ABSTRACT

A system for ensuring the convertibility of a currency into specified commodities is also, ipso facto, a system for stabilizing the prices of those commodities in terms of the currency in question. This connection is widely ignored in discussions of these two subjects, but it links the two specialised fields of monetary economics and commodity price stabilization tightly together. Unfortunately, despite much work on the topic spanning many decades, almost all such work is made within a single paradigm – that of establishing an international institution to stabilize commodity prices. However, for a number of reasons, no international agreement can achieve more than a very partial solution to this problem: most importantly it cannot directly stabilize more than a single currency, thereby losing the most fundamental benefit of a true solution for all but one of the participating countries. A different approach is therefore needed.

INTRODUCTION

The discussion of commodity-based currency convertibility brings us to a key issue concerning the potential importance of this subject: guaranteeing the convertibility of a currency into a commodity necessitates announcing

DOI: 10.4018/978-1-7998-8302-9.ch007

prices at which the body implementing convertibility will exchange the commodity for currency. *Ipso facto* this guarantee keeps the price of the specified commodity between the prices at which convertibility is guaranteed. That is, implementing convertibility of a currency into a real commodity is *ipso facto* to stabilize the price of the commodity in terms of that currency. In "mainstream" economics the subject of commodity price stabilization is typically treated as a separate subject from currency convertibility, which is part of the separate field of monetary policy, although they are in reality inextricably interconnected – indeed, literally the same phenomenon.

The topic of commodity price stabilization is itself the subject of an immense and wide-ranging literature, accumulated over decades, involving detailed analysis of many different policies and plans such as domestic agriculture support policies, ways of stabilizing farm incomes, subsidies or tax-relief for increased stockpiling, and other related topics. Another major sub-topic on which there is a very extensive literature is how to stabilize the notoriously unstable prices in international commodity markets – as in the discussion by Keynes and Hayek described in the previous chapter. Unfortunately, the great majority of the work on this topic has been done under the influence of an *idee fixe*: namely that a solution to the problem can be achieved only through international negotiations. Although this idea sounds logical, it has in fact failed to produce a solution to the problem despite discussions continuing for more than a century to date.

Hayek's paper quoted above was titled "A Commodity Reserve Currency", which refers specifically to Benjamin Graham's 1937 proposal for the establishment of a system to maintain prices of a range of primary commodities above a "floor price" by buying market surpluses as required, and below a "ceiling price" by selling sufficient reserves at times of shortage. This basic idea is easy to understand and it or similar proposals have been supported by many others, including Keynes, his successor Nicholas Kaldor, and others. However, even if the principle is accepted, the precise details of realization are of extreme importance in order to confirm that the policy would be truly beneficial. This is because the idea of interfering with market prices is itself almost taboo among many economists, because long experience has shown that it is very easy for government intervention in a market to cause greater costs than the initial instability, disrupting markets and thereby actually aggravating the perceived problem. It is a sign of how important Hayek considered the stabilization of trade fluctuations that he supported what would have constituted major interference with the commodity market price mechanism.

Hayek's support for this idea proposed by Graham also attracted the criticism that it would expose governments to an open-ended liability, by promising to buy up any amount of commodities at the guaranteed floor price, and to supply any amount of the commodity at or below its guaranteed ceiling price. This is indeed the Achilles heel of this proposal. Moreover, as well as representing an open-ended commitment for the governments involved, it is inevitable that forcing commodity prices to remain within a fixed price-range would at times severely distort market prices, causing problems both for supply and for demand.

Nevertheless, due to the widely recognized importance of the objective of reducing the depth of cyclical trade fluctuations, emphasized by both Keynes and Hayek, discussion of different aspects of the problem continue to the present day. Roughly speaking, proposed means of implementing the plan comprise three different approaches: "buffer-stocks", some versions of which include a "commodity-basket", and "virtual systems". All of these ideas face serious problems, as discussed next.

7.1 BUFFER-STOCKS

This is the name given to systems in which a fund is established and used to keep commodity prices between a "floor price" and a "ceiling price". That is, a manager uses a fund provided by participating governments to buy and sell commodities as they judge to be most effective in order to keep market prices between fixed lower and upper limits. Buffer-stocks of various types are the subject of a large research literature, involving detailed analysis of many different possible policies, as well as mathematical analysis of various theoretical schemes. For this book there is no need to survey this body of work in detail, other than to recognize the problems which all buffer-stocks face, since the Grondona system does not use a buffer-stock, as discussed in following chapters.

A central role in international efforts to stabilize prices of commodities in world markets in this way has been played by decades of work sponsored by the United Nations Committee on Trade and Development (UNCTAD) as part of its "Integrated Program for Commodities". This aims to establish a number of separate International Commodity Agreements funded by contributions from UN member countries. Realising these plans depends on achieving detailed agreement between multiple countries on a host of details about the system to be established in respect of each commodity. Notably, this includes selecting a currency to be used, deciding the price-range within which each commodity's price is to be maintained, and establishing a system for buying and selling reserves as required to limit market price movements, which also involves arranging the use of warehousing facilities on the scale estimated to be needed, at chosen sites.

As an example of the continuing interest in this plan, Ussher has published detailed discussions of the Graham/Hart/Kaldor plan, emphasizing both the stockholding aspect and the value of linking the operation to the issue of a new international currency (Ussher, 2012, Ussher, 2016). In 2021 Woods published a detailed discussion of Benjamin Graham's 1930s proposal for a "commodity reserve currency" to be used in such an international system to stabilize the prices of a range of primary commodities (Woods, 2021). As Woods explains, Graham discussed three aspects, namely the "storage aspect", the "price–stabilization aspect" and the "monetary aspect" of his system. For Graham the storage aspect was primary, that is the macro-economic stabilizing effect of having larger-scale and more precisely counter-cyclical stock-holding of primary commodities, which would reduce the severity of the international business cycle. This is also the aspect which both Keynes and Hayek emphasized in their writings quoted above: the potential value of operating much larger, counter-cyclical stock-holding than commercial warehousing services provide, in reducing the severity of the fluctuations in trade between major producers of primary commodities and their major users, which hinders growth of the world economy. However, there are several reasons why these international negotiations have been unsuccessful, despite the theoretical benefits and the long-term efforts of UNCTAD.

7.1.1 Fixed Price Limits

Trying to keep a commodity's price between fixed limits creates an open-ended liability, both in guaranteeing to buy all supplies available at the lower price, and to guarantee that the market price never rises above the upper price. Such an open-ended liability is potentially so large that it puts such a fund beyond the ability of any single nation, necessitating an international system, with all the expense, complexity and geopolitical difficulties which negotiations for such an objective inevitably bring.

7.1.2 Discretionary Management

Having the funds managed actively makes the system's operation opaque, which is the opposite of a system aiming to enhance market stability. A buffer-stock plan also creates a problem of insider information: knowing in advance what the buffer-stock manager will buy or sell would create profit opportunities, thereby creating incentives for bribery, hacking and/or other forms of corruption. These are not trivial problems for a system that is intended to control commodity prices for the whole world market.

7.1.3 Only One Currency

An international system can operate only in terms of a single currency, whether an existing currency, the Special Drawing Rights (SDR) used by the IMF, or a new currency created for the purpose. This makes it quite unattractive for any country to participate, since participation requires a government to use money from taxpayers to contribute to the fund, while gaining no direct benefit in the form of a stabilizing influence on the real value of their own currency. Under the Bretton Woods system, only the US dollar was directly stabilized in terms of gold: other countries had to keep a fixed exchange-rate with the dollar (which they could, in principle, do without joining the system formally), for which it was necessary to establish the major international institution of the IMF. Another "solution" would be for participating countries to switch to using the new currency, which only keen supporters of globalization would consider.

7.1.4 Target for Speculation

Another weakness of a buffer-stock from the point of view of governance, is that it creates a target for attack by speculators who typically gamble on the buffer-stock manager running short of either funds or reserves. In view of the recognized difficulty, indeed periodic near-impossibility, of keeping prices between fixed limits, at times the system will become a very attractive target for speculators. Moreover, the huge scale of funds available for speculation in the present day would make the buffer-stock manager's job essentially impossible at times. The unavoidable possibility of the system failing periodically due to massive speculation against it would make it unattractive for policy-makers considering supporting it.

7.2 BASKET OF COMMODITIES

Another way to accommodate the need to permit wide flexibility in the prices of industrial commodities is to define a "basket" of commodities, and guarantee its collective price, in the hope that it provides sufficient scope for price movements of the constituent commodities within the basket. There have been multiple detailed proposals for how to implement this idea with different combinations of commodities, and statistical analysis of their probable cost and effectiveness, but all have failed to convince governments to adopt them. Although such a system could in theory offer more flexibility than a system of single-commodity buffer-stocks, an outstanding problem that remains is that the occurrence of a large movement in the market price of one commodity could exert a destabilizing influence on other commodities' prices. For example, if one commodity in the basket became scarce, so that its market price rose, traders would buy units of the defined "commodity basket" and sell the commodities which they did not want, thereby pushing down their prices and potentially aggravating the initial price divergence. The risk of initiating such a vicious circle of price instability is clearly an unattractive feature in a system intended to improve economic stability.

Graham himself favoured the use of a "basket" of commodities with a narrow guaranteed price-range, which would permit larger movements in the market prices of different commodities in the basket, of which the overall price would be fixed by the terms of convertibility. By contrast Keynes favoured treating each commodity separately (Woods, 2021). This is in fact economically preferable, since there is no benefit from linking different commodities' prices together. However, Keynes did not develop a fully detailed plan of implementation.

7.3 VIRTUAL SYSTEM

Even before the Internet, there were proposals for systems that would avoid physical movement and storage of actual commodities, but would use paper (or nowadays digital) contracts representing reserves of specified commodities, contracts for future supplies, options to purchase reserves at agreed prices, and other derivative financial instruments, which could be traded on specialized markets so as to stabilize commodity prices. With the growth of the Internet and more recently of Blockchain-based systems, there are many more such possibilities today. However, these ideas all suffer from the over-riding weakness of lack of trustworthiness or transparency. Moreover, the continuing lack of security against hacking or data theft of all internet-based systems is currently an insurmountable obstacle to acceptance. Other unattractive possibilities such as the existence of different levels of access, whereby larger countries benefited more than smaller countries would be hard or even impossible to disprove.

By contrast, possessing physical reserves of primary commodities in a system in which they are convertible into currency on guaranteed terms is an easy and entirely reliable way to be 100% sure of their availability. The well-known saying that "Possession is nine tenths of the law" is an additionally useful reminder of this. By being understandable by even the least educated people, as explained by J.S. Mill nearly two centuries ago, real convertibility is also clearly the most democratic system.

7.4 INTERNATIONAL NEGOTIATIONS NOT CAPABLE OF SOLUTION

It is clear from the above that the three main methods discussed as possible means of achieving international commodity agreements, all have serious weaknesses. In general, multi-lateral negotiations between producers and users of primary commodities expose the weakness of this approach, since their interests in relation to the commodity prices to be defended are clearly opposed in the short-term. The situation is made more complex by the fact that a major motivation of UNCTAD is to provide aid for poorer commodity-exporting countries, which is a separate issue from trying to improve the operation of commodity markets. In addition, there is inescapably great uncertainty about the longer term, especially concerning the potential for technological progress to both reduce production costs, and change the scale and pattern of demand, which makes producers, users and other market participants understandably reluctant to make a long-term commitment to any fixed prices. But leaving future prices to be renegotiated as needed at a later date avoids the central issue, and ensures problems arising in the future.

As a result of these difficulties there has been little concrete progress over nearly a century since Graham's proposal. Yet despite this, experts keep coming back to the idea of international negotiations, their urge to remedy the excessive volatility of world commodity markets being like a seemingly "irresistible force" against the apparently "immovable object" of their failure to understand that their efforts are based on a mistaken assumption. Creating an international commodity-backed currency, even if possible, would be only a small part of the detailed agreement that would be needed in order to stabilize the currencies of all the countries participating in the project, which could be achieved only by agreeing to fix their exchange-rates, like the role of the IMF in enabling Bretton Woods.

Moreover, although the growth of international trade since 1944 has brought many benefits, the far greater growth of financial markets has made any such agreement more difficult. In particular, daily turnover in foreign-exchange markets has grown to a hundred times the volume of the international trade for which foreign-exchange transactions are nominally needed. In order to participate in what is in effect a gigantic casino, financial companies use high-speed computers, attracting the justified criticism of "casino capitalism". These and other problems are a strong disincentive for governments of smaller countries to collaborate in establishing an international system which would face all these difficulties.

Hence, unfortunately, the various international plans that have been proposed to implement the concept of commodity-based convertibility have all been demonstrably impractical – that is, they would require an unrealistic degree of international cooperation, an unacceptable level of interference with market forces, excessive dependence on experts' discretionary judgement, lack of transparency, excessive scale of taxpayer funding, inadequate resulting benefits, and other problems.

Consequently none of these plans for commodity convertibility have been implemented, because they would not be able to achieve their stated objective, such as to keep commodity prices between fixed limits; would not provide commensurate benefits in return for participating countries' contributions; or would have required detailed international negotiations among multiple countries for their possible implementation for which there has not been the required political will.

In addition, by ignoring the inextricable connection of commodity price stabilization with the topic of currency convertibility, researchers have failed to sufficiently consider the most important potential benefit of stabilizing primary commodity prices. By considering this centrally important issue, the weakness of focusing exclusively on international agreements as the path to solving the problem of commodity price instability becomes clear. A nation's monetary system is at the heart of its economy, and so currency convertibility requires individual countries to be able to decide their policy independently, not to give away this responsibility to other countries. Hence a different approach to those discussed above for solving the problem of how to link the real value of money to commodities is needed. Fortunately such a system has already been designed in detail. It was widely known and discussed during the 1950s, and even favourably debated in the British parliament. It is described in the following chapter.

SUMMARY

In order to provide a permanently sound foundation for economic activities worldwide, stabilizing the real value of currencies by guaranteeing their convertibility into a range of primary commodities could be uniquely effective, if an economically and politically attractive system could be designed. However, discussions of the system needed nearly all fail to give sufficient attention to the fact that currency convertibility is in itself also a system for stabilizing prices of the commodities involved, which is generally treated as a separate topic from monetary policy. As the mechanism for implementing price stabilization, three main methods have been proposed: buffer-stocks, a "basket" of commodities, and a virtual system using paper or electronic contracts. Unfortunately, each of these faces intractable problems: buffer stocks require a literally open-ended financial commitment; a commodities "basket" would cause price distortions by linking the prices of unrelated commodities; and a virtual system could not be trusted, due to its unavoidable lack of transparency and reliability.

In addition, most economists studying the problem of commodity price stabilization start from the assumption that it can only be achieved through an international system. But if such a system was implemented, it would essentially lose most of the benefits of currency convertibility, because only a single currency could be directly stabilized by an international system, as only the US dollar was stabilized in terms of gold under Bretton Woods – while the major new global institution of the IMF also had to be established in order to enable the other participating governments to commit to preserving fixed exchange-rates with the dollar. Although the Bretton Woods system achieved many economic benefits for a while, for all but one of the forty-four participating countries, it was very far from being a true system of national currency convertibility, like the gold standard in its heyday under which the national money supply would rise and fall without need for taxation as the national gold reserves rose and fell. By contrast, each country participating in the Bretton Weeds agreement had to pay a participation fee to the IMF, and to obey their policy dictates when they wanted to borrow from the fund in order to preserve their dollar exchange-rate. This obedience to a global organization comprises a greater loss of sovereignty than accepting the impersonal pressure of market forces which operate in a true system of currency convertibility – such as falling gold reserves putting pressure on a government to raise interest-rates.

Consequently, as long as discussions on how to implement a system of commodity price stabilization, which is itself also a system of currency convertibility, remain trapped within the paradigm that it requires a centralized system established through international agreement, the problem simply cannot be solved. The different paradigm which provides a real solution is discussed in the next chapter.

REFERENCES

Graham, B. (1937). *Storage and Stability*. McGraw-Hill.

Ussher, L. (2012). *Combining International Monetary Reform with Commodity Buffer Stocks: Keynes, Graham and Kaldor*. Economics Department, City University of New York. http://www.global-systems-science.org/wp-content/uploads/2012/11/ussher_Bancor_19Dec12.pdf

Ussher, L. (2016). International Monetary Policy with Commodity Buffer Stocks. *European Journal of Economics and Economic Policies: Intervention*, *13*(1), 10–25. doi:10.4337/ejeep.2016.01.02

Woods, J. E. (2021). Benjamin Graham on Buffer Stocks. *Journal of the History of Economic Thought*.

Chapter 8
The Grondona System of Conditional Currency Convertibility Based on Primary Commodities

ABSTRACT

Taking a different approach to the problem, Leo St. Clare Grondona devised a system of conditional currency convertibility that individual countries can implement independently in terms of their own currency. For each of the durable, essential, imported commodities included in the system, instead of stipulating a price-range to be maintained, Grondona stipulated a "price-schedule" in which the price-range to be guaranteed for each commodity adjusts in proportion to the quantity of reserves held, falling as they rise and vice versa. In this way the maximum possible outlay that could be required, even under extreme market conditions, can be decided in advance. Consequently, a government establishing a Commodities Reserve Department (CRD) to implement such a system could legitimately pay for reserves through corresponding expansion of the national money supply, which would be reversed as and when the reserves were repurchased.

DOI: 10.4018/978-1-7998-8302-9.ch008

INTRODUCTION

As seen in the previous chapter, considerable efforts have been made, over more than a century, to design a practical system to link the value of money to real commodities other than precious metals. That is, to design a system that would be effective in improving the stability of the real value of money in terms of a number of industrial commodities, and which would also be politically feasible, that is, acceptable to a majority of the population and its political representatives. This is a problem for which "the best is the enemy of the good": plans for an international system of buffer-stocks to manage world commodity trade as a whole, which has been an *idee fixe* among economists for decades, try to do far too much. It is far from clear that any such plan could ever achieve its stated, extremely ambitious goal of a single organisation or set of organisations being responsible for stabilizing world prices of most major commodities – and it would surely be politically unacceptable to a large proportion of the general public, even in these days when many, including the mass media, support "globalization".

The solution to this problem, which is surprisingly simple, is to recognize that stabilizing commodity prices is not an "all or none" issue: even a limited stabilizing influence could be better than none – provided that the stabilizing influence was consistent and dependable, and could not suddenly fail (as a "buffer-stock" is prone to do when either its funds or its reserves run out). Another way of looking at the problem is to start from the position that any proposal must be feasible at the national level: the government of an individual country must be able to implement the proposed system independently, without needing to negotiate with, depend on or be overruled by other countries. Consequently, the system must be designed to make an incremental contribution to solving the problem – not try to solve it entirely in a single policy measure. This is indeed the approach which Leo St.Clare Grondona took during the 1940s and 1950s when he finalized the details of his system, having studied and written about the problem as early as during the 1920s and 1930s

To this end, the key innovative feature of Grondona's system of commodity-based currency convertibility is deceptively simple, but it has extremely far-reaching implications, making his system radically different from other proposed solutions to the problem, notably in giving a greater role to market forces, and no role for administrative discretion or political interference.

Unfortunately, most people who give the Grondona system any attention fail to appreciate the significance of how it differs from other proposals for "buffer-stocks", "commodity baskets" and others, and so merely dismiss it as presumably ineffective, without actually learning how it would work.

Instead of an international organization, which would inevitably be subject to innumerable unseen geopolitical and diplomatic influences, a system which an individual nation can implement independently must somehow be limited to a realistic scale, proportionate to the size of its economy and of its trade in and use of primary commodities. Consequently, its support for any one commodity's price must be limited, or in other words its guarantee of convertibility must be conditional. However, in order to increase the stability of commodity prices, rather than introduce uncertainties into the market, the rule defining the conditionality must be fixed, thereby making the system's operation entirely transparent and predictable. This requires that it's operation must not be subject to the discretion of a manager or anyone else, however powerful – exactly like the unconditional guarantee to provide gold in exchange for currency under a gold standard, which could not be tampered with in any way without immediate damaging publicity, and thereby operated reliably for centuries.

8.1 CONDITIONAL CONVERTIBILITY

In order to implement an effective system of real currency convertibility, a government agency is to be given responsibility for exchanging currency for reserves of specified commodities, on demand, on specified terms. In order to clarify the critical differences of the Grondona system from other proposals it is contrasted with two other systems.

8.1.1 Gold Standard

Under the gold standard, conversion of gold and paper notes was essentially a passive operation, in which selected banks responded unconditionally to requests from customers to sell or buy gold: anyone could freely change paper currency notes into gold coins. The range between banks' official buying and selling prices of gold – known as the upper and lower "gold points" in the case of the sterling system operated by the Bank of England almost continuously from 1717 to 1914 – was very narrow, just 0.16%, shown as a narrow band in Figure 1 a). For the gold standard, the critical feature was the upper point – which required banks, which ultimately relied on the central bank, to always hold enough gold to be able to redeem any quantity of British bank notes which were presented by customers. This in turn imposed a rigid constraint on the Bank of England to hold sufficient gold reserves, and if necessary to be prepared to raise interest-rates to whatever level was needed to make holders of sterling notes content to hold them rather than to demand that the bank convert them into gold, which does not earn interest. Consequently interest-rates (i-r) moved in inverse proportion to the level of gold reserves, rising when reserves were low or falling, and lowering when reserves were high or increasing, as indicated in Figure 1 a).

8.1.2 Buffer-stock

In the case of commodity buffer-stocks as advocated by UNCTAD and supporters, the range between the upper and lower prices within which the manager aims to maintain the market price is much wider than for the gold standard, as shown in Figure 1 b), typically about 20%. In addition, the buffer-stock manager uses discretion to buy or sell commodities as they judge to be effective in keeping market prices within their specified range: this requires both holding large enough reserves to be able to sell enough to keep the market price below its upper limit, and having sufficient liquid funds to always be able to buy enough reserves to keep the market price above the lower limit. Since the manager's plans are confidential, not transparent, this introduces a major element of uncertainty into the market. It also creates a problem of "insider information": someone who knows what sales or purchases the manager is going to make can profit in various ways. As described in the previous chapter, this of course provides a motivation for speculation, spying, hacking and corruption – the opposite of stabilizing the market through improving confidence about how market prices will move over the near- and medium-term. In addition, there is no link to interest-rate policy, which is not adjusted in order to preserve the buffer-stock's reserves above zero. In principle, this could be made a condition of the system, but it would be a major additional complication, and would depend on the currency being used, and on the intentions of the founding countries' governments.

8.1.3 Grondona System

Like the gold standard, but unlike buffer-stocks, the operation of the Grondona system is passive: it buys or sells reserves only on demand – that is, when someone asks to sell or buy a quantity of one of the specified commodities handled by the system, at its publicly stated prices. The system handles each commodity (or standard grade thereof) separately, and the prices at which it buys and sells reserves on demand differ from the "gold points" in three critical ways.

1. The range between these prices is significantly wider than the width of the "gold points", varying between commodities, and typically being about +/– 10%.
2. Both of these prices adjust in proportion to the level of reserves which the system holds of the commodity in question, following a fixed and openly published "price-schedule", falling as the quantity of reserves increases, and rising as the quantity of reserves decreases, as shown in Figure 1 c).
3. The highest upper point is not guaranteed unconditionally, but only so long as the system holds reserves – as shown in Figure 1 c) by the gap in the upper horizontal line representing the system's maximum upper price, when reserves are zero. The system also involves no link to interest-rate policy – although monetary authorities may choose to use the level of reserves as a guide for their interest-rate policy after some experience of how it operates.

Figure 1. Commodity reserve–price relations for different systems

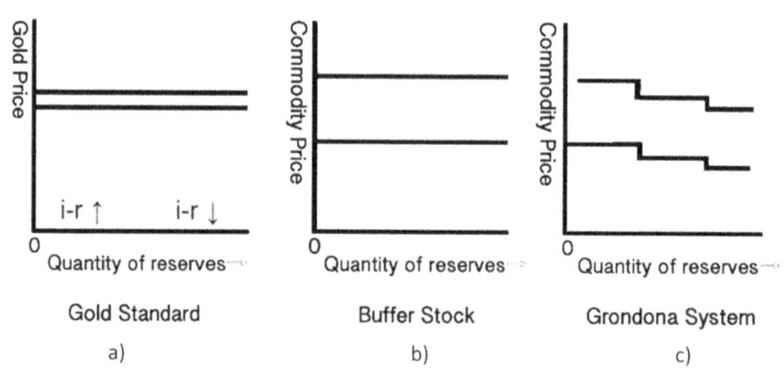

Clearly, not guaranteeing a maximum price for the commodities which the Grondona system handles makes its influence in preventing prices from rising weaker than a rigid gold standard. However, it does not eliminate the system's influence in restraining rising prices, but makes it partial rather than rigid, as discussed in more detail below. To recognize the soundness of this feature one need only consider that insisting that the system must guarantee a maximum price for any commodity would immediately create an open-ended liability for the implementing government, and make it likely that the country's monetary and other policies would become seriously distorted in the event of unusual conditions in commodity markets. By contrast, by entirely avoiding this problem, the government does not need to change its monetary or other policies in any way in order to establish the Grondona system, thereby eliminating any economic risk, and making the system politically far more easily acceptable.

Grondona named the organisation that would operate his system a Price Stabilizing Corporation (PSC). The author, with Grondona's agreement, names it Commodities Reserve Department (CRD). This is to emphasise the monetary aspect of its operation, which Grondona and his supporters discussed in their writings, but secondarily to the issue of stabilizing commodity prices, which was the more serious problem while monetary policies were still constrained under the Bretton Woods agreement. In recent years, as post-Bretton Woods monetary arrangements have become less and less satisfactory world-wide, the issue of how to improve the stability of the monetary system, and so the potential importance of currency convertibility, have assumed more importance, while commodity price stabilization has become a far less prominent topic in discussion of economic policy-making, although the damaging volatility of commodity prices continues.

To summarise: in the Grondona system, each commodity or standard grade thereof is treated separately. The Commodities Reserve Department (or CRD) is entirely passive, never entering the market, but standing ready to buy or sell reserves of the commodities it handles on demand, at prices stated in its price-schedule for each commodity, which depend on the current level of reserves which it holds. Because the CRD's pre-announced prices adjust automatically according to the quantity of reserves held, the convertibility which it provides is therefore *conditional*. This makes the Grondona system less ambitious than other proposals, but in this way the financial liability involved in establishing a CRD is limited by the government in advance, thereby avoiding the open-ended liability involved in commodity "buffer-stock" schemes that aim to keep commodity prices between fixed limits (which would in addition, severely distort commodity markets). This has the vitally significant implication that, in contrast to proposals for international systems, individual countries are able to implement the Grondona system independently in terms of their own currency. Moreover, and equally importantly, a CRD can legitimately pay for purchases of reserves through monetary expansion, as is also done under a gold standard, rather than needing to raise taxation or borrowing – the money supply contracting again when reserves are falling. These features of the Grondona system preserve the implementing country's sovereignty, and ensure direct national benefits from implementation, while avoiding the complex, difficult and unpredictable process of trying to negotiate different countries' shares of an international system. For these reasons the Grondona system is more politically practical, and its implementation is economically much more attractive than participating in international negotiations which, even if successful in some form, could never result in similar benefits.

Grondona described his system of partial price stabilization of primary commodities in detail in many speeches, articles and papers such as (Grondona, 1950) and (Grondona, 1964), and in a series of books which achieved endorsements from many journalists, politicians and economists (Grondona, 1952; Grondona, 1958; Grondona, 1962; Grondona, 1972 & Grondona,1975). Those books focused mainly on the practical issues of implementation. Various wider aspects are discussed in (Collins, 1985), which focused on OECD countries. Since these countries seem to be following globalist policies, implementation of real currency convertibility may be more promising for countries with smaller economies but which are in the process of industrializing. The book was also written at a time when "monetarist" control of the money supply was a priority of UK economic policy-makers, as a response to the "stagflation" caused by Keynesian policies which had loosened traditional constraints on government borrowing from the banking system. Consequently a major part of that book concerned the detailed effects on the British monetary system of implementing the Grondona system. A short description of the system is also available as an audio file (Collins, 2020).

8.2 DETAILS OF IMPLEMENTATION

In the following, the more important features of the Grondona system are discussed in more detail. Only by becoming familiar with the ways in which Grondona ensured the system's simplicity and reliability can the reader understand how Grondona's system solves the problems that proposals for much more complex and expensive international systems have not been able to solve over more than a century.

8.2.1 Durable, Essential, Basic, Imports

Grondona stipulated that only durable, essential, basic, imported commodities should be included, at least initially, and should be handled only in large units of quantity, in order to minimize operating costs and avoid problems of deterioration. This proviso also avoids political issues of subsidizing domestic primary production, which might arise with products for which the country did not depend on imports. (Grondona also suggested that, after some years of successful operation, equitable means of including domestic products within the system's scope might be implemented, but this would depend on national politics.)

8.2.2 Price-Schedules

For each of the durable, essential, basic, imported commodities selected, the CRD would publish a "price schedule", according to which the prices paid or accepted by the CRD in exchange for specified units of that commodity would adjust in proportion to the CRD's current level of reserves of the commodity.

This is illustrated in Figure 2 and Table 1, which show a simplified example. Having initially offered to pay 900 units per ton of a commodity of a standard grade used in world markets, if the CRD's reserves reach a level of 40,000 tons, then the price which the CRD offers will fall by 5% to 855 units per ton. The CRD's offer price and sale price (which Grondona called its "low point" and "high point", in parallel with the "gold points" under the gold standard) would continue to adjust by the same amounts, according to this "price-schedule" as the quantity of its reserves rose or fell.

8.2.3 "Gearing"

There are four parameters (which Grondona called the "gearing" of the system), which determine the scale of the system's monetary and economic influence, and also the scale of the government's financial commitment involved in implementing the system for each commodity. These parameters are 1) the initial price level for each commodity, 2) the size of "Blocks", being the maximum quantity which will be purchased at any one price, 3)

Figure 2. Illustrative price-schedule for a single commodity (Collins, 1985).

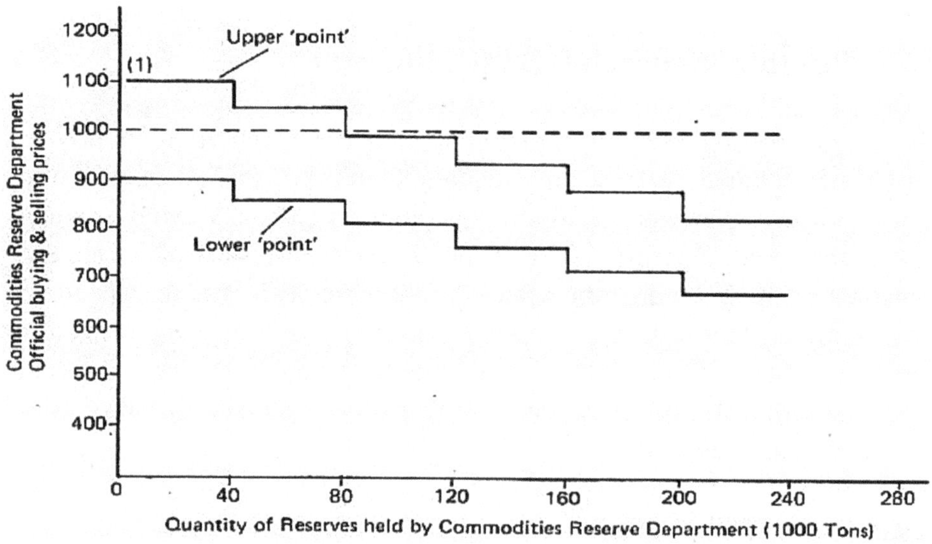

Table 1. Illustrative price-schedule for a single commodity

Quantity in CRD Reserves (Kt)	Current CRD Buying Price[1]	Quantity in CRD Reserves (Kt)	Current CRD Selling Price[1]
0 - 39.5[2]	900	0.5[2] - 40	1,100
40 - 79.5	855	40.5 - 80	1,045
80 - 119.5	810	80.5 - 120	990
120 - 159.5	765	120.5 - 160	935
160 - 199.5	720	160.5 - 200	880
200 - 239.5	675	200.5 - 240	825

[1]: arbitrary units; previous medium-term, average import price (c.i.f.) = 1,000.
[2]: minimum unit is 500 tons; "Block" of each commodity is 40,000 tons.

the width of the "price-band" for each commodity, and 4) the price steps between successive price-bands.

Generally, with a CRD in operation, when a commodity's market price was falling in terms of that country's currency (that is, when the value of that country's monetary unit was rising in terms of a particular commodity), market participants would sell commodities to the CRD in exchange for currency whenever the CRD's current buying price became attractive relative to current market prices. When the quantity of reserves of the commodity rose to the

Table 2. Grondona's Proposed "Gearing" of a Commodities Reserve Department (CRD)

Parameters	Grondona's Suggested Values
1. Initial Index	Average of recent annual import prices (c.i.f.) of each commodity (adjusted for inflation)
2. Width of Price Band	+/-10% of Initial Index
3. Block Size	10% of annual average import quantity
4. Size of Price-Step between Successive Price-Bands	5% of initial value

pre-specified quantity which Grondona termed a "Block", the CRD's official buying and selling prices for that commodity (i.e. its lower and upper "points") would fall by a pre-specified amount. If the value of the CRD's currency in terms of this commodity continued to rise, so that market prices fell to the new "lower point" and reserves continued to accumulate, the process would repeat, the lower and upper "points" would adjust downwards by the same amount again, and the cycle would continue until the CRD's buying price ("lower point") fell low enough to be unattractive to sellers. Later, when the value of the currency in terms of that commodity declined as market prices recovered, buyers would repurchase reserves from the CRD at the successively higher selling prices ("upper points") in its published reserve price-schedule, as each in turn became attractive relative to the current market price.

Once a CRD is established following Grondona's guidelines, the currency of the implementing country would thereby become convertible into a range of durable, essential, basic, imported commodities, at publicly known prices which would adjust according to the level of reserves held by the CRD, following each commodity's published "price-schedule". This form of conditional currency convertibility clearly provides a less rigid guarantee of the value of the currency than strict convertibility such as under a gold standard, and does not compel the government to prevent the level of reserves of any commodity falling to zero. However, in exchange, the maximum liability for the government is calculated in advance to be acceptable, thereby eliminating any unforeseen risk to the national budget.

Grondona also suggested that if a CRD obtains no reserves of a particular commodity for a certain specified period of time, say, two years (or more or less), then the upper and lower "points" for that particular commodity should automatically be increased by a certain stipulated percentage, say 5 percent (or other specified percentage) of the original initial levels. And they should be automatically increased by the same percentage each year until the CRD accumulates reserves of that commodity. Grondona argued that such an adjustment to the initial index is required to tailor the CRD's gearing to the inflation prevailing in the country, and medium-term conditions in each different commodity industry. As for the details of a CRD's "gearing", the most appropriate pace of adjustment will likely not be uniform, but should differ between different commodities according to their different market conditions.

Continuing inflation in the host country will eventually lead to loss of a CRD's reserves, even if world market prices are not rising. This can be partially compensated by Grondona's proposed remedy. However, rapid inflation of about 10% per year or more would considerably reduce a CRD's beneficial influence, by preventing it obtaining reserves of some or all commodities.

Before the CRD buys any reserves, their quality must be guaranteed by professional appraisers, and the reserves then physically delivered to the CRD's selected site, all such costs being paid by the customer. The CRD will prepare its own dedicated warehouses at sites convenient to domestic users of the imported commodities. The warehouses will be designed to be unattended, except when deliveries or collections are under way. At times of major surpluses the CRD may also pay to use commercial warehousing: this will depend on expectations for the commodity in question, and may lead to expanding the CRD's own storage facilities.

As a further detail, Grondona proposed that the sales premium that the CRD earned on all its sales should be used first to cover the costs of construction, maintenance and administration of the CRD's warehouses. He further suggested that any remainder could be transferred to a special account which could be used for poverty alleviation or other programs for enhancing public welfare.

In his writings Grondona discussed a number of other possible details, such as the CRD having the right to pay for reserves above a certain quantity with government bonds, which the customer could use as collateral for bank loans. Grondona considered this idea within the context of the CRD's budget for purchases of reserves coming from general government revenues, which he considered to be the "conventional" means of financing a "Price Stabilising Corporation" at the time when he was writing – in contrast to issuing new money against the reserves. Although that approach remains possible, the authors do not recommend it, since it would greatly reduce the economic benefits of establishing a CRD, of which the role as a means of reviving an element of real currency convertibility and corresponding counter-cyclical variations in the money supply is highly desirable. That is, from the point-of-view of economic policy, it is actually sounder to let variations in the level of a CRD's reserves adjust the money supply than to burden the national budget with paying for reserves – provided that the conditions of the CRD's initial establishment are reasonable, and balanced between different commodities.

8.3 COSTS AND RISKS

The balance of benefits and costs for a government implementing the Grondona system is greatly strengthened by the very low costs which Grondona's plan for CRDs would achieve. As a result, the main out-of-pocket cost of implementing the Grondona system comprises the cost of preparing and maintaining the warehousing needed to safely store the commodities that will be accumulated by a CRD. Grondona investigated these costs in great detail, obtaining and publishing estimates from construction companies for representative warehouses of different sizes and shapes as required for the main different types of commodities – metals, grains, fibres and foodstuffs. He included such details as the benefits of designing them, where suitable, with partitions to hold the single units of quantity which the CRD handles, and of siting CRD warehouses near ports and/or major users within the host country.

The construction cost of specialized storage facilities varies greatly as a percentage of the value of the commodities being stored, both due to the different density and other aspects of different commodities, and because of the wide swings in their market prices. For one of the commodities with low storage-costs, tin, the capital cost of storage is less than 1% of the cost of the tin stored, when at full capacity, while for one of the highest, wheat, this ratio may be more than 50%. Spread over the several decades of the buildings' lives, and including periodic maintenance costs, the effective annual cost of storage would be more than offset by the premium of some 20% or more that the CRD would earn on sales of reserves when prices were rising, which can be expected to occur every few years, as is typical of trade cycles.

The one case in which storage costs could become burdensome would be if large reserves were accumulated which were never repurchased from the CRD because market prices remained permanently depressed. At time of writing in 2021, this risk does not seem a serious threat, but the risk of deflation is obviously one factor to be considered by those planning the scale of implementation. Overall, the costs of preparing and maintaining the necessary storage facilities are determined primarily by the scale on which the system is established, and this will obviously be chosen to be acceptable from the point-of-view of its potential influence on the government budget.

All government policy-making involves political considerations: in the case of establishing a CRD, decisions on the siting of the CRD's warehouses could be used for other political purposes such as contributing to regional development, use of favoured contractors, and/or other purposes, as is common with public construction projects worldwide. Deciding the scale of the system's operation in respect to different commodities might also favour some commodities over others. However, provided that the central principle of the CRD's automatically-adjusting price-schedule is preserved, there are no complex or uncertain macro-economic or geo-political issues, such as politically controversial trade-offs typical of international negotiations, that need to be resolved. There is also no risk of losses due to misjudgement as is typical of stocks under discretionary management. Due to this, the author considers it appropriate to describe the Grondona system as "politically practical".

8.4 MONEY SUPPLY VARIATION

The second "cost" of implementing the Grondona system is that of permitting the money supply to increase and decrease in proportion to the CRD's reserves, within predetermined, conditional limits. That is, as under the gold standard, it is a fundamentally important aspect of the CRD's functioning that the money used to pay for the reserves should not be raised from taxation or government borrowing but should comprise "new money" released into the economy. Likewise, the proceeds of sales of the CRD's reserves should not be treated as government revenues to be used for other purposes, but should leave circulation. (NB This need not apply to the premiums which the CRD would earn on its sales. If not spent, these would comprise a net contractionary effect on the money supply.) This makes the reserves "costless", subject to the obvious condition that the scale of implementation is not excessively large or unbalanced between commodities (thereby causing significant "distortion" of the money supply). The variation in the money supply which a CRD's operation causes will in general be "counter-cyclical", increasing the money supply when commodity market prices are falling and economic activity is becoming depressed, and reducing the money supply when inflationary trends are worsening, in which case monetary contraction is beneficial. This is one of the fundamental strengths of currency convertibility which was responsible for its success over centuries in the past: the monetary changes to which it gives rise tend to smooth fluctuations in economic activity, both in individual industries due to changes in particular factors such as weather, technology or national capabilities, and overall in relation to national or international business cycles. Consequently, discussion of stabilizing commodity prices without including discussion of the merits of the counter-cyclical monetary variation that occurs in parallel is a serious failure of policy analysis, as discussed further in Chapter 16.3 below.

It should be added that an increase or decrease in the money supply caused by a CRD could be countered by the monetary authorities, if desired, without cancelling the CRD's beneficial stabilizing influence on each commodity trade and industry, due to the different route by which monetary policy acts on the economy (such as through changes in interest-rates, or the purchase or sale of government bonds). Moreover, *a priori* it is equally likely that the monetary authorities would wish to strengthen the monetary effects of the CRD operations rather than counteracting them, due to their counter-cyclical timing. It is for these reasons that Grondona's system was hailed as "epoch-making" when first published (Manager, 1958).

It is worth expanding on this point since, in the present era, direct currency convertibility is not a familiar policy. In particular, at a time when most new money entering the economy is no longer created debt-free by governments, but is created by banks as debt to themselves, the soundness of government issuing "new money" against such reserves may be questioned. For example, Prates describes the current situation in the following terms:

"Since the 1970s or the 1980s, the central bank has been prohibited to buy treasury bonds in the primary market in most countries, and the states have been under scrutiny of financial markets that are opposed to the idea of monetary financing of public debts, and attach great importance to restrain public borrowing within strict limits." (Prates, 2021)

That is, in addition to their loss of the role of creating the money supply, governments are required to borrow any funds which they need over and above their tax revenues from the private sector. As a result they are largely controlled by global financial markets which have usurped the historical right and duty of governments to provide a sufficient money supply. Unfortunately, Prates does not discuss the full implications of the fact that nearly all money is nowadays created by banks as debt to themselves, and how radical a change this is from the past. Bibow also discusses how unsatisfactory the associated "neo-liberal" tenet has been that the policy advice that comes with liberalised commercial financial inflows to industrialising economies will lead to better economic policy than the national government would otherwise implement (Bibow, 2021). The exchange-rate volatility caused by rapid foreign exchange flows in and out of such economies by foreign investment funds is one of the more obvious flaws in this viewpoint of the overgrown western financial sector.

The discipline which "... *financial markets that are opposed to the idea of monetary financing of public debts* ..." typically use against a government or central bank going against their opposition is to announce a loss of confidence in the currency in question, leading to a rapid fall in the exchange-rate. Notably, with a CRD in operation, this would automatically induce a corresponding stabilizing influence on the currency via purchases of reserves of various commodities from the CRD, thereby reducing the money supply proportionally. The scale of this effect would depend on the quantity of reserves held by the CRD, but would be a welcome stabilizing influence, as discussed further below.

8.5 NOT VULNERABLE TO SPECULATIVE ATTACK

Concerning potential risks, it is a major advantage that the Grondona system is not vulnerable to manipulation or attack by speculators, due to the "automatic" nature, that is the predictable conditionality, of its stabilizing operation. For example, a "speculative attack" on a CRD could involve one of only two possible actions: some organisation might buy all its reserves of one or more commodities, or conversely it might sell large quantities of commodities to it. But in either case the CRD would benefit – either by selling all its reserves at some 20% above the prices which it paid (as per its price-schedules), or by accumulating reserves of essential imports at ever-lower prices. Hence, except in case of actual fraud, the CRD is literally immune to speculative attack. From the point-of-view of a government considering implementing the system, this is an extremely important and attractive feature.

8.6 STABILIZING INFLUENCE ON EXCHANGE-RATES

By the same token, the operation of a CRD would help to strengthen a country's currency against speculative attack in foreign-exchange markets, due to its counter-cyclical response to major changes in domestic commodity prices (ie in its national currency) that could be caused by large exchange-rate movements. For example, if the value of the currency in foreign-exchange markets fell significantly, domestic prices of imported commodities would rise, and the CRD would be required to sell reserves, for which the customer would have to pay in the national currency, thereby creating demand for the currency in foreign exchange markets, and reducing the national money supply by the same amount. Any such stabilizing influence will depend on the scale of the CRD, which will generally be small compared to typical turnover on foreign-exchange markets – but any such influence is better than none, particularly at times of "panic" when market volatility is high, and "one way" trends are liable to arise in the foreign-exchange market. Prates notes the particular vulnerability of "peripheral currencies" to instability in foreign-exchange markets, due to their relative lack of liquidity (Prates, 2021). Hence this stabilizing influence of a CRD could be additionally beneficial for governments of relatively small economies, of which the currencies are unavoidably low in the "currency hierarchy" dominated *de facto* by the US dollar. Grondona envisaged that his system would be adopted by multiple countries, due to the obvious benefits for countries that implemented it, in which case their mutual exchange-rates would also be stabilized by their respective CRDs' operations, as discussed in more detail in Chapter 12 below.

8.7 NOT AT RISK FROM "COMPETITION"

Another strength is that a CRD would not be vulnerable to harm from "competition" from other countries' CRDs. Any "competition" between different countries' CRDs could only consist of their setting higher prices in their price-schedules in order to attract reserves, leading to their temporarily accumulating reserves ahead of other countries. However, provided that they use the central feature of the Grondona system, namely the market price-driven adjustment of its buying and selling prices according to its price-schedules, each CRD's buying prices would adjust downwards after accumulating a certain quantity of reserves, thereby making the price offered by other countries' CRDs more attractive (allowing for considerations of delivery cost, exchange-rate risk, & etc). Hence, there would be no need for coordination between different countries planning to establish CRDs, and any "competition" between different countries' CRDs would act to improve the stability of commodity prices and trade by increasing the quantity of reliably counter-cyclical stock-holding capacity in the world economy.

8.8 THEORETICAL SUPPORT

Despite vigorous support in the press and among politicians and economists during the 1950s, the Grondona system received little analysis or discussion by academic researchers. However, a theoretical analysis using a mathematical model was published by Nguyen in 1980 (Nguyen, 1980). In his paper Nguyen described related research to date on means of stabilizing commodity prices, and its inadequacy:

"The typical approach by writers in this field is to compare the instability of earnings under freely fluctuating prices with what it would be if prices were stabilized at some appropriate level . . . Underlying this approach is the assumption of a buffer-stock scheme which can operate successfully to maintain a perfectly stable price (i.e. "complete" price stabilization) by being able to buy or sell any required amount at the chosen price". (Nguyen, 1980)

Nguyen then explained that incomplete information and associated costs make it impossible in reality to achieve "complete stabilization" – for which the long history of failure of proposals for International Commodity Agreements provides much evidence. Nguyen then introduced his mathematical model designed to assess the effect of a system with

"... the objective ... to reduce, rather than to eliminate entirely, the fluctuations of prices." (Nguyen, 1980).

This is achieved by making the prices at which the system buys and sells commodities adjust continuously in inverse proportion to the quantity of reserves held. This model is not precisely the same as Grondona's system, but is a mathematical idealization, using a continuous function instead of a step function as used in Grondona's system. (NB Nguyen states that he received the idea from the Australian Wool Board (AWB): Grondona had discussed his system with AWB staff at length.) Nguyen's resulting conclusion was very positive:

"... in contrast to what is now widely believed, both objectives of price stability and earning stability can be achieved for almost all commodities ..." (Nguyen, 1980).

In view of this demonstration of an apparently promising new approach to the problem of commodity price stabilization, it is surprising that Nguyen did not himself pursue this research further. However, following Nguyen's positive result, a logical next step is to simulate a practical implementation of his theoretical rule. In particular, a system that bought and sold commodities at continuously changing prices, even if rule-based, could hardly be stabilizing, since traders would not be able to rely on continuously varying buying and selling prices. Consequently, Grondona's system in which a CRD's buying and selling prices adjust according to the level of its accumulated reserves in discrete, pre-announced steps, is a simple and practical realisation of Nguyen's approach.

The author considered that the best way to realistically assess the operation of the Grondona system is not another mathematical model of its non-continuous adjustment process, following Nguyen, but a simulation of its response to real commodity market movements, using actual past market data, since this is possible due to the simplicity of the system's operation. Using this approach, the author and colleagues have simulated the operation of the Grondona system in five different countries over periods of up to 10 years, as discussed in Chapters 9 and 10. Grondona designed his system specifically to make its operation as predictable as possible, driven by market prices, leaving no scope for discretionary management. This eliminates uncertainty among market participants about how the system would respond under different conditions, while also making it possible to simulate its operation reliably.

Being a simple mechanism to reduce instability of the real value of currencies, Grondona's system is not directly relevant to the discussions in earlier chapters about the relative advantages and disadvantages of different types of money, such as Blockchain-based crypto-currencies, some of which may be used as the basis of physical "coins". It offers a means of stabilizing the real value of any currency, independent of whether it is digital, Blockchain-based, private or government-controlled, and whether it is primarily a means of saving, a means to facilitate transactions, or a measure of value.

8.9 GREATLY PREFERABLE TO BUFFER-STOCK PROPOSAL

The revival in recent years of research on the feasibility and potential benefits of implementing the international "commodity reserve currency" originally proposed and advocated by Benjamin Graham in the 1930s is testimony to the continuing need to reduce the extreme volatility of commodity prices in international trade. This makes life difficult for both producers and users of commodities, and deepens the cyclical swings in the terms of trade between primary industries and manufacturing industries, and thereby hinders growth of the world economy.

Among others, Ussher has written detailed accounts of the evolution of these ideas, and concludes by supporting renewed efforts to implement an international buffer-stock system. Interestingly, Ussher refers to Grondona's work, and to his influence:

"Keynes was originally encouraged to create an international commodity fund for Bretton Woods by Roy Harrod who in 1939 also promoted the work of an Australian L. St Clare Grondona who advocated commodity buffer stocks as a tool of macroeconomic policy, as early as 1924 and as late as 1975" (see Grondona 1975, p.9) (Ussher, 2012)

Unfortunately, however, Ussher gives no sign of having read the book of Grondona's which she references, despite quoting from the laudatory six-page Preface which Sir Roy Harrod wrote for it. Presumably this oversight was due to the assumption that Grondona's approach, which did not include advocacy for an international buffer-stock system, was mistaken. Among many interesting points in a later paper, Ussher provides a useful discussion of nine criticisms of Graham's buffer-stock plan, and responses to them (Ussher, 2016). Of most interest for the present discussion, Ussher claims that international agreement is not required, as usually stated: a buffer-stock system could be established as a private venture, funded by the issue of a new currency backed by the system's reserves, referring to such a proposal by Lietaer (Lietaer, 2004). The recent rapid growth of crypto-currencies has increased the feasibility of opportunities such as this, as discussed further below in Chapter 14.10. However, any such system operated as a profit-seeking project could not achieve the same results as a government project to stabilize the value of its national currency, since these are different objectives. In addition, in order for existing currencies to benefit from such a system in the event that it was established, governments would have to link their currencies to the new currency via a fixed exchange-rate, which would involve imposing the major constraints on national monetary policy discussed above, and would provide no more than indirect benefits at best.

Although Ussher's discussion of many aspects of buffer-stock systems is very useful, the fact remains that establishing a global system involving the creation of a new global currency convertible into commodities based on operating buffer-stocks would be vulnerable to errors of judgement, manipulation or corruption by the managers – remembering that they would be targeted by special interests worldwide. In addition, the inevitable need to periodically adjust the prices at which the new currency is convertible into different commodities would make it the target of predatory speculators world-wide.

What Ussher's paper unfortunately does not include is a comparison of such a global system with the system designed by Grondona to achieve much the same goals, but through each country voluntarily establishing a separate system to partially stabilize their own currency. Fully as important as the weakness of depending on experts working in an international organization far beyond accountability to taxpayers, such a global system would do nothing to stabilize exchange-rates between the currencies of the participating countries and the newly convertible global currency.

More recently, Woods has written at length about the support by Keynes and his successor Kaldor for the Commodity Reserve Currency proposed by Graham in the 1930s. Keynes made proposals to include such a feature in the post-war economic system based on the US dollar, by establishing what he called a publicly funded "Commodity Control" for each selected commodity (Woods, 2021). However, there is no convincing evidence that giving each of these bodies the authority to control world markets for a major primary commodity would enable them to achieve a sufficiently fair and economically beneficial result that it would be preferable to the operation of existing markets.

Overall Woods makes a strong case for the importance of progress in this subject on which Graham, Keynes, Kaldor and others worked so hard and in such agreement over three generations. However, the paper founders on the difficulties discussed above that remain for any international system such as Graham's. In his "concluding remarks" Woods quotes Graham's question from 1937: "*Why has not the stockpile principle emerged as a fundamental factor in economic policy – both national and international?*" Yet the answer is surely very simple: the main reason is surely because the plan advocated for decades by Graham, Keynes, Hayek, Kaldor and others to implement a single, monopolistic global system to control the prices of most of the major traded primary commodities, is both economically and politically unattractive. As well as being a massive change for everyone involved in world trade, it would also introduce huge uncertainties, while putting the entire system in the hands of unaccountable international bureaucrats and giant corporations. It would be difficult for even the strongest supporter of the need for improvement in this part of the economic system to be optimistic that this would be an improvement over the present situation.

This risk is unintentionally clarified by Ussher, writing in favour of the Graham/Keynes/Kaldor plan without any apparent reservation:

"... price stabilization would be based on long-run averages, discerned by technocrats and experts in charge of running the buffer stock ... An alternative is to have no announced floor and ceiling, but just have an experienced technocrat act as a market maker ..." (Ussher, 2016)

This idea is contrary to centuries of successful experience among the developed countries of generally free worldwide trade. Although, as Woods and Ussher both discuss, international commodity markets as they operate today suffer from the major weakness that they do not prevent extreme price fluctuations, there is no evidence to suggest that switching to a centrally controlled, global monopoly system would be an improvement. The well-studied phenomenon of "regulatory capture" alone would make the prospect of such a system a target for bribery and corruption. In contrast to such a prospect, the fact that Grondona's system of partial commodity price stabilization is specifically designed to eliminate discretion, and therefore any possibility of error or corruption, like a gold standard, is an extreme, indeed unique strength.

Finally, it is ironic indeed that Woods ends his lengthy and detailed paper by quoting approvingly from Kaldor's two-page Preface to Grondona's last book (which follows Harrod's Preface to the same book referenced by Ussher):

"In the longer run, it is the supply of basic materials which would set the limit to the rate of growth of world industrial production and not, as now, the rate of growth of effective demand emanating from the advanced countries, which governed the trend rate of growth of investment and production of primary commodities." (Grondona, 1975).

However, Woods makes no other mention of Grondona's work, and gives no sign of having even read it, despite quoting from Kaldor's endorsing Preface, in which Kaldor also wrote:

"My ideas have been pretty close to those of Mr Grondona; the difference between us has mainly concerned the question of whether such an idea requires an international agreement among the leading importing countries

for its implementation, or whether, as Mr Grondona supposes, it would be possible for a country such as the UK to initiate such a scheme through its own action, without waiting for others." (Grondona, 1975)

It seems that we must deduce that, having read this comment of Kaldor's, Woods assumed that Grondona was mistaken. However, since Woods offers no critique of Grondona's system, he seems to be yet another victim of the *idee fixe* that only an international system could succeed in implementing a useful form of commodity price stabilization, which would also be a form of commodity-based currency convertibility. In other words, like Ussher, Woods too failed to recognise that, as he held Grondona's book in his hands, he was actually holding the answer which he was seeking to the fundamental problem he was writing about, which has baffled the economics profession for more than a century!

It is also noteworthy that Kaldor himself, after several decades of close involvement in planning an international system under UNCTAD auspices, conceded that the plan that prices should be adjusted as necessary through negotiations between the participating countries was not satisfactory, and that a more automatic system would be needed, in which "*... the adjustment of prices would be circumscribed by carefully laid down rules*" – exactly as Grondona had stipulated throughout his work (Kaldor, 1983). Indeed it does not seem too fanciful to think that, if Kaldor had lived longer, he might have come round entirely to advocating Grondona's system.

Although seemingly small-scale and not in itself international, the Grondona system in fact provides the blueprint for a much more realistic worldwide system, based on voluntary participation by individual countries which would each receive the direct benefits of partially stabilizing the real value of their national currency in terms of the commodities which they themselves selected to be most appropriate. Operating on a scale proportionate to the commitment which they made, this would also enable them to finance commodity purchases through monetary expansion rather than taxation. Moreover, the system's flexibility also ensures that different countries' systems will operate without mutual interference – indeed, to the contrary, they would benefit synergistically as other countries set up their own systems, as discussed in Chapter 12 below.

8.10 THE GRONDONA SYSTEM IS SHARIAH-COMPLIANT

It is a question of great importance for countries which encourage Islamic economic and financial policies whether the Grondona system is morally acceptable, that is "Shariah-compliant". Analysis by Jamil Ahmed has clarified that, provided that certain optional provisions which Grondona suggested are avoided, the operation of a CRD is indeed Shariah-compliant. Studies which describe why its operations are Shariah-compliant have been published in (Ahmed et al., 2014; Ahmed et al., 2018). This is important for clarifying that the Grondona system can also be implemented in the 57 countries which are members of the Organisation of Islamic Cooperation (OIC), comprising a fifth of the world population: hence the system could be adopted literally throughout the world, which would bring great synergistic benefits, as discussed in Chapter 12.

The underlying reason for the Grondona system's acceptability is that it is a simple and foolproof means of implementing the age-old policy of storing reserves of various essential raw materials at times when they are in troublesome surplus, in order to make them available for use when there is a shortage. This policy is recognised as an important precedent in Islamic economics, but Grondona himself also quoted from the Christian Bible in his books about this policy having been used in antiquity:

"Let Pharaoh do this, and let him appoint officers over the land ... And let them gather ... and lay up corn ... and let them keep food in the cities ... .And Joseph gathered corn as the sand of the sea, very much, until he left numbering, for it was without number ... .And when all the land of Egypt was famished, the people cried to Pharaoh for bread ... and Joseph opened all the storehouses, and sold unto the Egyptians, and the famine waxed sore in the land of Egypt ... And all countries came into Egypt for to buy corn, because the famine was so sore in all lands" Genesis xli, 34-57. (Grondona, 1958).

Such counter-cyclical stock-holding is a valuable function which is already provided to a certain extent by businesses on a commercial basis, and there is a substantial research literature concerning the conditions under which speculation may be either economically stabilizing or destabilizing. That is, in the simplest terms, trading which follows the traditional rule "Buy low, sell high" can help to support falling prices and to hold down rising prices. However, with or without speculation, market forces alone do not keep primary commodity prices stable: many commodity markets continue to experience rapid price increases of more than 100%, and rapid reductions in price of more than 50%. This means that commodity markets do not in fact stabilize the real value of money, which is a legitimate objective of government policy-making – indeed, it is a government responsibility, and so governments which fail to achieve this can be fairly criticized as failing in their responsibilities.

Another feature which Ahmed explained as Shariah-compliant is CRDs' custodial service. Grondona suggested that a CRD could offer to warehouse commercially owned reserves, at a cost to be paid by the owner, for which the CRD would provide conditional warrants, certifying the ownership of the reserves. The condition would be that, if the price of the reserves in any recognized commodity market rose to the current "high point", the CRD would take possession of the reserves, pay the owner their value priced at the "low point", and hold them for sale at the high point. The intended effect of such a service is to create a further incentive towards keeping market prices between the CRD's current low and high "points". Ahmed explained that such a contract is a genuine "Wadiah" contract of custodianship, and so is Shariah-compliant (Ahmed et al., 2018).

The feature of Grondona's system which is not Shariah-compliant was his proposal that a CRD might pay for some of its purchases with interest-bearing government bonds instead of cash, which would comprise usury. Although some countries might choose to use this option under certain circumstances, there is no need for Islamic countries to do so in order to successfully implement the system.

8.10.1 Not Riba

As a fundamental issue, it is clear that currency issued *de novo* to pay for the CRD's reserves is literally backed by the real commodity reserves which it is used to purchase, and which are purchased at prices below their long-term average trend. Moreover, if the CRD is required to purchase unusually large quantities of reserves, the price which it pays falls proportionately, minimizing any risk of loss in the future. When market prices rise once again, and so the quantity of reserves held by the CRD falls, the currency is retired from circulation (at a pre-announced premium to offset the costs of stock-holding, at least in part), thereby resisting any inflationary tendency connected with the rising commodity prices.

The importance of this is that, even while using one of today's *fiat* currencies, a CRD's actions in expanding the money supply cannot be criticized as "Riba", neither for issuing *fiat* money without real backing, nor for being debt-based, like all OECD currencies today (and many others), which are largely supplied via privately owned, fractional-reserve banking systems. A concomitant benefit, discussed further in Chapter 12 below, is that the exchange-rate of a currency used by a CRD would experience a stabilizing influence as a result of the CRD's counter-cyclical operation, increasing the money supply when the real value of the currency is rising (and so commodity prices are falling), and reducing the money supply when the value of the currency is falling (as commodity prices rise).

Among other implications, this means that implementing the Grondona system in terms of their national currencies could be a means by which members of the Organisation of Islamic Cooperation (OIC) could independently improve their macro-economic stability in the face of sometimes destabilizing external influences. A common argument used by supporters of "globalization" is that there is no better alternative: smaller countries inevitably depend on larger countries' economic policies, and this extends to monetary matters as well. However, participation in the Euro has been very costly to smaller EU member-states, as the loss of their ability to adjust their exchange-rate with stronger currencies has led to high unemployment, loss of political independence, and falling indigenous populations through emigration. The feasibility of the larger "D-8" members of OIC taking this initiative to introduce real currency convertibility, while also reducing the volatility of commodity prices, trade and exchange-rates by establishing CRDs, is discussed further in Chapter 12.

8.11 SUMMARY OF GRONDONA SYSTEM STRENGTHS

The following list summarises the main strengths of the Grondona system, as a result of which its implementation could make a valuable contribution to improving the stability of economic systems world-wide, while helping to preserve the sovereignty of implementing nations.

8.11.1 Minimal Costs

The only actual cost to be paid from government revenues is the cost of storage, since payments for purchases of reserves are made by issuing new money against the reserves.

8.11.2 Liability Limited

The scale on which the system is to operate is decided in advance by the implementing government to be optimal for its needs.

8.11.3 National Systems Independent

By using only the national currency, the system is exclusively under the control of the implementing government.

8.11.4 Markets Not Distorted

The operation of the system reduces fluctuations in commodity prices in the national currency, but does not prevent prices moving as markets need.

8.11.5 Neither Inflationary nor Deflationary

Unlike "Keynesianism" which is inflationary in practice, and "Monetarism" which is deflationary in practice, as also was the gold standard, the Grondona system resists both problems.

8.11.6 Monetary Policy Not Distorted

The operation of the Grondona system does not necessitate changes in monetary policy like a strict gold standard, but facilitates sound policy.

8.11.7 No Conflict Between National Systems

By using the same operating principle, the stabilizing effects of different countries' systems would be synergistic and cumulative.

8.11.8 Shariah-Compliant

By issuing currency in exchange for reserves of commodities, CRDs operate to reduce the role of *fiat* money, and do not involve government debt.

8.11.9 Possible to Simulate Accurately

The simplicity of the Grondona system enables realistic simulation of its operation in order to examine its potential effects under different conditions.

8.12 SIMULATION OF THE GRONDONA SYSTEM

Finally, expanding on this last point, it is a further consequence of the operation of Grondona's system being "automatic", activated by market forces rather than by political or "expert" judgement, that its operation can be simulated realistically. That is, by using historical market price data it is possible to estimate how a country's CRD would have operated over past time periods, which can be considered realistic with a high degree of confidence. In this way, simulations of how it would have operated in different countries are useful to help understand the effects of the counter-cyclical timing of the system's automatic functioning in relation to each commodity industry separately, and thereby its broadly counter-cyclical influence relative to the overall trade cycle.

In the following chapter, the timing and scale of changes in the national money supply that would have occurred in Japan during the 1990s, if a CRD had been established on representative terms, are estimated and discussed (Collins, 1996). In Chapter 10, parallel simulations of the Grondona system operating in the four countries Indonesia, Malaysia, Turkey and Pakistan are shown.

SUMMARY

This chapter has described Grondona's system of conditional currency convertibility in detail. As readers will understand, it is modeled closely on the classical gold standard – notably in its "automaticity", so that it operates without discretion on the part of active managers, thereby offering an entirely reliable service to market participants. Most notably, it differs critically from a gold standard in permitting much greater flexibility in the guaranteed prices of the commodities involved, by maintaining a publicly announced "price-schedule" for each commodity, rather than a fixed price-range, whereby the system's guaranteed buying and selling prices adjust according to the level of reserves held. In addition, by explicitly not guaranteeing a maximum price for any commodity, the system thereby enables the implementing government to limit its maximum possible liability in advance to a scale appropriate for its economy.

In this way the system is politically much simpler than buffer-stock systems based on international negotiations and requiring international funding to guarantee a fixed price range for commodities involved. In addition, implementing governments receive the direct benefit of having the real value of their currency directly stabilized in terms of these commodities, thereby exerting a counter-cyclical stabilizing influence on the economy as a whole – a highly desirable result which an international system such as that supported by many economists from Graham in the 1930s to Ussher and Woods in the 2020s, can not achieve.

REFERENCES

Ahmed, J., Collins, P., & Meera, A. K. (2018). Analysis of Commodity Reserve Currency System from Siyasah Shariyyah Perspective. *Journal of Islamic Accounting and Business Research*, *9*(3), 222–250. doi:10.1108/JIABR-05-2015-0018

Ahmed, J., Meera, A. K., & Collins, P. (2014). An Analysis of Yusuf (AS)'s Counter-Cyclical Principle and its Implementation in the Modern World. *Tazkia Islamic Finance and Business Review, 7*(2). Retrieved from https://www.tifbr-tazkia.org/index.php/TIFBR/article/view/13

Bibow, J. (2021). Evolving International Monetary and Financial Architecture and the Development Challenge. In Emerging Economies and the Global Financial System (pp. 101-115). Routledge.

Collins, P. (1985). *Currency Convertibility: The Return to Sound Money*. Macmillan. https://link.springer.com/book/10.1007/978-1-349-07058-9

Collins, P. (2020). *Resisting Economic Crises with the Grondona System of Currency Convertibility*. https://www.scipod.global/resisting-economic-crises-with-the-grondona-system-of-currency-convertibility

Graham, B. (1937). *Storage and Stability*. McGraw-Hill.

Grondona, L. (1939). *National Reserves for Safety and Stabilization*. Allen & Unwin.

Grondona, L. (1950, July 21). Insurance Against Slump: A Way to Price Stability. *The Manchester Guardian.*

Grondona, L. (1952). *A System for Commodity-Price Stabilization*. Economic Research Council.

Grondona, L. (1958). *Utilising World Abundance*. George Allen & Unwin.

Grondona, L. (1962). *A Firm Foundation for Economy*. Anthony Blond.

Grondona, L. (1964). A Built-in Stabilizer for Commodities. *Westminster Bank Review.*, (May), 15–29.

Grondona, L. (1972). *A Built-in Basic-Economy Stabiliser*. Economic Research Council.

Grondona, L. (1975). *Economic Stability is Attainable*. Hutchinson-Benham.

Kaldor, N. (1976). Inflation and Recession in the World Economy. *Economic Journal, 86*(344).

Kaldor, N. (1983, July). The Role of Commodity Prices in Economic Recovery. *Lloyds Bank Review*.

Lietaer, B. (2004). *The Terra TRC White Paper*. https://www.scribd.com/document/31636027/The-Terra-TRC-White-Paper-2004

Manager. (1958). Editorial. *The Manager, 26*(3).

Nguyen, D. (1980). Partial Price Stabilisation and Export Earning Instability. *Oxford Economic Papers*, *32*(1), 340–352. doi:10.1093/oxfordjournals.oep.a041483

Prates, D. M. (2021). Monetary sovereignty in the Post Keynesian perspective: In the search of a concept. In Emerging Economies and the Global Financial System (pp. 230-244). Routledge.

Ussher, L. (2012). *Combining International Monetary Reform with Commodity Buffer Stocks: Keynes, Graham and Kaldor*. Economics Department, City University of New York. http://www.global-systems-science.org/wp-content/uploads/2012/11/ussher_Bancor_19Dec12.pdf

Ussher, L. (2016). International Monetary Policy with Commodity Buffer Stocks. *European Journal of Economics and Economic Policies: Intervention*, *13*(1), 10–25. doi:10.4337/ejeep.2016.01.02

Woods, J. E. (2021). Benjamin Graham on Buffer Stocks. *Journal of the History of Economic Thought.*

Chapter 9
Illustrating the Grondona System in Operation

ABSTRACT

While working in Japan during the 1990s, the author took the opportunity to collect data on past Japanese commodity imports and recent commodity market prices and to use them to simulate how a CRD would have operated over the decade 1987 – 1996 using a computer spreadsheet. The graphs showing the results are easy to understand: the CRD would have bought reserves when Yen prices were falling and sold them when Yen prices were rising, thereby exerting a stabilizing influence on the prices and quantities of these imported commodities. In parallel, by expanding and contracting the money supply counter-cyclically, the system would have helped to stabilize the overall economy.

INTRODUCTION

As described in the previous chapter, the Grondona system is not complex, but readers need to thoroughly familiarize themselves with its key features, in order to be able to visualise how its automatic price adjustments would operate, and to understand how critically this differentiates it from other proposals. Fortunately, as described in the previous chapter, once a Commodities Reserve Department (CRD) was established, its operation would be very simple, following fixed rules. As a result, it is possible to reliably predict how a CRD would behave under different market conditions, and so also to

DOI: 10.4018/978-1-7998-8302-9.ch009

accurately simulate how it would have operated in the past, by using historical commodity market price data. That is, because the system follows clear rules, it can be simulated as being literally activated by market prices, since market participants use market prices to decide when and where to buy or sell commodities. Hence, by collecting past data on market price movements of selected commodities it is possible to estimate accurately what quantities of reserves of different commodities a CRD would have accumulated as prices fell, and what quantities would have been repurchased from the CRD as market prices rose again.

Performing such a simulation requires making assumptions about the terms on which the system might have been implemented, but once these assumptions are made, the results are driven by market data. This enables a simple visual illustration of how the system would have operated over any time-period for which the necessary market price data is available. As more and more countries collect and publish reliable statistical data on their international trade using standard definitions, it has become easier to illustrate how the system would have operated in each of them.

A computer model can speed up the process of simulating how a CRD would have reacted to past market price conditions – and could even be made to operate in near-real time using daily market price data. However, this is not a use of "big data", since the calculations involved are quite simple: the sequence of a commodity's price data over time is compared regularly with a CRD's current prices, resulting in either purchase or sale of reserves, or – most of the time – no action. Typically, "big data" systems are used to search for significant patterns of behavior in large masses of data about some economic phenomenon in order to predict some aspect of the future pattern. This can be a valuable function for businesses, but is not needed in order to understand or simulate the operation of a CRD.

Grondona explained that, in practice, each country would decide the details of the initial conditions of implementation of a CRD to suit their own conditions, but he offered some preliminary guidelines. For simplicity, in the following we use his uniform guidelines, as suggested in (Grondona, 1975), namely that only durable, essential, basic, imported commodities are handled; the CRD's initial buying and selling prices are 10% below and above the previous average c.i.f. prices (adjusted for inflation if necessary); the maximum quantity that the CRD would purchase or sell at a given price (a "Block") is 10% of previous average annual imports; and the buying and selling prices would adjust downwards or upwards by 5% of their initial levels on the purchase or sale of each full Block of reserves.

The first such simulation was performed manually for the case of Japan by the author, by looking up historical data on import quantities in annual volumes of trade statistics in a specialised library, and using a computer spreadsheet to facilitate calculations. The results shown below illustrate how the system would have operated on the above assumptions.

9.1 ILLUSTRATION OF CRD OPERATING IN JAPAN

Based on these ideas, the initial simulation was of how the Grondona system might have operated in Japan over the decade 1987 – 1996. This necessitated deciding the conditions on which the Japanese CRD might have been set up, including selecting which commodities to include in the simulation: those chosen were copper, nickel, aluminium, lead, zinc, tin, sugar, coffee beans, cocoa beans, cotton, wool, rubber, wheat, barley, maize and soy beans.

It was necessary next to use Japanese national import data from the years before the start of the simulation to calculate the average import quantities of each commodity and average Yen price; to decide the quantity in a Block of each commodity; and to estimate initial buying and selling prices for each commodity, as well as the price-steps by which they adjust on the purchase or sale of each Block of the commodity.

After having decided the CRD's "gearing" for each commodity in this way, following Grondona's suggested guidelines, quarterly Yen market prices of the commodities involved were calculated from actual market prices published in US dollars and the dollar-Yen exchange-rate in each quarter, in order to then simulate the CRD's operation.

Finally, for each commodity, for each quarter of the period of the simulation, the following calculation was made: if the Yen market price was below the CRD's current "low point" for that commodity, it was assumed that the CRD would have been required to purchase a whole Block. In practice the CRD's standing ready to purchase at its current lower point might have prevented the market price falling so far, or less than a Block might have been purchased. However, as an approximation, it was assumed that the CRD would have no significant influence on the Yen market price, and would be a simple "price-taker". In truth, a CRD could well have a significant stabilising influence on the market price on days when the quantity traded on the spot market was either less than, or not much more than, the quantity in the CRD's Block

Figure 1. Movements in Yen commodity import prices

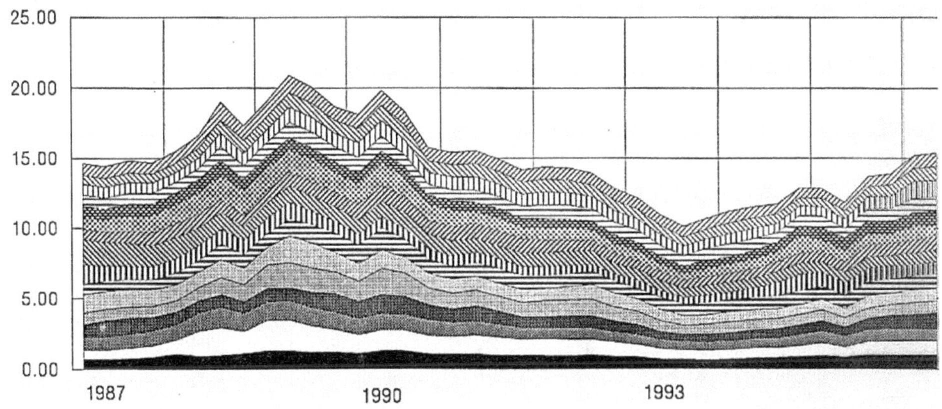

of that commodity. However, the assumption that the CRD would have no influence can be seen as conservative, and it probably leads to larger quantities of purchases and sales than would have actually occurred.

In following quarters, if the Yen market price fell below the next lower point, the same assumption was made, that the CRD would purchase another full Block of reserves of that commodity, and the same process would repeat for as long as market prices continued to fall.

The starting level of reserves would in practice depend on the timing of the CRD's establishment relative to the commodity price cycle. In the present simulation it is assumed to have already accumulated reserves of each commodity proportionate to the level of market prices at the start of the simulation relative to the previous average import prices.

This simulation was presented at the annual autumn meeting of the Japanese Monetary Society in 1996 (Collins, 1996). Figure 1 shows the commodities' market price data from those years, which were used to estimate how the Japanese CRD's reserves would have risen and fallen counter-cyclically over that period.

The units on the vertical axis are prices of the different commodities, expressed as an index number, while the horizontal axis represents the ten years of the simulation. Figure 1 shows that, after being roughly stable for one year, commodity prices rose for two years, after which prices fell for four years, and then rose again over the last three years. The pattern shows how commodity market prices tend to move together, and to move substantially:

over this period they initially rose by about 50%, then fell more than 50%, and finally rose again by about 50%.

Figure 2. Changes in money supply and CRD operating profits

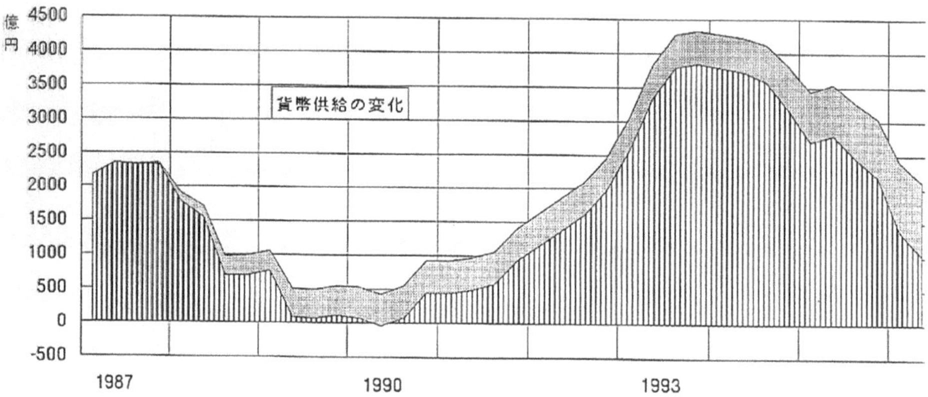

Figure 2 shows the effect which the movements in commodity market prices shown in Figure 1 would have had on the Yen money supply via changes in the CRD's reserves. (The units are 100 million Yen, or about $900,000 at time of writing in 2021.) Starting at a position of expansion of more than 200 billion Yen (about $1.8 billion), and remaining roughly stable for the first year, the expansion of the money supply caused by the CRD fell for the next two years, actually going slightly negative in 1990, before rising again for four years to reach nearly 400 billion Yen (about $3.6 billion), and finally falling again to about 100 billion Yen (about $900 million) over the last three years. (NB Since all sales from the CRD in this simulation are assumed to earn a fixed premium of 22%, the net effect on the money supply of selling most of the CRD's reserves would be contraction.) The darker band in the graph shows the growth of the cumulative profits earned by the CRD due to the fixed premium on all its sales, reaching a little more than 100 billion Yen (about $900 million) by the end of the ten years of the simulation.

Figure 3 shows another view of the monetary effects of the CRD's operation: the darker areas show net purchases (positive) or sales (negative) of reserves in each quarter, and the paler areas show the CRD's cumulative profits. In the second and third years the CRD's reserves fell, which led to it earning profits on its sales. This was followed by four years of net purchases, during which the CRD earned almost no profits, and finally three years of sales again, when the CRD's cumulative profits rose again.

Figure 3. Monetary movements caused by CRD operation

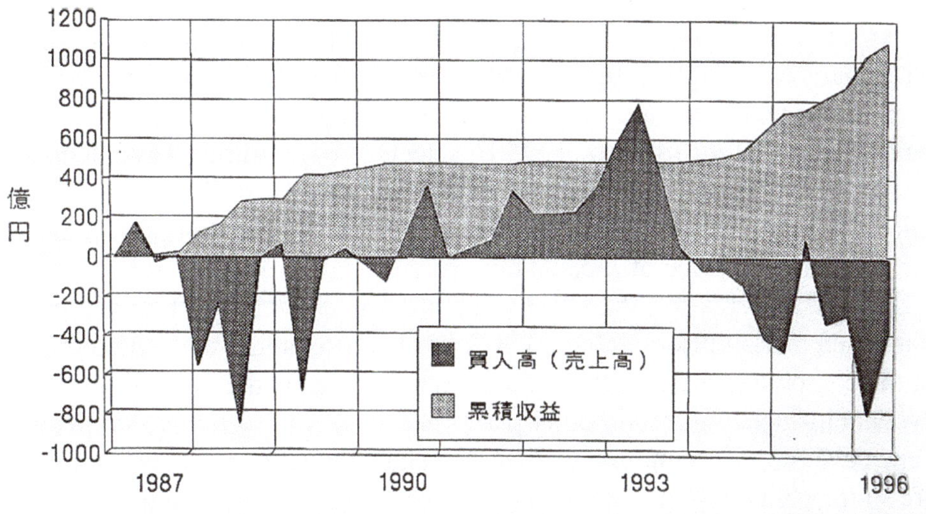

Figure 3 also shows that the CRD's accumulated premiums from selling reserves would have reached a little more than 100 billion Yen (about $900 million) over the 10 years of operation illustrated. This would have covered most of the cost of warehousing the reserves over a decade, depending on the shares of different commodities. The resulting net reduction in the Yen money supply also represents savings to the national balance of payments on its imports of commodities.

Overall, the CRD's counter-cyclical operation would have helped to stabilize domestic prices of each commodity, as well as the annual quantities of Japan's imports. In addition, the automatic price adjustment mechanism of the Grondona system, by partially stabilising the real value of the Yen in real terms, would have thereby helped to insulate the domestic economy from fluctuations of the business cycle and other external shocks.

Based on this initial simulation, the author has collaborated with colleagues in recent years to create a computer model to systematically simulate the operation of the Grondona system in other countries for which the required trade data is available. In Chapter 10 the results of using this model to illustrate the Grondona system's operation are shown for four more countries.

SUMMARY

This chapter has shown the first simulation of how the Grondona system would have operated in response to real market price data. It was assumed that a CRD was established in Japan in 1987 on the scale suggested by Grondona in his guidelines. A Block of each of the 16 selected commodities was calculated as 10% of average imports in the three years preceding 1987, and the CRD's initial buying and selling prices were calculated as 10% below and above the average c.i.f. price of Japan's imports of each commodity over the same three years. Thereafter, the CRD's operation was calculated by hand using published market prices and the US dollar-yen exchange-rate. Three graphs of the combined results of the simulation clearly show the system's counter-cyclical influence on commodity prices and trade, on the money supply and hence also on the economy as a whole. The calculations needed to do this are simple, but time-consuming by hand: using a computer simulation model will make it possible to greatly speed up this process.

REFERENCES

Collins, P. (1996). Conditional Currency Convertibility and its Applicability in Japan. *Japanese Society of Monetary Economics Spring Conference.*

Grondona, L. (1975). *Economic Stability is Attainable.* Hutchinson-Benham.

Chapter 10
Simulation of Four National CRDs' Operations

ABSTRACT

This chapter introduces simulations of how CRDs might have actually operated in the four different countries of Indonesia, Malaysia, Turkey, and Pakistan if they had been established in 2009. Two types of data are used, all from publicly accessible databases. The first is data on the annual quantity and cost of imports to each country for three or more years prior to the start of the simulation, from which each CRD's initial "Index" price for each commodity is calculated, as well as the size of the CRD's "Block" of reserves. The second type of data is quarterly market prices of each commodity, and the national exchange-rate where needed, through the period of the simulation, from which changes in the CRDs' reserves are calculated. For each country the level of reserves of the different commodities held by the CRD are clearly seen to automatically vary counter-cyclically as traders sell to or buy from the CRD at the prices in its price-schedule for each commodity.

INTRODUCTION

As discussed in previous chapters, the Grondona system is a way to make a currency directly but conditionally convertible into a range of primary commodities, modelled on the gold standard, but permitting market prices of the commodities involved to move over a much wider range than the price of gold moved under the gold standard. Although this may seem paradoxical, it

DOI: 10.4018/978-1-7998-8302-9.ch010

is analogous to a mechanism that damps oscillations in a machine, but without preventing the machine from moving as required to perform its function. Conveniently, the simplicity and automaticity of the Grondona system make it possible to accurately simulate how it would have operated under different conditions, using economic data from past time-periods. Chapter 9 showed an example of such a simulation, performed using Japanese economic data from the 1980s and 1990s. In this chapter the results of the same calculations are shown for four different countries: Indonesia, Malaysia, Turkey and Pakistan. These countries were chosen as being members of the D-8 group of major OIC countries, as part of a longer-term project: similar simulations are to be performed of representative members of other international groupings, including ASEAN, Mercosur and the African Union, as discussed further in Chapter 12.

10.1 SIMULATION METHODOLOGY

Simulations are a valuable tool for the government of any country either considering or planning to implement the Grondona system, enabling the operation of a national CRD to be evaluated over a range of scales and other conditions. In order for a government to decide the optimal conditions of implementation, it is clearly very valuable to be able to simulate the system's operation in advance, including under a wide range of different conditions. Deciding the "gearing" of the system, which determines how it will operate, includes deciding

1. which commodities and grades to include,
2. the CRD's initial price-levels for each,
3. the maximum quantity of reserves to hold at each price level, and
4. the steps in the price-schedule for each commodity.

The following simulations are based on the same principles and guidelines as discussed in Chapter 8, using Grondona's suggested values of the system's parameters. That is, the initial conditions of implementation were decided not with hindsight to try to achieve an optimal result, but based on the information that was available at the time of implementation, in order to produce a more realistic, although likely less than optimal, result. For this, past data on the annual quantities and costs (in domestic currency) of each of the four countries' imports of the selected primary commodities were used to decide the conditions for establishing each CRD. Thus, for the following simulations starting as of 2009, data from 2006 through 2008 was used to decide the terms of implementation. The simulations then use quarterly or monthly commodity market prices, combined with data on the national exchange-rate where necessary to calculate commodity prices in the national currency, to calculate how the CRD would have responded. Notably this would have included what quantities of which commodities it would have been required to buy and/or sell each quarter over the time-period of the simulation.

For all four countries it is assumed that the CRD would have no substantial stabilizing influence on world commodity market prices. In reality, CRDs could have a significant stabilizing influence on some commodity prices at some times, in which case their purchases and sales, matched by the expansion and contraction of the money supply which they cause, would be reduced proportionately. Hence the following simulations somewhat overestimate the scale of the CRDs' likely transactions, and so of their direct effect on each country's national money supply.

For each simulation, past data on the annual quantities and costs of each country's imports of selected primary commodities were collected, and the average annual quantities and prices of each were calculated. These were used as an "Index" price for each commodity, which becomes the centre-point between the buying and selling prices which the CRD uses initially. Second, a commodity's market price for a particular date is looked up and compared with the current buying-price and selling-price in the CRD's price-schedule for that commodity. From this the quantity of commodities that would have been bought or sold is calculated, as well as any change in the levels of the CRD's "points", following the system's fixed rule. The outputs of the simulations were then processed in a computer spreadsheet to generate the graphs in Sections 10.3 – 10.6 below.

10.2 DATA DESCRIPTION

The primary commodities included in the simulations were selected based on the attributes recommended by Grondona in his last book, "Economic Stability is Attainable" (Grondona, 1975), namely durable, essential, basic and imported. Grondona explained that essential imports are strategically different from domestic products, since their supply is not under national control, and interruption in supply could be economically disruptive and even dangerous. By contrast, domestic producers are ultimately under national control, and often receive government support of some kind, making it more complex to decide whether and on what terms the commodities which they produce should be stockpiled. Hence, although domestically produced commodities could, in principle, be included in the operation of a CRD at a later stage, Grondona recommended that they be excluded initially.

Based on these attributes, a list of candidate primary commodities was created using the Harmonized Commodity Description and Coding System (HS) of 6-digit product codes, which is one of the standard forms of trade statistics, and has been widely used for recording trade data in 160 countries since 1988. These 6-digit HS codes were then used to retrieve annual quantities and costs of each country's imports of the selected commodities from the World Integrated Trade Solution (WITS) database managed by the World Bank (WITS, 2021), and to select the most suitable primary commodities for each country from the full list of imports. Table 1 shows the complete list of imported primary commodities selected as candidates for inclusion in the Grondona system.

On examining these commodities' data for each country, it was found that for some countries some commodities were imported only in small quantities, or they had missing values for a few years: these commodities were excluded from the present simulations. The annual quantities and costs of most commodities obtained from WITS are given in kilograms and U.S. dollars respectively, so the annual quantities were converted into tonnes, and the costs into the appropriate national currency, using contemporary exchange-rates obtained from the World Bank website (World Bank, 2021). Annual data on each country's Consumer Price Index (CPI) were also retrieved from the World Bank database, in order to adjust the commodities' average import prices for inflation, where required, in order to establish realistic initial Index prices, as suggested in (Grondona, 1975). (Without such adjustment, where inflation had been relatively fast the initial Index prices would be too low, and so the CRD would obtain reserves only when market prices fell very substantially.) Finally, in order to activate the simulation, quarterly market prices of the primary commodities selected to be handled by each country's CRD were retrieved from the Index Mundi website through the period of the simulation (Index Mundi, 2021).

Table 1. List of Primary Commodities Selected to be Handled by CRDs, with their HS 6-digit Product Codes.

S. No	Product Description	HS Product Codes
1.	COFFEE NOT ROAST, NOT DECAFEINATED	090111
2.	DURUM WHEAT	100110
3.	BARLEY	100300
4.	SOYA BEANS, WHETHER OR NOT BROKEN	120100
5.	COCOA BEANS, WHOLE, BROKEN, RAW OR ROAST	180100
6.	RAW SUGAR, NOT CONTAINING ADDED FLAVOURING OR COLOURING MATTER: CANE SUGAR	170111
7.	COTTON, NOT CARDED OR COMBED	520100
8.	RICE IN HUSK (PADDY OR ROUGH)	100610
9.	JUTE AND OTHER TEXTILE BAST FIBRES, RAW OR RETTED	530310
10.	NATURAL RUBBER LATEX, WHETHER OR NOT PRE-VULCANISED	400110
11.	REFINED COPPER, CATHODES & SECTIONS	740311
12.	NICKEL, NOT ALLOYED	750210
13.	ALUMINIUM, NOT ALLOYED	760110
14.	REFINED LEAD	780110
15.	ZINC CONTAINED BY WT>99.99% NOT ALLOYED	790111
16.	ZINC CONTAINED BY WT<99.99% NOT ALLOYED	790112
17.	TIN, NOT ALLOYED	800110

Worked Example

The simulations of the four countries described in Sections 10.3 – 10.6 below do not use or generate complex data-series or mathematical manipulations that would require careful scrutiny. They operate simply by first calculating a 3-year average of the quantity and cost of imports of each commodity for each country. Secondly, they compare one number (i.e. the selected commodity's market price in the national currency at the appropriate times) with two other numbers (i.e. the CRD's current buying and selling prices for that commodity in that time-period), and decide whether the CRD either made a purchase or made a sale or did nothing. In the event of the CRD making a purchase or sale, the number of Blocks held by the CRD is changed, and the CRD's current buying and selling prices are updated to match the new number of Blocks. (NB this is a simplification of the process in a real case, since the simulations below assume that all transactions are for a whole Block of the commodity in question. In practice, most transactions would be substantially less than a whole Block, so the changes in reserves would be smoother than in this simulation.)

Rather than including the pages of tables of all the simulations, a representative example of these calculations is shown in the following case of Indonesia's imports of aluminium, thereby enabling readers to easily repeat such calculations for any commodity for any country.

In order to calculate the initial Index price for aluminium (HS 760110: aluminium; unwrought, not alloyed) for Indonesia, the annual quantity and cost (in US dollars) of imports for the year 2006 are available at:

https://wits.worldbank.org/trade/comtrade/en/country/ALL/year/2006/tradeflow/Imports/partner/WLD/product/760110

(Data for 2007 and 2008 are available at the same URL, but with the year changed appropriately.) From this, the average quantity over the three years 2006 through 2008 can be found as: (76,625 + 96,436 + 83,375) / 3 = 256,436 / 3 = 85,479 tonnes. On the same pages, the annual costs of aluminium imports for the same three years were $196.6 million, $203.4 million and $226 million. US dollar: Rupiah exchange-rates are available at https://www.indexmundi.com/xrates/graph.aspx?c1=IDR&c2=USD&days=5475

The earliest figure is for Nov 8, 2006, so this figure, and those for the same dates in 2007 and 2008 were 9,120 Rupiah/$, 9,160 Rp/$ and 10,800 Rp/$ respectively. Consequently annual import costs can be estimated as 1,793 billion Rupiah, 1,863 billion Rupiah and 2,441 billion Rupiah. The average price of imports over the three years can therefore be estimated as (1,793 + 1,863 + 2,441) billion Rp / (76,625 + 96,436 + 83,375) = 6,097 billion Rp/ 256,436 = 23.8 million Rp/tonne. (An additional step that may be taken is to adjust the calculation of this initial "Index price" by including adjustment for inflation.)

Calculating the Size of a Block of Aluminium for Indonesia

Following Grondona's guidelines, the quantity in a Block of aluminium is to be 10% of average annual imports, which is 85,479/10 = 8,548 tonnes. Grondona recommended that, in practice, for simplicity, such a figure could be rounded – so in this case it is rounded to 8,500 tonnes.

Calculating the Indonesia CRD's Initial Buying and Selling Prices for Aluminium

From a) above, the average price paid for aluminium imports during the three years 2006-2008 was 23.8 million Rupiah/tonne, which can be rounded to 24 miilion Rp/tonne. Following Grondona's illustrative guidelines, the CRD's initial buying and selling prices are set at 90% and 110% of this price respectively, namely 21.6 million Rupiah/tonne and 26.4 million Rupiah/tonne. (Another possible adjustment would be to note the weakening trend of the US$: Rupiah exchange-rate in a) above, and so to decide a somewhat higher initial Index price when rounding the figures above.)

Creating the Indonesia CRD's Price-Schedule for Aluminium

Starting with the figures of 21,600,000 and 26,400,000 Rupiah/tonne for the CRD's initial buying and selling prices, we can produce a price-schedule for aluminium by using Grondona's suggestion that these prices should both fall by 5% of their initial value on the acquisition of each Block, that is by 1,080,000 and 1,320,000 Rp/tonne respectively, as shown in Table 2.

Estimating Initial Number of Blocks Held by Indonesia CRD

Having prepared the price-schedule based on previous years' import prices, as would have been done by following Grondona's guidelines, we can deduce the number of Blocks that would be held at the start of the simulation, if the system was already in operation. Aluminium market prices for the period 2009 – 2118 are found at https://www.indexmundi.com/commodities/?commodity=aluminum&months=300

The price in January 2009 was approximately $1,410 /tonne, while the January US$: Rupiah exchange-rate was 11,210 Rp/$. Hence the January aluminium price in Rupiah can be estimated as (1,410 x 11,210) = 15,806,100 Rp/tonne. This is less than the buying price of 16,200,000 Rp/tonne of the CRD's 6th Block of aluminium in the price-schedule estimated above, and so we estimate that the CRD would be holding 6 Blocks of aluminium at the start of the simulation in 2009.

Table 2. Illustrative Rupiah price-schedule for aluminium.

Current CRD Buying Price (Low Point) Rp/tonne	Current CRD Selling Price (High Point) Rp/tonne	Quantity in Indonesia CRD's Reserves (tonnes)	Number of Blocks
21,600,000	26,400,000	8,500	<1
20,520,000	25,080,000	17,000	<2
19,440,000	23,760,000	25,500	<3
18,360,000	22,440,000	34,000	<4
17,280,000	21,120,000	42,500	<5
16,200,000	19,800,000	51,000	<6
15,120,000	18,480,000	59,500	<7
14,040,000	17,160,000	68,000	<8
12,960,000	15,840,000	76,500	<9
11,880,000	14,520,000	85,000	<10

Calculating Indonesia CRD's Actions in 2009 and 2010 for Aluminium

From Index Mundi, through the four quarters of 2009 the US dollar prices were approximately $1,410 /tonne in January, $1,420 /tonne in April, $1,670 /tonne in July, and $1,880 /tonne in October. The corresponding US$: Rupiah exchange-rates were approximately 11,210 Rp/$, 11,380 Rp/$, 10,240 Rp/$ and 9,646 Rp/$. Hence the four quarterly aluminium prices in Rupiah can be estimated as (1,410 x 11,210) = 15,806,100 Rp/tonne, (1,420 x 11,380) = 16,159,600 Rp/tonne, (1,670 x 10,240) = 17,100,800 Rp/tonne and (1,880 x 9,646) = 18,134,480 Rp/tonne, as shown in Table 3.

In Table 3, in each quarter the Rupiah market price is compared to the CRD's then buying and selling prices, the CRD's buying and selling prices having been read from Table 2. For January the market price of 15,806,100 Rp/tonne is less than the buying price of 16,200,000 Rp/tonne of the CRD's 6th Block, and so we assume that the CRD would have previously bought 6 Blocks (though this would depend on market conditions at the date of implementation). The second quarter price of 16,159,600 Rp/tonne is somewhat higher, but it is well below the CRD's corresponding selling price of 19,800,000 Rp/tonne. Although market prices continue to rise, the third and fourth quarter prices are also below 19,800,000 Rp/tonne, and so the number of Blocks would not have changed through 2009.

Table 3. Indonesia CRD's actions in 2009 & 2010 for Aluminium (prices in millions of Rupiah per Tonne)

Time period	**2009 qtr. 1**	**2009 qtr. 2**	**2009 qtr.3**	**2009 qtr.4**
Market Price	15.806	16.160	17.101	18.134
CRD buying price	15.120	15.120	15.120	15.120
CRD selling price	19.800	19.800	19.800	19.800
Number of Blocks	6	6	6	6
Time period	**2010 qtr. 1**	**2010 qtr.2**	**2010 qtr.3**	**2010 qtr.4**
Market price	19.286	21.344	18.109	19.891
CRD buying price	15.120	17.280	17.280	17.280
CRD selling price	19.800	22.440	22.440	22.440
Number of Blocks	6	4	4	4

In the four quarters of 2010, aluminium prices were approximately $2,050/ton, $2,320/tonne, $1,990/tonne and $2,220 per tonne (Index mundi, 2021). The corresponding US dollar: Rupiah exchange-rates were 9,408 Rp/$, 9,200 Rp/$, 9,100 Rp/$ and 8,960 Rp/$ (Index mundi, 2021). These give Rupiah prices of 19,286,400 Rp/tonne, 21,344,000 Rp/tonne, 18,109,000 Rp/tonne and 19,891,200 Rp/tonne for the four quarters of 2010, as also shown in Table 3. From these it can be seen that while 19,286,400 Rp/tonne is still less than the CRD's selling price at 19,800,000 Rp/tonne, and so no one would have bought reserves from the CRD, the second quarter market price of 21,344,000 Rp/tonne is higher than 19,800,000 Rp/tonne and also than the 21,120,000 Rp/tonne of the fifth Block's selling price. Consequently, we deduce that the CRD would have been required to sell 2 Blocks of reserves during the second quarter. The market prices of 18,109,000 Rp/tonne in the third quarter and 19,891,200 Rp/tonne in the fourth quarter remained between the CRD's corresponding new buying price of 17,280,000 Rp/tonne and its selling price of 22,440,000 Rp/tonne, and so no further movements in the CRD's reserves would have occurred in 2010.

This same sequence of calculations can be used to simulate the operation of a CRD for any commodity for any country over any time-period for which data is available. The following sections show the results of comparable simulations for each of four countries.

Table 4. Commodities Included in Indonesian CRD Simulation.

Country	Agricultural Commodities	Metals	Total Primary Commodities
Indonesia	Soybeans, Coffee, Cocoa Beans, Sugar, Cotton, Rice in Husk, Natural Rubber Latex	Copper, Nickel, Lead, Tin, Zinc Aluminium	13

10.3 SIMULATION OF INDONESIAN CRD

For the following simulation of a CRD operating in Indonesia, 13 commodities were selected, as shown in Table 4.

The initial Index and price-schedule, which were prepared for each of the primary commodities selected for simulation, used the data described above, adjusted as necessary for inflation. The quantity in a Block of each commodity was also decided following Grondona's suggested guideline of 10% of the average annual quantity of imports over the years preceding the start (rounded as appropriate).

After development of the price-schedules for all 13 commodities, simulations were performed for each commodity for the decade 2009–2018, following the procedure also described above. The results of the simulations show that, on the assumptions made above, the Indonesian CRD would have accumulated reserves of Copper, Nickel, Lead, Zinc > 99%, Zinc < 99%, Aluminium, Coffee, Cotton, Sugar and Rice during the period of the simulation. However it was found that the CRD's initial prices for some primary commodities (namely Tin, Cocoa beans and Rubber) were too low, so that the CRD purchased no reserves throughout the simulation period: consequently the initial Index of each of these commodities should have been set at a higher price – that is, by basing them on different calculations than the other commodities. (This is an example of what Grondona had in mind when he advised that each country should use discretion for setting the CRD, and not follow his suggested guidelines rigidly.)

Figure 1 shows the simulation results for Nickel, Zinc, Aluminium, Coffee, Cotton and Sugar.

In the graphs of Nickel, the Indonesian CRD accumulated reserves during the first few months of 2009 rising to 5 Blocks, due to a fall in Nickel prices, causing an expansion in the Indonesian money supply of Rp 39,079 million. Subsequently, as a result of the 100% rise in Nickel market prices during June–July 2009, the CRD's accumulated reserves of Nickel were all purchased

Figure 1a. Operation of Indonesian CRD

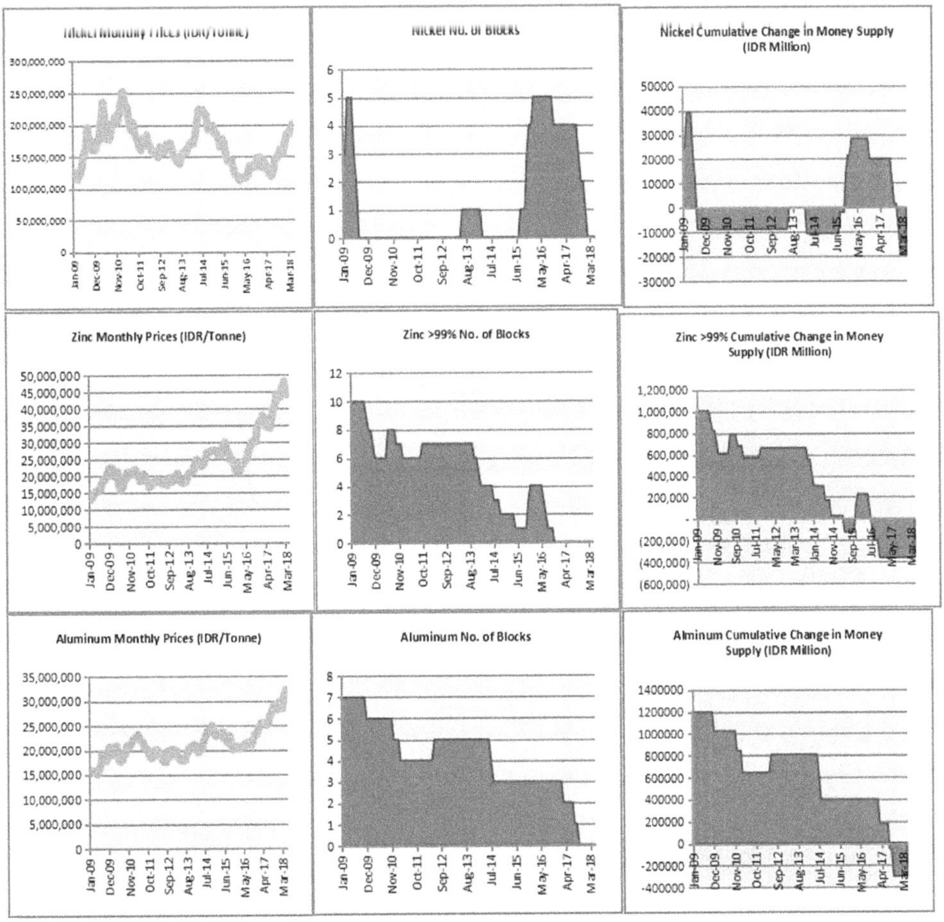

from the CRD, which caused a contraction in the Indonesian money supply of Rp 47,745 million.

The initial expansion of the Rupiah money supply in this case was 18% less than the subsequent contraction, due to the sales premium, namely the difference between the buying and selling prices offered by the CRD. In the case of Nickel, the sales premium earned by the Indonesian CRD during that period of the simulation was (Rp 47,745 million – Rp 39,079 million) = Rp 8,666 million.

As another example, the CRD accumulated 10 Blocks of reserves of Zinc >99%, thereby expanding the Indonesian money supply by Rp 1 trillion. Later, the purchase of Zinc >99% Blocks by traders, as domestic prices doubled during August–December 2009, contracted the Indonesian money supply by

Figure 1b. Operation of Indonesian CRD

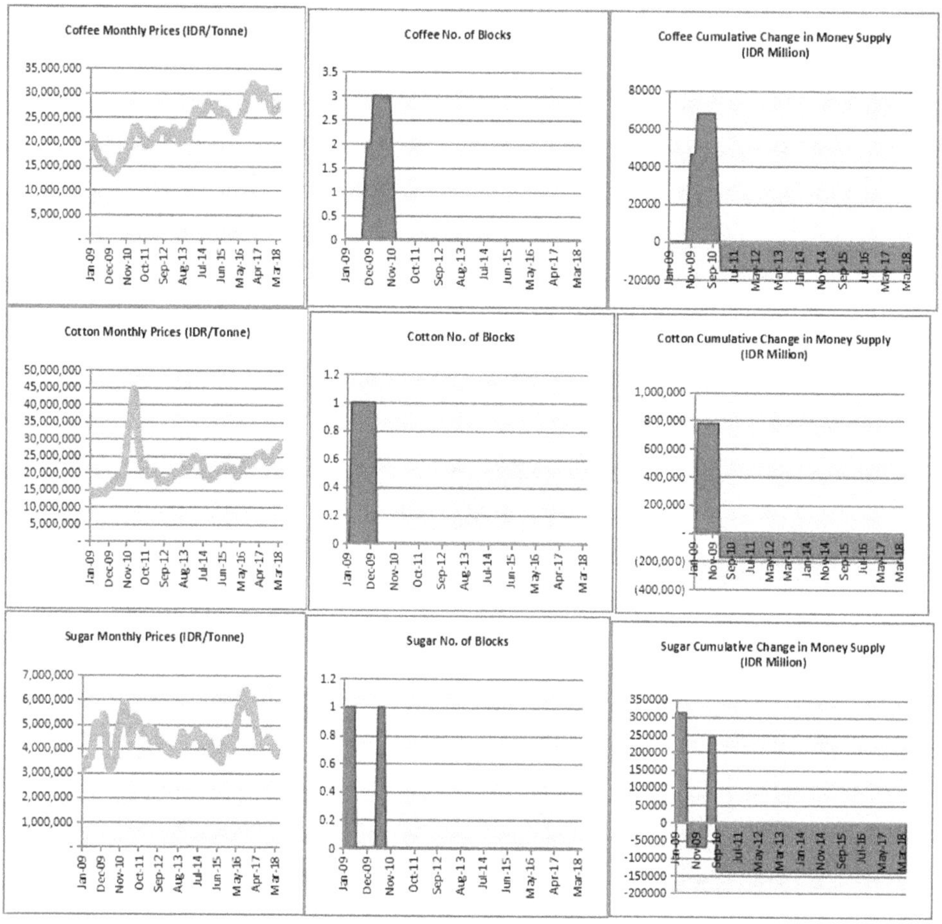

Rp 400,000 million. Subsequently, as market prices rose to nearly 400% of their initial level, the CRD's reserves were sold out in 2016.

Likewise, a fall of some 30% in the market price of coffee led to the Indonesian CRD accumulating 3 Blocks of reserves in 2009 and early 2010, which had an expansionary effect on the money supply of nearly Rp 70 billion. However, the market price then rose to 50% above the price in January 2009, and so the money supply contracted by more than Rp 80 billion in late 2010.

In this way, the CRD helped to stabilise the Rupiah prices and trade quantities of the primary commodities which it handles, and thereby lessen the volatility of primary commodity market prices to some extent during both slump and boom periods. As a result, the operation of the CRD would have simultaneously exerted a corresponding stabilising influence on the real value of the Indonesian Rupiah in terms of these commodities.

The overall pattern of financial flows resulting from the Indonesian CRD's operations is to disburse additional Indonesian Rupiah abroad at times of falling commodity prices, and to withdraw Indonesian Rupiah from the domestic economy (which would otherwise flow abroad) at times of rising commodity prices. This pattern of financial flows is clearly seen in the graphs in Figure 1 and would tend to reduce the volatility of prices paid by domestic users of commodities, of the prices received by foreign commodity producers, of the quantities of imports, and as a second-round effect, of the demand for exports from Indonesia.

10.3.1 Overall Monetary Effects

The collective effects on the Indonesian money supply of the changes in the quantities of all the commodity reserves held by the Indonesian CRD through the ten years of the simulation are summarized in Figure 2.

The monetary effect of the CRD's purchasing reserves is similar to an increase in government payments to the private sector. Consequently, the Indonesian CRD's payments will appear as an increase in banks' deposits at the Bank of Indonesia, which will influence the "reserve progress ratio of reserve deposits" and, if not counter-acted by the monetary authorities, the call-rate. In this case it could lead to a further expansion of bank deposits over the following months by some multiple of the CRD's payments.

Sales to the CRD would, either directly or indirectly, be made by primary commodity exporters in foreign countries, and so the increase in the money supply would comprise an increase in Rupiah bank accounts held by foreigners. Foreign-held Rupiah bank deposits may be used in three ways, of which the relative amounts could be estimated to some extent from past statistics, if needed.

1. They may be exchanged for the national currency of the exporter, in which case there could be some downward influence on the Rupiah exchange rate relative to the currency in question, which is generally appropriate when commodity prices are falling (and so the real value of the Rupiah in terms of those commodities is rising).
2. They may be used to purchase goods and services from Indonesia, in which case they could increase Indonesian exports.
3. They may be used to invest in Indonesian securities.

Figure 2. Changes in Indonesian Money Supply Caused by CRD Transactions

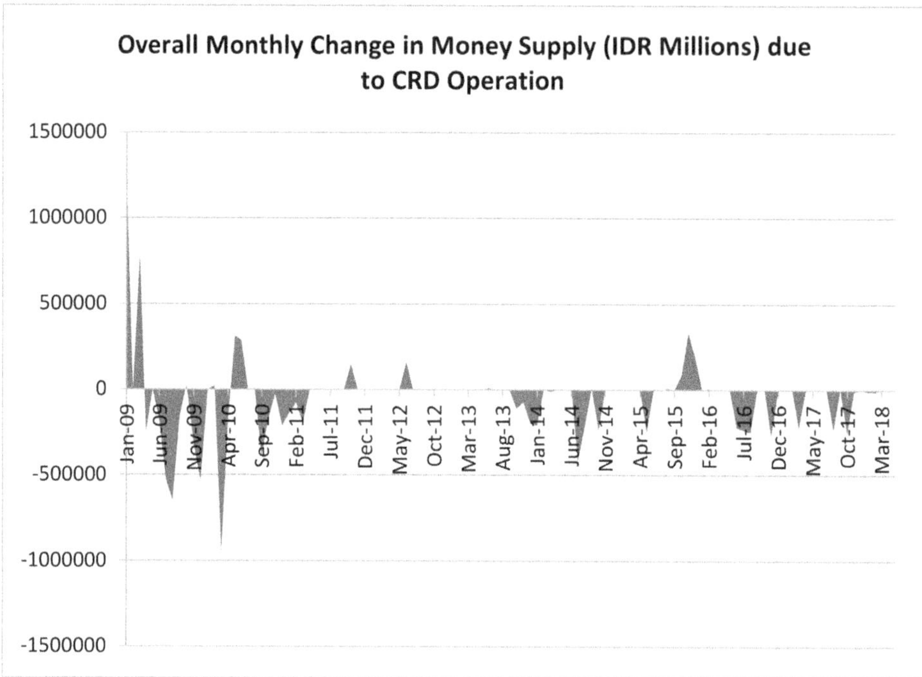

To the extent that the Indonesian CRD's operations had the effect of maintaining Rupiah-denominated import prices of the commodities involved higher than the level to which they would have fallen in the CRD's absence, this will maintain the flow of commercial payments abroad above the level to which it would otherwise have fallen. Thus, the flow of Rupiah abroad resulting from the CRD's operations, and the commercial activities which this supports, can be expected to be somewhat larger than the amount disbursed by the CRD itself, due to companies' imports also continuing at prices higher than they would have otherwise been.

When commodity prices rise again, the financial flows resulting from payments to the CRD for purchases of reserves will reduce bank deposits at the Bank of Indonesia, similar to receipts by the public sector. The fall in bank deposits at the Bank of Indonesia will alter the "reserve progress ratio of reserve deposits" and, if not counter-acted, the call-rate. In this case it could lead to a further reduction in bank deposits to some multiple of the CRD's transactions, which is generally appropriate when commodity prices are rising (and so the real value of the Rupiah in terms of those commodities is falling).

Table 5. Commodities Included in Malaysian CRD Simulation

Country	Agricultural Commodities	Metals	Total Primary Commodities
Malaysia	Wheat, Soya beans, Coffee, Maize, Cotton, Wool	Copper, Lead, Zinc, Aluminium	10

Purchases from the CRD will generally be made by domestic users of the commodities concerned. That is, although the CRD will operate without national discrimination, Grondona proposed that the sites of its reserves should be chosen to be convenient for domestic users, who will as a result generally find the CRD's selling prices more attractive than foreign buyers, by the difference in cost of transportation. For foreign buyers this will typically include transport from a CRD warehouse in Indonesia to a dock, and loading onto a ship.

Purchases of reserves from the CRD, by displacing imports, will lead to a reduction in the flow of Rupiah abroad to some extent below what it would have been in the CRD's absence. In addition, primary commodity imports by domestic users will be purchased at prices lower than they would have been in the CRD's absence, due to its influence in resisting rises in Rupiah-denominated import prices. Consequently, the reduction in the flow of Rupiah abroad resulting from the CRD's activities, and in the commercial activities which this supports, will be somewhat larger than the value of purchases from the CRD itself, due to companies' imports continuing at somewhat lower prices.

10.4 SIMULATION OF MALAYSIAN CRD

For the following simulation of a CRD operating in Malaysia, ten commodities were selected, as show in Table 5.

The operating conditions of a Malaysian CRD were based on calculations similar to those used for the simulation of an Indonesian CRD, and described in some detail in Section 10.2 above. National import data from 2005 through 2008 were used to decide the initial operating conditions. Based on these assumptions, the simulation was performed over the five years from 2009 through 2013. Figure 3 shows the results of the simulation for Aluminium and Wheat.

Figure 3. Monthly Commodity Prices, Changes in Reserves and Financial Outlays of Malaysian CRD

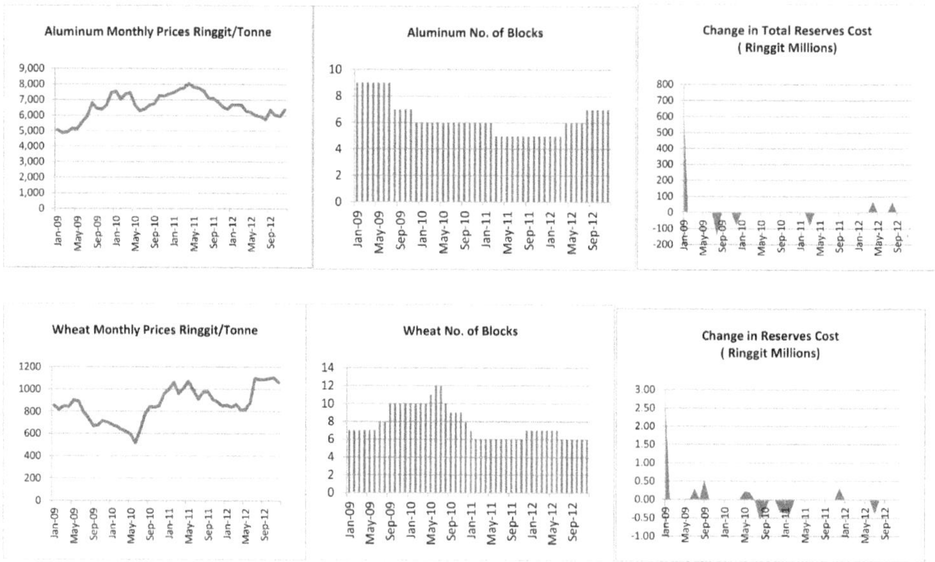

In the case of Aluminum, market prices in Malaysian Ringgit rose until mid-2011, leading to a continuing fall in the initial level of reserves from 9 blocks down to 5 Blocks. Thereafter market prices fell again, leading to a rise in reserves to 7 Blocks by early 2013. Wheat market prices showed a different pattern, falling until mid-2010, so that the CRD's reserves rose from7 Blocks to 12. After this, prices rose through 2011 to a level higher than at the starting-point, leading to a reduction in the CRD's reserves to 6 Blocks. The third graph for both commodities shows the net increase or decrease in the money-supply due to the CRD's transactions, being counter-cyclical to the pattern of price-movements.

Figure 4 shows the overall level of reserves of all ten commodities handled by the CRD, and the overall changes in the money supply resulting from changes in them. As the above cases of Aluminium and Wheat show, market prices of individual commodities do not move strictly together. However, as Figure 4 shows, as a group, commodity prices move largely together, which causes the CRD to exert a stabilizing, counter-cyclical influence on the money supply: as reserves of most commodities fell together until 2011, due to rising market prices, the money supply is reduced significantly, as is appropriate to combat this inflationary influence. Thereafter, in the present short simulation, it remained more-or-less steady.

Figure 4. Changes in Overall Reserves and in Malaysian Money Supply Caused by CRD Transactions

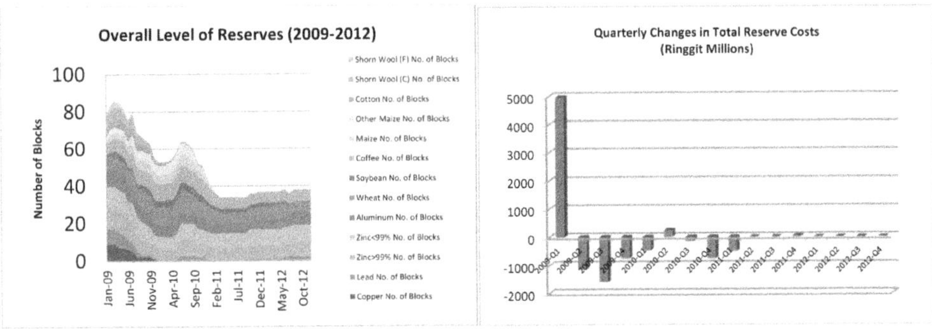

10.5 SIMULATION OF TURKISH CRD

For the following simulation of a CRD operating in Turkey, fourteen commodities were selected, as shown in Table 6.

The results of the simulation over the years 2009 – 2018 are shown in Figure 4 for nine of the commodities, using the same format as for Indonesia and Malaysia above: the change in each commodity's market price in the domestic currency is shown, followed by the resulting changes in the level of the CRD's reserves of that commodity. In addition, the effects of these changes on the money supply are shown for Nickel and Barley.

The graphs in Figure 5 show that the Turkish CRD's holdings of Copper fell to zero over the first year, as its market price tripled, and did not recover by the end of the simulation period. Reserves of Lead and Zinc also fell to zero through 2013 as their market prices rose. Reserves of Coffee beans and maize rose initially, due to a fall in market prices, followed by a decline to zero in 2011. Reserves of Barley fell to zero in 2014, while Wheat reserves lasted until 2018.

As examples of the effects on the money supply, in 2009, the CRD held 13 Blocks of reserves of Nickel, of which the purchase had expanded the

Table 6. Commodities Included in Turkish CRD Simulation.

Country	Agricultural Commodities	Metals	Total Primary Commodities
Turkey	Wheat, Soybeans, Coffee, Cocoa Beans, Maize, Cotton, Barley, Rice in Husk	Copper, Nickel, Lead, Tin, Zinc Aluminium	14

Figure 5a. Monthly Commodity Prices, Changes in Reserves and Financial Outlays of Turkish CRD

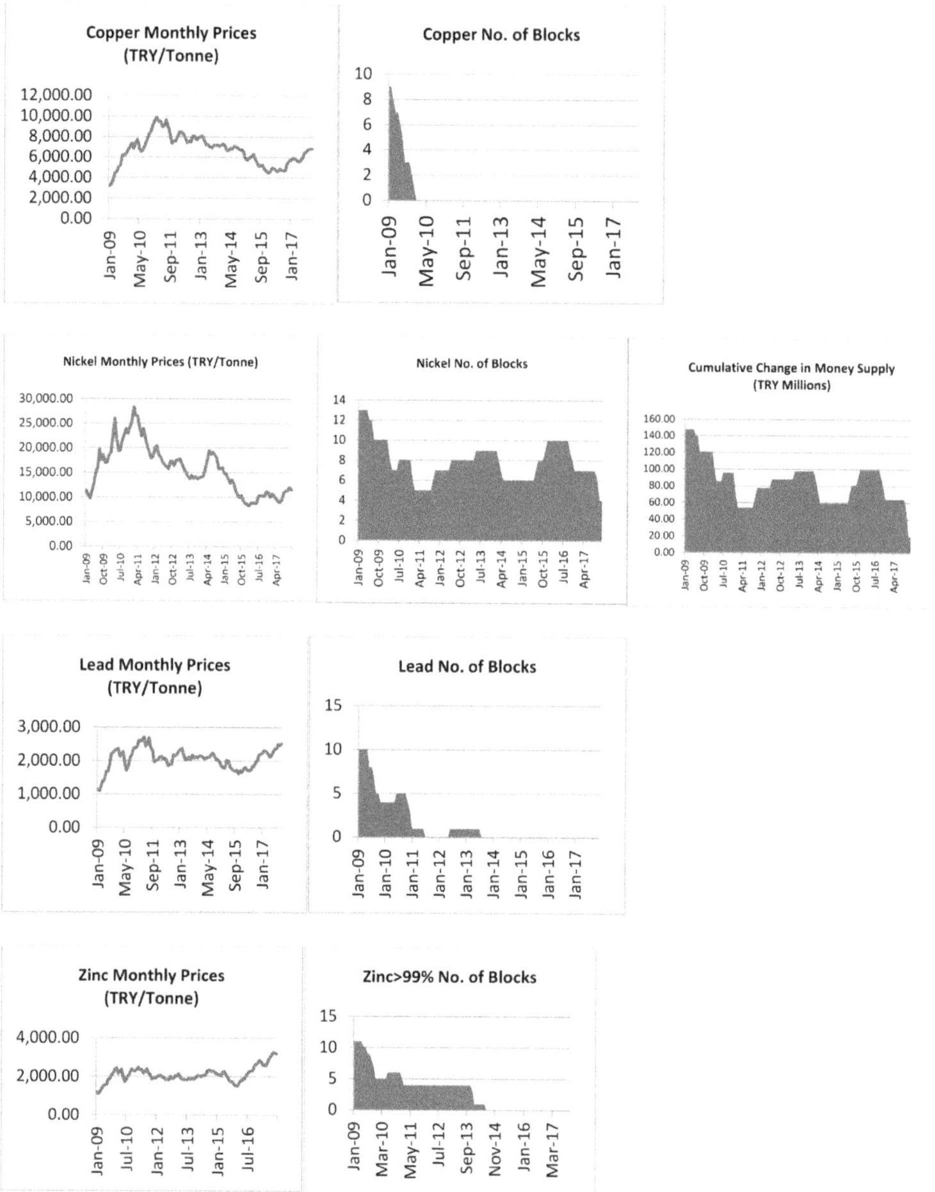

Turkish money supply by 148 million Turkish Lira. These reserves fell to 5 Blocks in 2011, thereby reducing the money supply by about 100 million Lira as the price nearly tripled. Thereafter reserves varied from 5 to 10 Blocks. In

Figure 5b. Monthly Commodity Prices, Changes in Reserves and Financial Outlays of Turkish CRD

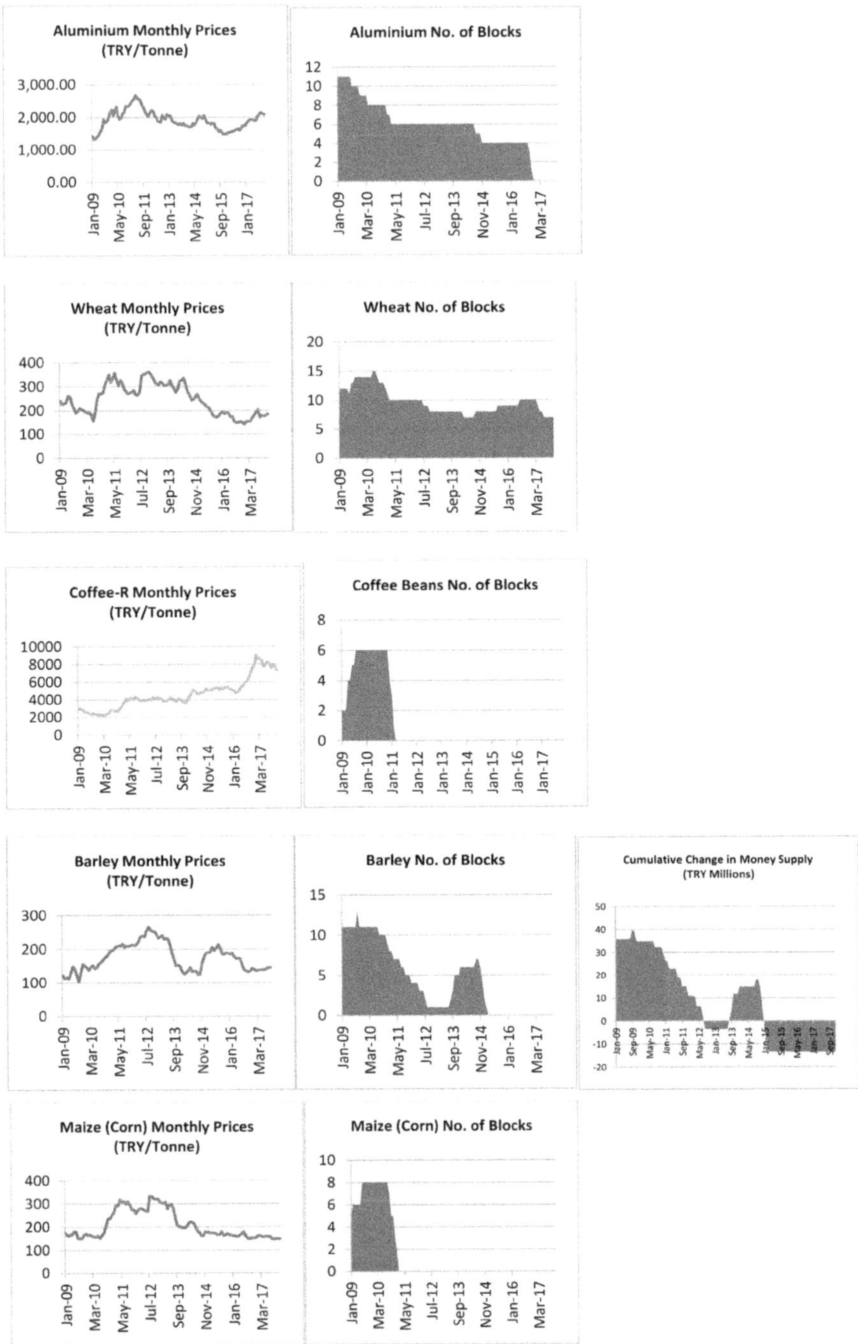

Figure 6. Changes in Overall Reserves and in Turkish Money Supply Caused by CRD Transactions

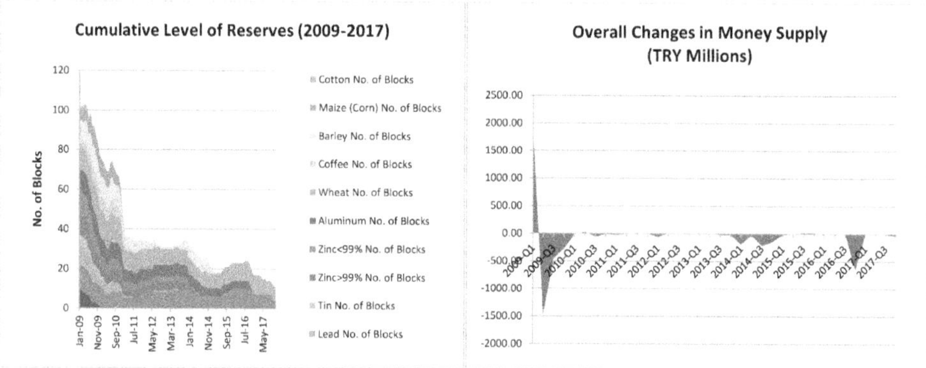

the case of Barley, the CRD initially held 36 million Turkish Lira of reserves, which were all purchased from the CRD by the end of 2014 as a result of the increase in their market-prices. This caused a corresponding reduction in the Turkish money supply, being net negative once all reserves were sold, due to the CRD's selling prices being set at levels higher than its buying prices.

As a result of the Turkish CRD's transactions during the period of the simulation, overall changes in the CRD's reserves and in the Turkish money supply occurred as shown in Figure 6. It is notable that the level of reserves of most commodities fell to zero through the period, due to the rising trend in domestic prices. This shows how continuing inflation will reduce the influence of a CRD, unless its buying and selling prices for any commodity are raised progressively in response to holding no reserves for a period of time, as Grondona proposed.

10.6 SIMULATION OF PAKISTAN CRD

In the following simulation, a Pakistan CRD is assumed to handle the eight commodities (9, including different grades) shown in Table 7.

Institutionally it is assumed that a Pakistan CRD would be established as part of the State Bank of Pakistan, which is responsible for maintaining monetary and economic stability through the regulation of the national monetary and credit systems, among other responsibilities. The institutional innovation needed to do this would be relatively easy for the State Bank to accommodate, since the CRD would have no discretion in its operation, but

Table 7. Commodities Included in Pakistan CRD Simulation.

Country	Agricultural Commodities	Metals	Total Primary Commodities
Pakistan	Wheat, Maize, Barley	Copper, Nickel, Lead, Zinc (2 grades), Aluminium	8

would merely respond "automatically" according to the fixed rules described above. That is, when approached by either sellers or buyers of the commodities which it handled, it would simply oversee the physical exchange of Rupees for commodities – all transaction costs being paid by the client – essentially like the operation of gold convertibility under a gold standard.

The simulation is for the period 2009-2018, and the operating conditions of the CRD are based on Pakistan trade and macro-economic data from the preceding period of 2006 – 2008, as described in Section 10.2 above. The CRD's "gearing" follows the rule-of-thumb proposed by Grondona for illustrative purposes. Consequently, a CRD established in Pakistan today would likely have considerably different terms of operation from that simulated here, and would operate on a substantially larger scale, due to Pakistan's economic growth over the past twelve years. The results shown in Figures 7 and 8 are based on actual, commodity-market price-movements over the decade of the simulation.

On inspection, it can be seen that as commodity market prices rose in the first two years of the simulation, most of the CRD's initial reserves were purchased from it. Although a CRD holding no reserves continues to support falling commodity prices by standing ready to buy at its announced prices, its influence in resisting rising prices is clearly ended until it accumulates reserves once again. However, most commodity prices fell again from about 2014, whereupon reserves of most of the commodities accumulated once again, reinstating the CRD's selling prices for these commodities. The fact that reserves of Copper, Lead and Zinc did not recover after falling to zero shows how inflation reduces the CRD's influence.

As in the three previous simulations, the counter-cyclical changes in the Pakistan money supply shown in Figure 8 would have been appropriate in response to the major changes in prices of the essential imported commodities which caused them. However, the monetary authorities would have been free to either ignore, enhance or counteract these changes, depending on their judgement of other conditions in the economy.

Figure 7a. Changes in CRD Reserves of Commodities and Money Supply by Pakistan CRD over the Period 2009-2018.

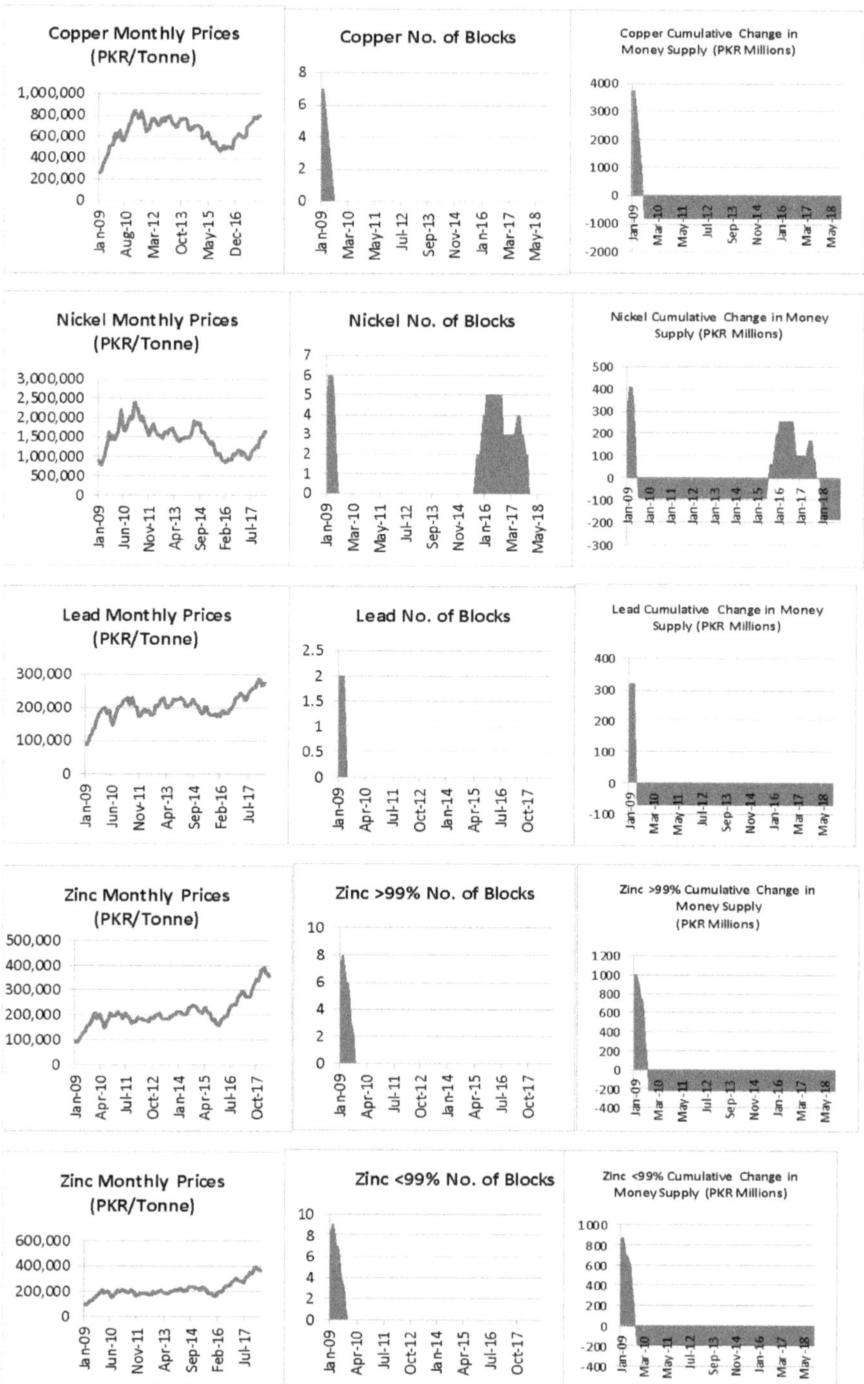

Figure 7b. Changes in CRD Reserves of Commodities and Money Supply by Pakistan CRD over the Period 2009-2018.

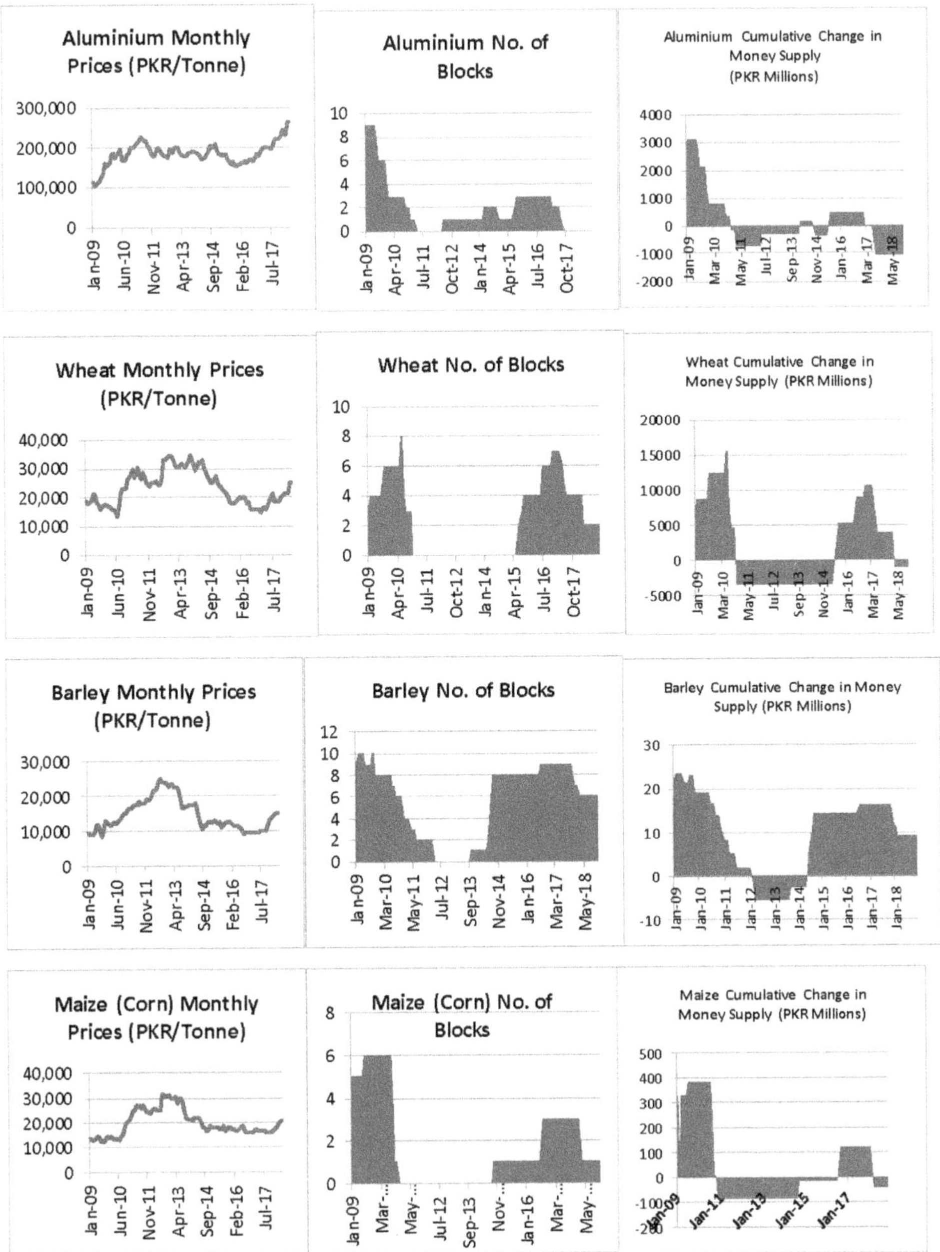

Figure 8. Changes in Overall Reserves and in Pakistan Money Supply Caused by CRD Transactions

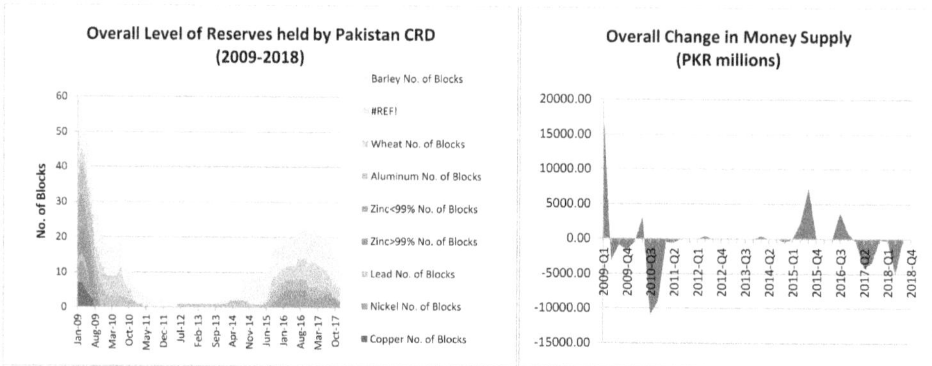

10.7 LIMITATIONS AND POTENTIAL FOR FUTURE SIMULATIONS

It is important to note that the above simulations represent only a first step in using this method to evaluate the policy of implementing the Grondona system for monetary and macro-economic stabilization, based on Grondona's own proposals. That is, all four simulations face the limitation that they were performed using the same rule-of-thumb to decide the initial terms of operation of each country's CRD for each commodity. Despite this, the results are clearly very promising, showing a consistent pattern of counter-cyclical commodity stockholding, of which the combined effect is an overall counter-cyclical variation in each country's money supply. So we can see that Grondona's suggestion for reasonable starting conditions was indeed sound – essentially because the system's flexibility makes the precise conditions less important. However, Grondona explicitly stated that this rule-of-thumb was only a starting-point for discussion, since it would clearly not be an optimal arrangement for every commodity in every country.

In practice, consultation with a range of related experts would enable more nearly optimal decisions concerning the initial conditions than the results of using the same simple, fixed rule used here. Using such advice, much valuable simulation work could be done in order to optimise the system for each country. Nevertheless, it is also a very important strength of Grondona's system that, due to its inherent flexibility in response to market forces, such less-than-optimal "gearing" of the system does no harm (unless perhaps it was implemented on a much larger scale). That is, the stockholding activity may start at a higher or lower level than optimal, and/or be smaller or larger than optimal, and so the system's stabilizing influence may be less than it could safely be, but it will not act perversely, nor pro-cyclically.

In practice, each country would decide the terms of operation of their CRD independently, based not only on past trade data, as in these simulations, but also on such matters as expected growth in the country's industrial activities, and collaboration with other countries, such as agreeing to establish CRDs simultaneously. Different countries also have very different ratios of imports to GDP, and so it could be useful to use simulations to investigate on how large a scale a CRD might be established without causing inconveniently large changes in the money supply – up to perhaps several times larger than Grondona's guidelines.

The combined, synergistic effects of multiple CRDs operating simultaneously are considered in Chapter 12. It could be valuable also to simulate these in detail in order to learn ways in which the stabilizing effects on their mutual exchange-rates might be enhanced, such as perhaps through different countries having their CRDs handle the same commodities in the same proportions. This would tend to synchronise the effects of the different CRDs on the rate of growth of their respective money supplies.

Another possibility which could be simulated would be collaboration by different countries' governments and monetary authorities in adjusting their monetary policy response to their CRDs' actions in order to maximise the benefits of their counter-cyclical influence. Yet another potentially useful topic would be to simulate one or more CRDs' operation, and to use relevant data from past financial crises to insert a representative exogenous shock to the economy, such as a sharp fall in the exchange-rate, and then to calculate the system's response, and analyse the impact on the economy. The use of such preparatory simulations might be particularly appropriate for preparing joint implementation by member-states of the regional groupings of countries working to improve their collective policies, such as OIC, ASEAN, Mercosur and the African Union, as discussed in Chapter 12.

SUMMARY

This chapter has presented the results of simulating the operation of the Grondona system in the four countries of Indonesia, Malaysia, Turkey and Pakistan. The operating conditions were decided on the basis of the simple guideline suggested by Grondona, and each country's CRD handles a somewhat different group of commodities, based on their different level of dependence on imports of each. The four simulations clearly show the counter-cyclical timing of the rise and fall in the CRD's level of reserves of each commodity, which tends to stabilize their domestic prices. Although there are many reasons why international market prices of different commodities fluctuate independently, the simulations also show the roughly coordinated timing of the combined effect of the partial stabilization of the different commodity industries on the national money supply. In doing so, the CRDs each exert some resistance to the macroeconomic fluctuations in the overall economy, on a scale chosen in advance by the government of each implementing country. The same process tends to stabilize the real value of the currency in terms of each of the commodities handled by the CRDs. Such an automatic, market-driven, damping influence on fluctuations in various aspects of the economic system is a fundamental effect that arises when the value of a currency is preserved by being convertible on demand into real commodities, but is lacking in any national economy which is based on a purely *fiat* currency.

REFERENCES

Grondona, L. (1975). *Economic Stability is Attainable*. Hutchinson-Benham.

Index Mundi. (2021). https://www.indexmundi.com

WITS. (2021). *World Integrated Trade Solution database*. https://wits.worldbank.org/

World Bank. (2021). *Gross Domestic Product*. https://databank.worldbank.org/data/download/GDP.pdf

Chapter 11
Discussion of CRD Simulation Results

ABSTRACT

The results of the simulations shown in Chapter 10 clearly show the consistent pattern of operation of the Grondona system, buying and selling reserves of commodities in response to changes in market prices as reliably as under a gold standard. This has a range of direct and indirect effects which are discussed in this chapter, including the reliably counter-cyclical timing of changes in the quantity of the CRD's reserves, and the parallel changes in the national money supply, the system's contribution to resisting inflationary pressures, and the effect of a CRD's reserves of a commodity falling to zero. Some remaining uncertainties about the system's operation are also discussed, notably about the foreign exchange market's likely response to the system expanding the money supply when commodity prices are falling.

INTRODUCTION

The simulations of four different national CRDs described in Chapter 10 showed how the Grondona system would have operated if it had been established in each country on the stated terms, based on actual market data from 2009 onwards. These simulations are made possible by the fact that CRDs operate "automatically", that is, according to fixed rules very like the department of a central bank responsible for exchanging bank notes for gold coins under the gold standard. Because of this, there is no scope for discretion in a CRD's

DOI: 10.4018/978-1-7998-8302-9.ch011

operation, and so no uncertainty about what the CRD would have done in response to any change in market prices.

This relative certainty in simulating the operation of the Grondona system has enabled the author to analyse the probable results of the system's implementation in different countries in some detail. Most immediately, the results of the above simulations clearly show how the CRDs would have stockpiled reserves of selected primary commodity imports in response to a drop in their domestic market prices, and/or in response to a rise in the exchange-rate that reduces import prices – and would have released those reserves during the following period of domestic price rises, whether due to market price rises or a fall in the exchange-rate. Such a mechanism would have helped to stabilize the domestic prices and quantities of primary commodity imports, and so lessen overall fluctuations in the country's primary commodity trade over the business-cycle. Further implications of this behavior are discussed in turn.

11.1 RELIABLY COUNTER-CYCLICAL FOR COMMODITY INDUSTRIES

The simulations in Chapter 10 illustrated how a CRD's purchases and sales of primary commodities vary over the trade cycle, but are always precisely counter-cyclical for each commodity-importing industry, thereby helping to stabilize that industry's materials costs and flow of funds abroad to producers. This also ensures the converse – that the Grondona system's automatic adjustment mechanism would exert a stabilizing influence on the real value of the national currency in terms of each of the commodities included in the system. This stabilizing influence comprises direct stabilization in the form of convertibility of the currency on demand into any of the commodities handled, as well as indirect stabilization through counter-cyclical changes in the money supply, expanding it when commodity import prices are falling and so the currency's real value is rising, and contracting it when import prices are rising and so the currency's real value is falling.

In addition, although the price-cycles in individual commodity industries differ somewhat in their timing, the collective changes in the CRD's overall reserves are largely counter-cyclical for the country's economic cycle. Because of this, it will generally be neither necessary nor desirable for monetary authorities to counteract or neutralize the Grondona system's monetary effects.

Indeed, it is likely that, after some experience of the system's operation, monetary authorities might choose to enhance the changes in the money supply caused by the CRD, using the timing of its overall outlays and receipts as a natural measure of the true business cycle.

It is important that, even if the monetary authorities decided to take steps to reduce, neutralize or even reverse the system's influence on the national money supply, this would not undo the system's direct stabilizing influence on each domestic commodity-utilising industry through counter-cyclical stock-holding. That is, monetary policy is typically implemented by raising or lowering interest-rates, in order to reduce or increase business activity respectively, and by sales or purchases of government bonds to reduce or increase cash holdings in financial markets. While these actions have a generally depressive or expansive effect on business activities, including on the costs of stockholding, none of them has a direct effect on individual commodity markets like a CRD's operations.

Prices of many primary commodities tend to rise and fall largely together in synchrony with world economic growth, as shown by various indices of primary commodities that are prepared and used in financial markets. Commodity prices expressed in a single national currency may at times differ significantly from international market prices due to movements in the national exchange-rate. Consequently, since changes in a CRD's reserves occur in response to changes in domestic commodity prices, its effects may at times not be closely correlated with the business cycle in other countries. For example, in a country suffering from accelerating inflation, the CRD will reduce the money supply as its reserves are purchased from it. If at the same time, the world economy is heading into recession, such monetary influence might be considered politically undesirable. In such a case, the national monetary authorities might choose to loosen overall monetary conditions, even though this would not be necessary, since no country is expected to implement self-destructive economic policies in order to benefit the world economy. The US decision to abandon gold convertibility of the dollar in 1971 is an example of a national government implementing policy that was considered domestically beneficial, despite being damaging to much of the rest of the world.

11.2 SUPPORT FOR ANTI-INFLATION POLICY

It is an important fact that the Grondona system does not compel governments to follow non-inflationary monetary policies, like a traditional gold standard, which guaranteed the maximum price of gold unconditionally. Making such a rigid guarantee in the case of primary commodities would make implementation of the system politically almost impossible, due to the unlimited liability that is inevitably involved. (This is consistent with UNCTAD's failure to establish buffer-stocks with fixed prices, despite decades of effort.) However, the Grondona system's conditional operation would nevertheless help governments to implement non-inflationary monetary policy in important ways. First, the system would itself alter the national money supply, to a predetermined extent, in the direction of stabilizing the real value of the currency, notably reducing the money supply when commodity prices were rising and/or the exchange-rate was falling.

Second, and perhaps more importantly, the level of reserves held by the CRD would provide an objective, public measure of the real value of the currency in terms of imported commodities essential for the country's industries, and of its current trend. Hence, a decline in the CRD's reserves that was seen to continue for months or years could help to persuade the public to support government policies to prevent inflation by raising interest-rates, and implementing other restrictive policies, as necessary to preserve the CRD's reserves of most or at least some commodities above zero.

That is, the CRD would publicise in real time – such as through a website and through news services which report economic data – the quantity of reserves it currently held of each commodity, as well as the price-schedule for each, showing its current buying and selling prices. Consequently, when domestic prices were rising, and the quantity of reserves of different commodities were gradually falling, well before they were all purchased the public would be aware of the growing risk of increasing inflation if they were permitted to fall to zero. This would add a transparent, objective measure, and hence persuasiveness to moves by the government or central bank to raise interest-rates in order to resist inflation.

It hardly needs to be said that governments need public support in order to be able to tighten monetary policy and/or other economic conditions as required to prevent inflation, regardless of the electoral cycle. This depends in turn on public trust in government statements. The level of the CRD's reserves, and trends in them, would be effectively incorruptible evidence of real economic conditions – more reliable than official measures of inflation expressed as price indices, for example, which are notorious for being manipulated in many, if not most, countries. By contrast, the levels of a CRD's reserves are determined by world commodity prices, which are set in world markets activated by buyers and sellers in all the countries of the world. Although all markets are subject to distortion and corruption to some extent, commodity markets are generally so large that they are driven mainly by supply and demand (including market participants' expectations), which is the most appropriate basis for adjusting CRDs' reserve levels. This is the point made by Mill as quoted above in Chapter 6, that the operation of real convertibility of a currency creates undeniable, objective facts in the form of changes in physical reserve holdings, in a way that numerical movements in a calculated index do not.

11.3 MACRO-ECONOMIC INFLUENCE FULLY COUNTER-CYCLICAL

A notable advantage of the Grondona system over the gold standard is that it is fully counter-cyclical: that is, it is automatically stimulatory under deflationary conditions, as well as contractionary under inflationary conditions, thereby stabilising both phases of the business cycle. It was a major weakness of the classical gold standard that it obliged countries experiencing a trade deficit and/or inflation to raise interest-rates and so contract domestic demand in order to prevent its gold reserves from falling to zero, but it did not oblige countries experiencing a trade surplus and/or deflation to reduce interest-rates and so expand domestic demand, and thereby reduce "excessive" reserves of gold. As a result, the governments involved tended to keep interest-rates higher than necessary, and so the system generally had a net deflationary tendency, leading to unnecessarily slow economic growth and correspondingly high unemployment. This is a serious weakness also of the operation of the IMF, which remains from the Bretton Woods gold exchange standard system, as discussed at length by a number of economists, including Joseph Stiglitz (2002) and Ann Pettifor (2003), among others.

By contrast, under the Grondona system a fall in commodity prices in the domestic currency, and/or a rise in the exchange-rate, would automatically expand the money supply and the flow of national currency abroad, thereby stimulating economic activity, and particularly demand for exports, automatically in response to deflationary market pressure. As discussed in Chapters 6 and 7 above, it was this benefit of a system of commodity-based currency convertibility that was discussed with approval by both Keynes (Keynes, 1938) and Hayek (Hayek, 1943). They both saw it as a means of stabilizing the world trade cycle, which is aggravated by the extreme volatility of commodity prices, as they both agreed was a fundamental flaw in the world economic system which economic policy-makers should aim to correct. Support for this objective continued among the many later advocates of the international "commodity reserve currency" advocated by Graham (Graham, 1937), such as Hart, Kaldor and Tinbergen (Hart et al, 1964) and more recently still, Ussher (Ussher, 2016) and Woods (Woods, 2021) – though still without being able to offer a solution to the inherent problems facing an international buffer-stock system.

11.4 RESERVES FALLING TO ZERO

In the simulations in Chapter 10, reserves of some commodities fell to zero within just a few years, such as nickel, coffee, cotton and sugar in the case of Indonesia, and all the metals in the case of the Turkish CRD. At such times the maximum domestic price of these commodities is no longer limited. Nevertheless the CRD still stands ready to purchase reserves on its stated terms, and so when market prices fall again, it will support them to some extent, while accumulating reserves once again.

In anticipation of this potential problem, Grondona proposed the additional rule that, if reserves of some commodity were not held for, say, 18 months, then the CRD's buying and selling prices would automatically increase in successive steps of, say, 5% per year until reserves accumulated again. Grondona stressed the importance of not making unexpected changes in the CRD's operation: improving the stability of commodity prices requires such changes in a CRD's terms to be announced well in advance. Consequently, any such changes should be made only after at least one year's prior warning. At a time of relatively rapid inflation, a CRD's holdings of reserves will be repurchased relatively rapidly, and so this provision will be important in order to preserve the value of the CRD's operation as far as possible, while also helping to reduce inflation.

As mentioned above, in order to be conservative, the simulations all assumed that the CRDs would have no stabilising influence on world commodity market prices. However, in practice the CRDs' effect would likely not be zero, particularly at times of more than average volatility. This influence could be improved over time by governments increasing the scale of their CRD, and/or by tightening its gearing. It would also improve progressively as more governments established CRDs, as discussed in Chapter 12.

11.5 REPEATED SIMULATIONS USEFUL

The simulations in Chapters 9 and 10 also show how useful it would be to be able to perform repeated simulations with different initial values for any commodity, in order to estimate optimal conditions for national implementation. This is needed since the simulations in Chapter 10 also show that, as Grondona himself recommended, the uniform rule that was used to determine the initial conditions for all commodities was too simple: market prices of some commodities never fell low enough for the CRD to accumulate reserves, thereby limiting the CRD's stabilizing influence. In practice, the different conditions of each commodity's production, trade and utilisation would need to be considered by each country in deciding the most appropriate details of the system's gearing. These include the typical range of price fluctuations of each commodity, longer-term trends in prices, trends in the quantities imported and used annually, the domestic inflation-rate and future prospects, technological changes affecting each industry's outlook, and other countries' related activities. Consulting with experts in each industry would surely enable more nearly optimal conditions of implementation than simply using a single fixed rule for all commodities.

The ability to simulate in detail how the system would operate is a very important advantage of the Grondona system over other proposals for commodity-backed currency systems, including international plans, which leave many important matters to be decided through negotiations, and/or discretionary decisions. These unavoidably make the operation of any actively managed scheme unpredictable, and subject to a range of difficulties, including mismanagement, as well as creating scope and incentives for corruption. By contrast, none of these are possible with the Grondona system – unless its publicly guaranteed operating rules were actually broken, which would be as clearly apparent as if a central bank operating a gold standard suspended gold payments – which would immediately become headline news.

11.6 REMAINING UNCERTAINTIES

It is important to note the following three uncertainties that remain about the influence of a CRD's operation, and so also about the simulations in Chapter 10.

11.6.1 Influence of Market Expectations on Exchange-Rate

Until implemented, a significant uncertainty will remain about markets' likely reaction to a CRD's operation during periods of exchange-rate volatility (possibly including movements to unprecedented levels or at unprecedented speed). This is because, when a CRD's reserves increase, the money supply would increase proportionately, which might be expected (on theoretical grounds) to reduce the value of the currency through markets' loss of confidence – particularly in view of the modern-day situation in which financial markets are expected to "discipline" governments which use their power of money creation. However, at the same time, the real value of the currency, in terms of the commodities stored by the CRD would be increasing proportionately as their prices fell, and reserves of the country's essential imports purchased at lower than recent average prices would be growing, thereby clearly improving the prospects for the economy in the future. As a result of this, by contrast, the currency could be expected to strengthen, thereby leading to even lower commodity prices in the domestic currency. In advance of implementation it is not possible to know for certain which of these considerations will have the stronger influence on market sentiment on different occasions.

11.6.2 Price-Stabilizing Influence

As already noted, the simulations in Chapter 10 assume the "worst case", namely that the CRDs had no stabilizing influence on world commodity market prices. In practice, a CRD of even a relatively small economy might well have a significant stabilizing influence on prices of some commodities under some circumstances, particularly after a few years of operation. This is because the quantity of commodities actually traded in "spot" markets (in contrast to trade based on longer-term contracts, of which prices are agreed in advance) is generally only a small percentage of total world trade, and so the quantity of any commodity in a "Block" of even a relatively small

CRD could at times be large relative to a single day's spot market trade (as discussed in more detail in (Collins, 1985).

One effect of a CRD exerting a significant stabilizing influence on world market prices would be to reduce the quantities of purchases and sales by the CRD to some extent, thereby also reducing the size of changes in the national money supply caused by the CRD. In one sense, this can be thought of as reducing "risk" to the national economy. However, since the timing of a CRD's changes in the money supply will be strictly counter-cyclical for each commodity, larger movements will often be desirable, thereby acting as an "automatic stabilizer" for the economy. Hence, to the extent that a CRD had a stabilizing influence on world market prices, a government might even decide to further strengthen its influence by increasing its scale &/or tightening its gearing, in order to increase its economically stabilizing influence on the money supply.

It would also be possible to simulate CRD operations based on the assumption that it would have some significant stabilizing influence on commodity market prices, although this would introduce some uncertainty into the results. This would arise because assumptions would have to be made about the size of this influence, which would depend on the scale of daily trading in spot markets, about which detailed data might not be available.

Despite these uncertainties, the "worst" case assumed in these simulations, which is the simplest and least uncertain case to simulate, is useful for planning purposes. NB in practice a CRD having no influence on world commodity market prices might not be "worst" from the point-of-view of national economic policy, since wider price fluctuations would lead to the CRD providing opportunities for greater profits from resale of greater quantities of reserves bought at lower prices. As commodity prices became more stable, a CRD would have less opportunity to earn profits from sales in order to offset the cost of holding reserves. In response to this, governments might make the range between their CRD's buying and selling prices narrower, so that sales would be more easily triggered. The ultimate case would be where no more sales occurred, and so the entire cost of maintaining the storage facilities would become a government cost: this would be offset by the numerous benefits of having unprecedented stability of imported commodity prices.

11.6.3 Extreme Market Movements

A third uncertainty about establishing a CRD is the unavoidable uncertainty concerning future extreme movements in commodity market prices. Market prices of many primary commodities show movements of −50% or more during recession and +100% or more during economic boom, as seen in Chapter 10, which are disruptive for trade and industry. In addition, both the demand for and supply of primary commodities are also subject to major changes due to technological progress which may either raise or lower prices. Hence a government establishing a CRD would need to make precautionary arrangements for potential "emergency" conditions. For example, in preparation for the possibility of a severe fall in the market price of one or more commodities, the implementing government might arrange for the CRD management to be able to lease commercial storage space at short notice if reserves of some commodity increased beyond the scale for which it had already prepared its own dedicated storage facilities.

These three uncertainties concern the scale of the influence that a CRD may exert on the economy, and so may lead to some caution. However, they do not represent sufficient uncertainty to suggest that implementation would be inadvisable. At worst they might lead a government to initially establish a CRD on a smaller scale than otherwise, accompanied by the intention that, if any such undesirable effects were smaller than feared, the scale or other aspects of the CRD's gearing could be adjusted in order to increase the system's effects, or to alter the balance of effects between different commodities (after sufficient notice).

SUMMARY

The "automatic" operation of the Grondona system – that is, passive, rule-based operation without discretion – makes it similar to the gold standard from the point of view of users, who can thereby rely on any country's CRD to keep its promise to exchange currency for commodities on its stated terms. The same features also make it easy to simulate the system's operation accurately and reliably, using past market data, in a way that a system operated by an activist manager could not be. As seen in the simulations in Chapter 10, another important result is that the timing of the rise and fall in a CRD's reserves, and the concomitant changes it causes in the national money supply, are always accurately counter-cyclical for each commodity handled by the CRD, and for its associated industry, from primary producers to manufacturers. Since large cyclical movements in primary commodity prices are also generally correlated to a considerable extent, in time with the business cycles in the major industrialized countries, this ensures also that the overall effect of the CRD's response to changes in each commodity's price on the national money supply is generally appropriately counter-cyclical for the economy as a whole. To the extent that it might be considered less than optimal, however, those responsible for monetary policy could implement their usual counter-measures without disturbing the CRD's counter-cyclical influence on each of the individual commodity industries.

The system's influence in resisting inflation is also discussed: although a CRD's influence in slowing a rise in commodity prices would in theory be less than that of a system with a fixed price range, and so reserves of some commodities could fall to zero, guaranteeing a maximum price would require a politically unrealistic and economically very costly open-ended commitment. Instead, a CRD's influence is spread over a range of prices, and continuing public loss of reserves would be an important signal to government and citizens that the danger of inflation was increasing, thereby facilitating timely counter-measures from economic policy makers.

Finally, three important uncertainties are discussed. Of most interest is the question of whether the expansion in the money supply which a CRD causes as commodity prices are falling will weaken the currency or strengthen the currency. Any such effect will depend on market expectations, and so is hard to predict. The remaining uncertainties about the stabilizing effect on world commodity prices of one or more smaller CRDs, and the potential effect of extreme price movements as occur periodically in commodity markets are also of interest. However, none of these uncertainties would prevent a CRD from operating reliably according to its published rules.

REFERENCES

Collins, P. (1985). *Currency Convertibility: The Return to Sound Money*. Macmillan. https://link.springer.com/book/10.1007/978-1-349-07058-9

Graham, B. (1937). *Storage and Stability*. McGraw-Hill.

Hart, A., Kaldor, N., & Tinbergen, J. (1964). The Case for an International Commodity Reserve Currency. *United Nations Conference on Trade and Development*.

Hayek, F. (1943). A Commodity Reserve Currency. *The Economic Journal, 53*(210/211), 176-186.

Keynes, J. (1938). The Policy of Government Storage of Foodstuffs and Raw Materials. *Economic Journal (London)*, *48*(191), 449–460. doi:10.2307/2225437

Pettifor, A. (2003). *Real World Economic Outlook. The Legacy of Globalization: Debt and Deflation*. New Economics Foundation.

Stiglitz, J. (2002). *Globalization and Its Discontents*. Penguin.

Ussher, L. (2016). International Monetary Policy with Commodity Buffer Stocks. *European Journal of Economics and Economic Policies: Intervention, 13*(1), 10–25. doi:10.4337/ejeep.2016.01.02

Woods, J. E. (2021). Benjamin Graham on Buffer Stocks. *Journal of the History of Economic Thought*.

Chapter 12
Multi-National Implementation

ABSTRACT

It is an extremely important feature of Grondona's system that, just as any country implementing it would do so independently on a scale appropriate to their economy, many different countries could establish a CRD without any need for coordination and without in any way hindering each other. On the contrary, as the number of CRDs increased, their collective stabilizing influence on commodity markets would increase proportionately. Moreover, the stabilizing influence on their mutual exchange rates would increase more than proportionately as the number of their mutual exchange rates grew. This contrasts sharply with the proposed international system of buffer stocks which could stabilize no more than a single currency and would become increasingly cumbersome as the number of participating countries increased.

INTRODUCTION

As discussed above, apart from the Grondona system, most if not all proposals for linking currency-values to real commodities comprise systems to be established through international negotiations. For nearly a century this has been an *idee fixe* among those who have considered the problem, the main reason for this thinking being as follows. The scale of world markets dwarfs the trade of any single country, and so huge stocks of commodities would be needed in order to guarantee convertibility of a currency unconditionally at fixed prices. Hence, the cost of stabilizing commodity prices in this way would need to be shared between the different countries wishing to implement

DOI: 10.4018/978-1-7998-8302-9.ch012

such a policy, which would necessitate international negotiations through which appropriate contributions to a central fund would be agreed.

However, although this reasoning sounds logical, it then faces the problems discussed in Chapters 6 and 7. Not least is that it is generally not desirable to keep commodity prices between fixed limits decided *a priori*, as is proposed for UNCTAD-sponsored buffer stocks. Both demand for and supply of many commodities vary considerably over time, for a variety of reasons beyond the control of policy makers, and it is important that market prices should be able to adjust to reflect this. By contrast, such adjustment is automatically accommodated under the Grondona system, which does not attempt to place any rigid limits on commodity prices, but to reduce their volatility. For this, individual CRDs operated independently by different countries offer a far more attractive solution to the problem of stabilizing real currency values and commodity prices – simple, foolproof, effective, low-cost, and open to progressive improvement.

Another critical weakness of the international approach is as discussed in Chapters 6 and 7: only one currency would be made directly convertible into commodities under such a system, and so the benefits to all the other participating countries from such a system would be very much less – and very unclear, unless a further treaty was agreed by members to preserve fixed exchange-rates with the newly convertible currency. This would require no less than "a new Bretton Woods", in fact, for which the IMF was established in order to help preserve fixed exchange-rates among the member states – and even so that system collapsed after less than 30 years.

Alternatively, proponents of globalization would nowadays urge participating countries to all use the single currency stabilized through real convertibility. However, this would raise another range of major problems including particularly that of loss of control over national monetary policy, and more widely of national sovereignty, against which there is understandably strong political resistance. Consequently it is not surprising that this dilution of benefits for most participants in an international system has prevented a successful outcome even after decades of negotiations. This failure surely makes continuing hope for such an international solution unrealistic, despite wide recognition of the potential benefits of real convertibility, if achievable in reality rather than theory. That is, the experience of more than half-a-century of fruitless talks about UNCTAD's Integrated Program for Commodities is evidence that these problems make such an international system unattractive to the governments which would be required to fund it. It is unfortunate that in recent years, while considering the potential benefits of reviving efforts aimed at realising an international buffer-stock system, Ussher and Woods both failed to study Grondona's system in sufficient detail to understand how it avoids these problems, although they both referred to his work, as discussed in Chapter 8.9 above (Ussher, 2016; Woods, 2021).

12.1 ADVANTAGES OF MULTI-NATIONAL RATHER THAN INTERNATIONAL IMPLEMENTATION

By contrast to the extreme difficulties facing plans for an international system of buffer stocks, the reliable and predictable manner in which the Grondona system operates in the simulations shown in Chapter 10 is striking. Seeing that this result is simply achieved by each country acting independently, it is clear that it represents a radically different approach to solving the problem of how to share the costs of implementing currency convertibility and the concomitant stabilization of commodity prices. Importantly, in contrast to the international approach, each country's own currency is made directly convertible into commodities, and its real value directly stabilized to a predetermined extent in terms of the commodities involved, with the corollary that the domestic prices of each country's imports of the selected commodities would also be partially stabilized.

Table 1 shows how the commodities handled by each of the four countries' CRDs in the simulations in Chapter 10 are different, as appropriate for each country's different economic conditions. (NB the choice of commodities shown in Table 12.1 is based on trade data from before the start of the simulations in 2009, and so may be far from optimal more than a decade later.) That is, there is no need for uniformity between countries: provided that they implement the automatic price-adjustment rule, their operations will not impede each other, but will rather have a cumulative stabilizing effect, as discussed further below.

Even more importantly, because of the Grondona system's conditionality, each CRD could legitimately pay for its purchases of reserves through expansion of the money supply lasting for as long as the reserves are held, thereby avoiding the need for increased taxation or borrowing in proportion to the quantity of reserves held, while benefiting from economically desirable counter-cyclical variation in the national money supply, to a predetermined extent.

Table 1. Commodities handled by each country's simulated CRD

	Indonesia	Malaysia	Turkey	Pakistan
Copper	Y	Y	Y	Y
Nickel	Y		Y	Y
Aluminium	Y	Y	Y	Y
Lead	Y	Y	Y	Y
Zinc	Y	Y	Y	Y
Tin	Y		Y	
Cotton	Y	Y	Y	
Wool		Y	Y	
Rubber	Y			
Sugar	Y			
Coffee beans	Y	Y	Y	
Cocoa beans	Y		Y	
Wheat		Y	Y	Y
Rice	Y		Y	
Barley			Y	Y
Soya beans		Y	Y	
Maize		Y	Y	Y

These differences between the balance of benefits, risks and costs under the two different approaches of multi-national versus international implementation, are extreme. Multi-national implementation is simple, effective, safe and "costless", in contrast to the theoretical idea of international implementation which, even if it was possible, would achieve far less benefit – and arguably none for most participating countries – while imposing a greater financial burden, as well as severely distorting commodity markets, and being at risk of periodic crises due to insufficient budget or reserves to ensure its guaranteed lower and upper prices.

It is important to also note that, even without any coordination, each country would benefit from the operation of the other countries' CRDs, due to both the increase in scale of their cumulative stabilizing influence on commodity prices, and to the stabilizing effects on each country's mutual exchange-rates. That is, with the different countries' systems operating simultaneously, the degree of commodity price stabilization achieved would have been greater due to the greater total quantity of reserves that could be sold to or bought from CRDs by market participants over any price-range in their publicly known price-schedules. In addition, since the changes in multiple countries' money supplies caused by their CRDs' operations would be largely simultaneous, due to being driven primarily by world commodity market prices, their mutual exchange-rate pairs would also be stabilized to some extent, as discussed further in Section 12.2 below.

Moreover, these benefits for participating countries increase as the number of CRDs increases – in contrast to increasing complexity, difficulty, rigidity and lack of transparency as the number of participants in an international system increased. In addition, if instead of being entirely independent, multiple countries coordinated their implementation to some extent, for example in order to balance the relative quantities of different commodities, the collective benefits could be improved further.

Discussions to establish International Commodity Agreements have low priority today, presumably due to the failure to establish a single agreement after half-a-century of efforts. However, instead of acknowledging the superiority of Grondona's multi-national approach, which enables all countries to preserve their existing currencies while stabilizing them directly, the alternative being promoted by globalists is to double down by trying to make every country use the same global digital currency. Economic instability in the form of volatility of exchange-rates is claimed to be inevitable – and since it cannot be prevented, then it must be avoided by eliminating different currencies. But this is a self-fulfilling argument: large countries and financial corporations which largely control world financial markets can destabilize smaller countries' currencies. Moreover, the US federal government currently operates a policy to "punish" governments of countries of which it disapproves, for example by shutting them out from US dollar financial services, which can be very costly to victims in today's largely dollar-based world trade system.

However, for the great majority of countries, to give up their national currency to participate in such a "Great Reset" would be to "jump from the frying-pan into the fire": it would surely bring even worse consequences, since they would then have little or no say in the management of the global currency. That is, their needs would inevitably be ignored by the larger countries which would certainly dominate the management of the system, as in the IMF. As a recent example, Greece has suffered massive economic and social costs due to using the Euro, of which the management is inevitably dominated by Germany and France, and so interest-rates and other policy measures do not match the needs of the Greek economy. These costs, including historic levels of unemployment, could have been avoided if Greece had continued to use its own currency, the Drachma.

In sharp contrast, it is a major strength of the Grondona system that, as discussed above, it requires no international negotiations or agreements in order to be implemented multi-nationally. That is, the system is designed for individual countries to implement independently, and Grondona expected that many countries would adopt it because of the direct benefits that would result, once governments and their advisers understood the system's advantages.

The obvious desirability of such an outcome, and its contrast with the failure of all attempts over half a century to devise an international solution to the problem, can perhaps best be appreciated as being due to the superiority of market forces over political decision-making in this field. This is because CRDs are passive, their operations following simple rules activated by market participants responding to movements in prices, as reliably as a gold standard. Consequently, provided that each country's CRD is set up as Grondona planned, so that the prices at which it buys or sells commodities on demand adjust "automatically" in proportion to the quantity of reserves held, then, as market prices fall, reserves will be automatically spread among the different CRDs in operation. That is, when market prices are falling, each different CRD's current buying price will periodically become the most attractive to sellers of commodities. This influence is increased by the fact that each CRD will operate in a different currency, and hold its reserves of commodities within its own territory, and so sellers will face a variety of different costs in different currencies to deliver to or collect from each CRD. As a result, it might be that several different CRDs might be asked to purchase or sell reserves simultaneously.

Although it is not hard to imagine, it is useful to also illustrate how the operations of different countries' CRDs would complement each other. Figure 1 illustrates, in a somewhat simplified form, this synergistic effect of three different CRDs operating simultaneously.

In this illustration of three CRDs' actions, the simplifying assumption is made that the three countries' mutual exchange-rates are fixed, so that the relation between the three CRDs' buying and selling prices is shown as fixed, although this would not be likely in reality, in the contemporary world of floating exchange-rates. Hence Figure 1 shows how, when prices are falling, each of the current buying prices of the three countries' CRDs, which are all different, would in turn become the highest, and so the most attractive to sellers of the commodity in question, after another CRD with a higher buying-price accumulated a full Block of reserves, and its buying-price fell automatically by a few %.

Figure 1. Synergistic operation of 3 national CRDs
(Collins & Grondona, 1976)

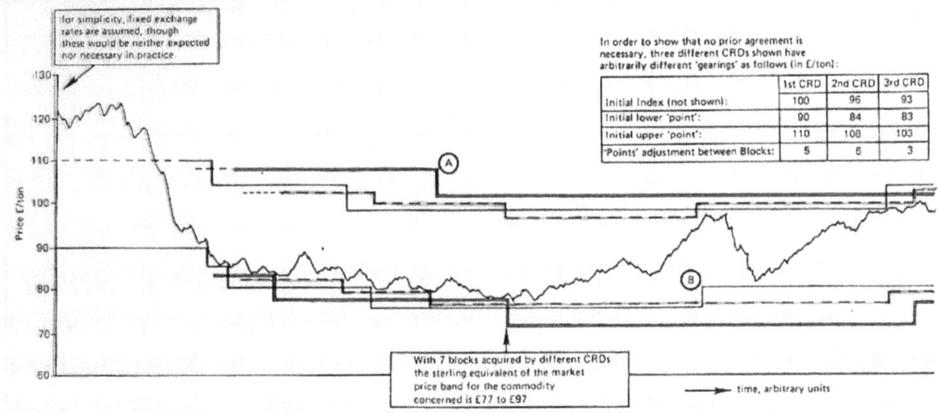

In the case shown in Figure 1, three CRDs absorb 7 Blocks of reserves while the price falls from 90 to 77. By contrast, if only the CRD with the highest initial lower point was in operation, it would have absorbed only 3 Blocks of commodities as prices fell this far. (NB in practice, the different CRDs' Blocks would be likely to contain different quantities of each commodity.)

Figure 1 also shows how the more different countries implemented the Grondona system using their different national currencies, the more stable that world commodity market prices would become, since the effective market "floor price" at any time would be the highest of the various CRDs' then buying prices, while the effective market "ceiling price" would be the lowest of the multiple CRDs' then selling prices.

This synergistic effect would occur in the absence of any coordination or even communication between the three countries' CRDs or governments. As more countries established CRDs, whether or not they coordinated their plans through consultations in advance of implementation, the stabilizing influence of the multiple CRDs' operations would increase proportionately.

The simulations in Chapter 10 provide real examples of how four countries' CRDs would have collectively exerted a much greater stabilising influence than any of the CRDs operating alone. For example, the maximum number of Blocks held during the 10 years of the simulations by the four countries' CRDs, of the three commodities, nickel, aluminium and coffee are shown in Table 2.

Table 2. Maximum number of Blocks of selected commodities held by each CRD

	Nickel	Aluminium	Coffee
Indonesia	5	7	3
Malaysia	-	9	9
Turkey	13	11	6
Pakistan	6	9	-
Total	**24**	**36**	**18**

Since the total number of Blocks held by all four CRDs was much larger than any one country's holdings, the overall stabilizing influence on commodity prices and so on the four national currencies' real value would also have been much greater – although each country only paid for its own reserves. Clearly the stabilizing effects of multiple CRDs are much greater than any one alone, and there is no need for uniformity or negotiations between countries in order for all four countries to achieve these cumulative benefits. Of course, to the extent that commodity market prices were stabilized, other countries without CRDs would also benefit. This would impose no costs on countries operating a CRD, and would avoid the need for all countries to feel obliged to establish a CRD.

12.2 EXCHANGE-RATE STABILIZING INFLUENCE

As each country's CRD increased and reduced its national money-supply to some extent, in proportion to changes in its holdings of commodities, the several countries' CRDs would act roughly in synchrony, increasing their respective money supplies together when commodity prices were falling, and reducing them together as commodity prices rose again (though with some differences between countries due to the different CRDs' different operating conditions, and to exchange-rate movements). In this way, the multiple CRDs would exert a direct stabilizing influence on their mutual exchange-rates, since their respective money supplies would be expanding and contracting in response to the same movements in commodity market prices. This complementarity would arise even though different countries' CRDs would handle different quantities of different commodities in different ratios, as appropriate to their annual import requirements.

Importantly, this exchange-rate stabilizing influence would benefit from the "network effect" which has become famous from the rapid growth of successful Internet-based services: the more people who use a particular service, the more attractive it becomes for new users to join. Likewise, the more different countries that implemented the Grondona system, the wider will be the stabilizing influence on the exchange-rate of each additional country that implements the system *de novo*. Moreover, the size of the network effect is an exponential function of the number of participants, as each country has pair-wise exchange-rates with every other country. So, for example, if 25 countries each established a CRD, the number of mutually stabilized exchange-rate pairs would reach 300.

Like Internet-based services, this mutually beneficial stabilizing influence would grow continually, with no inherent limit to prevent it spreading world-wide. It is also noteworthy that this influence would be a spontaneous result of the multiple CRDs operating essentially "automatically" in response to market forces, and would not depend on any discretionary policy-making.

Figures 2 and 3 illustrate how far the actions of three of the CRDs simulated in Chapter 10 in expanding and contracting their national money supplies would have been complementary. (The simulation of a Malaysian CRD was over only five years, and so is excluded.) The simulations in Chapter 10 were performed separately, and the scale of each of the CRDs' influence on their national money supply was calculated and shown in the last graph of each simulation. This data for the three countries simulated over 40 quarters was normalized by showing the increase or decrease in the money supply for each quarter as a fraction of the CRD's initial stockholdings, and aggregated in Figure 1 to show the overall cyclical pattern of the CRDs' collective monetary influence.

The same data is plotted for each CRD separately in Figure 2, thereby showing the changes in the three countries' money supplies separately, and how they generally parallel each other, but with small differences in timing due to their different terms of operation.

During most of the first three years, the CRDs reduced the money supply, as market prices of most commodities rose. After several years of only small changes, the last two years see simultaneous reduction by Pakistan and Turkey, though not by Indonesia. Other things being equal, this rough overall coordination of the CRDs' monetary influence would have tended to stabilize the three countries' mutual exchange-rates, although this was not an explicit objective of the Grondona system. It is, however, an inherent feature of systems of real currency convertibility: by linking the values of currencies

Figure 2. Collective monetary influence of three CRDs

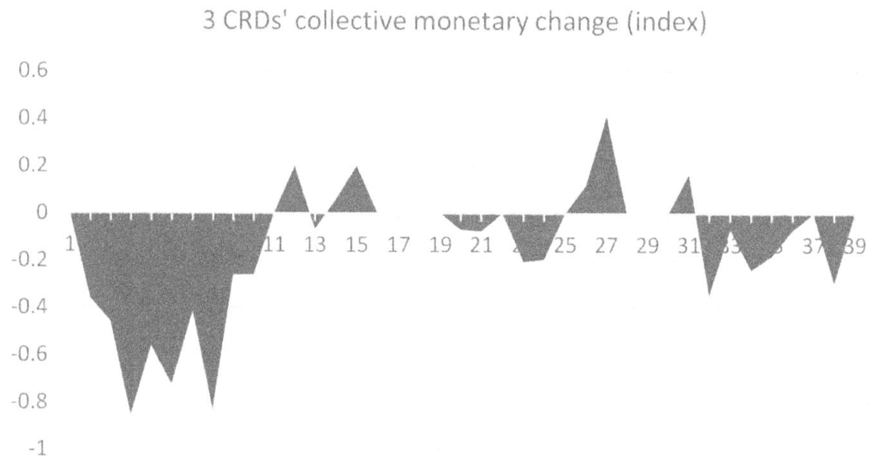

to real commodities, their relative values are stabilized in similar real terms. Further details of the different effects of a CRD in cases where its influence on the exchange-rate is greater or less than its influence on commodity prices are discussed in more detail in (Collins, 1985).

Figure 3. Rough coordination of monetary expansion and contraction by three different CRDs

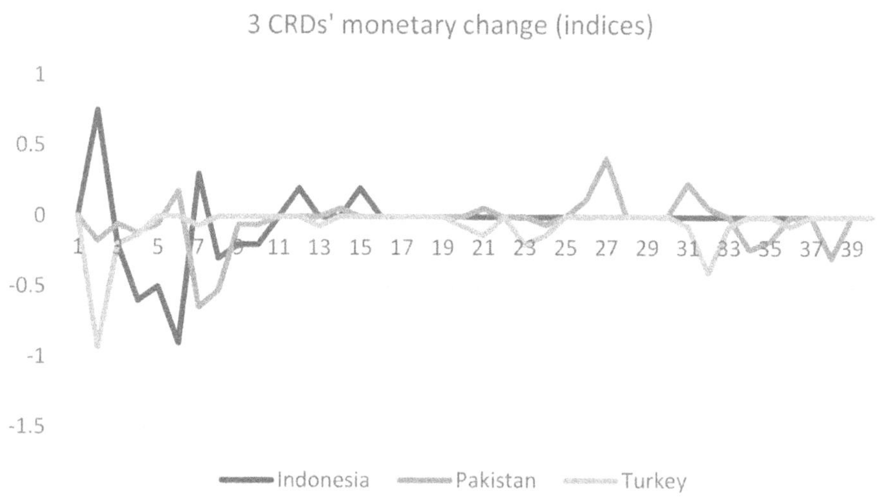

12.3 FURTHER EVOLUTION OF MULTI-NATIONAL ADOPTION

The benefits of the economic stabilizing influences experienced by a group of countries which each implemented a CRD could lead to their coordinating their policies in various ways in order to enhance the benefits further. Such actions as exchanging information about their CRD's operations and commodity markets, collaborating in constructing specialized warehouses, sharing information about possible policy responses to the monetary influence of CRD operations (eg concerning whether and how to magnify or reduce their influence, using CRD reserve movements as a guide), exchanging related monetary and macro-economic information, and others could all enhance the collective stabilizing influence of a group of independent countries' CRDs.

In view of these possibilities, more simulations of several different countries' CRDs' operations over a common time-scale could be valuable. Simulating how the combined monetary impact of several different CRDs responding to movements in primary commodity market prices could exert a cumulative stabilizing effect over the business cycle, and also in response to external shocks, would be a promising extension of such work. In addition, increasing the extent of overlap in the commodities handled by the different countries' CRDs could improve their synchronization, thereby increasing their stabilizing influence on their mutual exchange-rates. This could be an important topic for joint investigation by various groupings of countries, since the greater the degree of synchronisation in the operation of several different CRDs, the greater would be their mutually stabilizing influence.

The gradual enhancement of these stabilizing influences might eventually lead to a group of countries making moves towards forming a currency "bloc", for example by implementing other policies to further stabilize their mutual exchange-rates, in order to facilitate mutual trade and to better pursue like-minded policies. Such a group of implementing countries might adopt additional policies to enhance the system's spontaneous stabilizing effects, such as narrowing the price-ranges and price-steps in their CRDs' price-schedules for selected commodities in order to further reduce movements in their mutual exchange-rates. Such actions might ultimately lead to some countries even agreeing to merge their currencies. If so, this would happen as the result of progressive reduction of movements in their exchange-rates, and improved trade relations, rather than being due to external pressure to adopt a common currency managed by another country.

12.4 GEO-POLITICAL CONSIDERATIONS

A situation in which many different countries independently operated their own CRD tailored to the structure and trade requirements of their own economies would manifestly be a far better solution to the problem of reducing volatility in world foreign-exchange markets than many different countries being bullied into using a single global currency, thereby making them all subservient to a single group of "experts" who controlled "global monetary policy".

Implementing a market-driven mechanism that reduces the volatility of exchange-rates between different currencies, whether national, regional or private, is a logical, non-partisan policy that will help the worldwide network of different countries' currency and trade systems to evolve naturally towards ever-improving cooperation. Avoiding rigid convertibility makes the system much easier to initiate, both organizationally and politically, while smoothing rather than preventing the adjustments in commodity prices that are needed due to ever-changing economic, technological and other conditions. And as the different participating currencies' mutual exchange-rates become more stable, there will become less need for them to use a third-party currency for their mutual trade.

Politically and economically powerful advocates of a centralized global system will try to bully other countries into agreeing to join. But present-day problems show how this is a mistaken approach: public trust in political leaders is at historically low levels in many countries, perhaps particularly in the OECD, and so the scope for leaders to sign binding international treaties to implement policies with which the public do not agree is limited. As part of this trend, the USA is clearly no longer as capable of leading much of the world, either politically or economically, as it was in 1944, or even in 1971. Moreover, implementing CRDs will facilitate natural incremental change, whereby each country's government will have the option of improving their policy by adjusting their CRD's operating terms, as well as by waiting for the benefits from other countries implementing a national CRD *de novo*.

In this way, establishing a CRD will help governments to resist external political-economic pressures. As an example, deliberate destabilization of a country's exchange-rate would lead to wider movements in its domestic commodity prices, which would increase the scale of the CRD's transactions and hence the premiums which it earned from commodity purchases and sales, while making larger stabilizing changes in the money supply. Hence, for example, countries targeted for destabilization, as occurred during the

1997-8 South East Asian currency crisis, would be better able to withstand such political pressure with a CRD in operation than without.

12.5 POTENTIAL FOR D-8 COUNTRIES' INITIATIVE

The Organisation of Islamic Cooperation (OIC), founded in 1969, is the second largest political grouping of countries in the world after the United Nations, comprising 57 countries with combined GDP of $5 trillion. It is therefore of interest to consider to what extent implementing the Grondona system might contribute to their economic growth and development. A key objective of Islamic economics is to design effective policy measures that will help to free Islamic and other countries from the international system of privately controlled, debt-based *fiat* money which is used throughout the world today. Muslims consider this system to be "*Riba*" and therefore immoral, and moreover responsible for most of the problems in the world.

A particularly relevant example of this viewpoint was stated at the 7th Islamic Economics Workshop, which was organized in 2019 by the Research Center for Islamic Economics (IKAM), the Turkish Scientific Studies Association (ILEM), and the Turkish Entrepreneurship and Business Ethics Association (IGIAD), on the theme of "Monetary Issues in Islamic Economics". The Final Declaration of the workshop included the following summary statements, among others:

1. "*... few reserve currencies are ruling over international markets with exorbitant advantage over others, leaving the weaker ones exposed to daily artificial fluctuations of exchange-rates ...*"
2. "*... countries should reduce their dependence on reserve currencies and vehicle currencies, specially the US dollar, in their bilateral trade ...*"
3. "*... the need for devising pragmatic policies towards achieving an Islamic monetary system was accentuated ...*" (IKAM, 2019)

The simulations in Chapter 10 of how the Grondona system might operate in four different OIC countries show that establishing CRDs has the potential to contribute substantially to each of these major goals.

1. It will help to insulate the economies of countries which establish a national CRD from "*daily artificial fluctuations of exchange-rates*", through its automatic stabilizing influence on the real value of each

country's national currency in terms of the commodities handled by the CRD, thereby making them less susceptible to market volatility or manipulation.

2. It will facilitate wider use of the currencies of countries which implement a CRD in their mutual trade, by stabilizing the mutual exchange-rates between implementing countries' currencies, as discussed above. This benefit will increase progressively with the number of CRDs, and could be further enhanced by governments agreeing to coordinate their policy responses. This will reduce the need to use "*reserve currencies and vehicle currencies*" such as the US dollar in their trade.
3. Establishing a CRD will clearly be a "*pragmatic policy*", due to the ease with which each country could implement the system independently, with no need to negotiate or even discuss it with governments of other countries, either friendly or threatening (although some such discussions could be beneficial in optimising the conditions of implementation). By deciding the most appropriate scale of implementation in advance, governments will be able to avoid any risk of shock to the economy, such as could be caused by trying to implement a more rigid system, or by depending on a global initiative beyond national control.

The potential contribution of CRDs to solving these three problems is made even greater by the possibility of including gold and silver in their operations, as discussed in Chapter 13 below, albeit on somewhat different terms from other commodities. In view of these considerations, it seems clear that implementing the Grondona system could contribute greatly towards preparing and creating the foundations needed to achieve a sound and stable Islamic monetary system, distinct from the *Riba* system used in most countries today.

Hence, a possible initiative could be for the "D-8" group of leading OIC countries – Bangladesh, Egypt, Indonesia, Iran, Malaysia, Nigeria, Pakistan and Turkey – to each implement the Grondona system on approximately the same scale relative to their national economies. In this case the total quantity of reserves held by the eight CRDs would be several times larger than any country alone, leading to a proportionately much greater stabilizing influence on their primary commodity trade and prices.

In addition, the mutual exchange-rate stabilizing influence of the eight CRDs would also be proportionately greater, since it will benefit from the "network effect". In the case of adoption by the D-8 countries, the overall quantity of reserves of each commodity held by the eight CRDs will be eight times the average quantity held by each country's CRD, while the number of exchange-rate pairs experiencing a mutual stabilizing influence will be twenty-eight, as each country will have seven such relationships.

These benefits will in turn facilitate agreements such as the sharing of data and use of currency swaps between central banks as measures to resist and/or ameliorate currency crises and other problems. Further still, as experience of the eight national CRDs' operation accumulated, their growing stabilizing influences on the D-8 currencies would evolve naturally towards acting as an informal currency "bloc", as they came to make the same policy responses to external shocks.

Finally, these stabilizing influences would extend beyond the D-8 countries to other OIC member states, many of which could also implement the Grondona system, even if on a limited scale. Depending on many unpredictable future events, it is surely within the bounds of possibility that such cumulatively strengthening relationships might later even develop into the basis of a common, Shariah-compliant, commodity-backed currency.

12.6 POTENTIAL FOR ASEAN INITIATIVE

Another major economic grouping which could benefit from collectively implementing the Grondona system is the Association of Southeast Asian Nations (ASEAN), which was established in 1967. The ten Member States are Brunei Darussalam, Cambodia, Indonesia, Lao PDR, Malaysia, Myanmar, Philippines, Singapore, Thailand and Viet Nam. These countries have 10% of the world population, and a combined GDP of more than $3 trillion (putting them between Germany and India). They also handle nearly $3 trillion/year of international trade, which is a high proportion relative to GDP, and are industrialising rapidly. This makes the volatility of imported commodity prices of particular importance for them, and so increases the benefits they would receive from operating CRDs. Moreover, the severe instability of exchange-rates which they experienced in 1997-98 has given them a strong collective incentive to adopt policies that reduce their vulnerability to destabilization by giant corporations or foreign governments. As one possibility, the potential benefits for ASEAN countries of implementing the Grondona system in collaboration with Japan are discussed in (Collins, 2002).

12.7 POTENTIAL FOR MERCOSUR INITIATIVE

Known as "the Southern Common Market", Mercosur is an economic cooperation bloc started in 1991, and currently comprising the countries of Argentina, Bolivia, Brazil, Paraguay, Uruguay and Venezuela, with a combined population of 300 million, and combined GDP of $2 trillion. Six more south American states are associate members. The countries of South America have long suffered from a lack of collective geopolitical influence, due to being relatively disunited by comparison with the USA in North America. In this situation, an initiative by major members of the group to establish CRDs could help to stabilize Mercosur trade relations, and facilitate the use of their own currencies for intra-Mercosur trade. Although Mercosur members are major exporters of some primary commodities, their economies are also increasingly industrialised, and so they each import growing quantities of commodities. Consequently, as for the D-8 and ASEAN international groupings, an initiative by Mercosur countries to perform a feasibility study of implementing the Grondona system, which would include simulating a number of national CRDs established on different scales, could be very valuable.

12.8 POTENTIAL FOR AFRICAN UNION INITIATIVE

The African Union (AU) is a grouping of all 55 countries of the African continent, established in 2002 as the successor organization to the Organisation of African Unity (OAU) founded in 1963 to promote development in Africa. The AU comprises several Regional Economic Communities (REC), which collectively have 1/6 of the world population, and $3 trillion GDP. If CRDs were established in the five largest AU economies, Nigeria, South Africa, Egypt, Algeria and Morocco, with a combined GDP of $1.5 trillion, they could become a useful "island of stability" which could facilitate mutual trade and trade with other AU countries. It need hardly be said that African countries have suffered great costs from imperialist and neo-imperialist intervention by richer and more powerful countries over several centuries. Consequently, a network of CRDs could surely help to strengthen the continent's economic independence. It could be a promising first step for these countries to investigate the likely effects of their CRDs operating through simulating their operation, both separately and collectively, under different conditions.

SUMMARY

This chapter has explained and discussed the unique feature of the Grondona system that, due to its flexibility, many different countries' CRDs could be established, with no prior coordination or negotiation. The conditionality of each different CRD's operation ensures that their separate influences are compatible, and their stabilizing influence is cumulative and indeed synergistic, growing as the overall number of CRDs grows. In view of the cost, time, complexity, difficulty and unavoidable uncertainty of international negotiations, it is a striking advantage of the Grondona system that relations between different countries' CRDs do not need to be planned in any way in order to ensure their compatibility. That is, although each country can freely decide their own share of the "burden" of holding counter-cyclically managed stocks, they all benefit from each other's contribution. By contrast to such a multi-national system, if the four countries simulated in Chapter 10 had tried to negotiate shares in an international system of buffer stocks, as well as being time-consuming and frustrating, they would have been unlikely to achieve agreement, while only one their currencies could have benefited directly from the system's stabilizing influence. Instead, each country does what they consider optimal from their national point of view, and receives the benefits of both direct and indirect stabilization of their currency greater than their national commitment alone.

This could be particularly valuable for the member states of such international groupings as the D-8 members of OIC, ASEAN, Mercosur and the African Union, which are all going through the stresses of industrialization, by helping to stabilize their mutual exchange-rates, their mutual trade and their overall economic growth. Monetary agreements between different countries to support each other's currency, such as through currency swaps at pre-agreed prices, would also be easier to negotiate as their mutual exchange-rates became more stable.

REFERENCES

Collins, P. (1985). *Currency Convertibility: The Return to Sound Money*. Macmillan. https://link.springer.com/book/10.1007/978-1-349-07058-9

Collins, P. (2002). The Grondona System of Conditional Currency Convertiblity: a basis for Conflict-Free Monetary Cooperation. *Proc. 1st International Conference of Japan Economic Policy Association (JEPA).*

Collins, P. & Grondona, P. (1976). *Illustration of multi-national implementation of Grondona system*. Submitted to House of Lords Select Committee on Commodity Prices.

IKAM. (2019). *Final Declaration*. https://ikam.org.tr/images/pdf/Final_Declaration_-_IEW_7.pdf

Chapter 13
Potential for Further Evolution of CRDs

ABSTRACT

Although Grondona prepared detailed guidelines that his system should be implemented in relation to durable, essential, basic imported commodities, he also understood that, once established successfully, CRDs' operations could evolve in various ways in order to achieve greater benefits. For example, the inclusion of precious metals such as gold and silver, albeit on a somewhat different basis than industrial commodities, is an interesting possibility. Grondona also recommended that other products such as basic manufactured components like standardised steel or aluminium strip could be included. Another potential evolution is a CRD's role in a currency crisis: a sudden change in the exchange rate would be countered to some extent by a CRD being asked to sell or buy commodities, which would tend to resist the initial change. A CRD's terms of operation might be adjusted in order to strengthen its influence as such a countermeasure.

INTRODUCTION

As different countries' experience of the Grondona system's operation increases, they will naturally seek ways to improve its influence. Most simply, this can be done by increasing the quantity of commodities contained in a CRD's "Blocks", which would increase the CRD's stabilizing influence proportionately, as also would various means of tightening its "gearing", such

DOI: 10.4018/978-1-7998-8302-9.ch013

as narrowing the range between its buying and selling prices, or reducing the price-steps between successive Blocks of reserves in its price-schedules for certain commodities. As the number of countries implementing the system increases, the different CRDs' combined stabilizing influence will also increase, as discussed in the previous chapter. To the extent that this stabilized commodity market prices, it would benefit all countries, not only those with a CRD operating in their own currency. There are a number of other ways in which the system's overall stabilizing influence could be improved over time, as discussed in the following.

13.1 CONDITIONAL GOLD AND SILVER CONVERTIBILITY

Grondona did not include gold in his system, because it is not a major industrial commodity, and is not imported in large quantities, so that partially stabilizing its market price and trade would not in itself have a major stabilizing influence on the economy of a country operating a CRD. In addition, gold has an important monetary role and so is unlike other industrial metals. Notably, large fluctuations in the market price of gold are less correlated with the cyclical movements in industrial primary commodities, which generally move broadly together. Consequently, movements in gold prices which caused a CRD to make significant changes in the money supply would be less likely to be appropriate from the point of view of monetary policy. So, for example, if the price of gold increased substantially for geo-political reasons, it would lead to market purchases of reserves from the CRD, thereby reducing the money supply, even if other commodity prices were at low levels.

However, there is no fundamental problem preventing gold's inclusion within a CRD's scope, although the conditions on which it should be included would need to be decided according to somewhat different considerations than for industrial commodities. For example, deciding the most appropriate quantity of gold to be included in a Block, and the size of the price-steps between successive Blocks of reserves, should include monetary considerations, rather than being simply based on historical data about past import quantities.

A potentially major benefit of introducing conditional gold convertibility within the Grondona system is that it would be a low-risk step towards strengthening the monetary role of gold. As experience of its operation accumulated, a CRD's "gearing" could be progressively tightened, narrowing the range between the CRD's lower and upper "points" and/or increasing the size of its Blocks. This would have the effect of progressively stabilizing the domestic price of gold in countries including it in their CRD's operation, which would facilitate its monetary use. This process could continue as far as a government chose, enabling it to obtain most of the benefits of resuming strict gold convertibility, but without needing to take the final, high-risk step of unconditionally guaranteeing a maximum gold price, which would immediately impose strict constraints on monetary policy.

Much the same considerations apply to the possibility of including silver among the commodities handled by a CRD. Compared to gold, silver is a "hybrid" metal in that it has important industrial as well as monetary uses. Silver is also subject to large price movements, but again there is no insurmountable reason why it could not be included in a CRD, perhaps on a relatively small scale initially in order to enable the monetary authorities to gain experience of the effects of its volatility.

It should be noted that, like other commodities, a CRD would handle gold and silver entirely separately from each other, thereby avoiding any of the problems of "bimetallism", which arise when gold and silver coins are used in parallel. CRDs' operations would thereby permit the relative prices of gold and silver to move to whatever extent required by supply and demand. In order to preserve its stabilizing influence, the CRD's holdings of gold and silver should also be kept entirely separate from any monetary reserves held by the central bank. The use of these is typically not based on fixed rules, but may be decided for different objectives arising from monetary policy, trade, geopolitics or other reasons.

The start of one or more CRDs' handling of gold and silver would probably be welcomed by market participants, since the market prices of both metals suffer from severe manipulation through trade in futures markets of contracts for "paper gold" and "paper silver" – that is, promises to supply the metals at a future date at pre-specified prices. The value of open positions in futures markets is often far greater than the physical supply available, of which they frequently drive the price – giving rise to the criticism of market manipulation. In particular, this "paper trading" has long been used to suppress gold and silver market prices. Hence, having supplies reliably available through CRDs' predictably counter-cyclical operations could help to reduce such manipulation, which is facilitated by uncertainty about supply availability, among other factors.

13.2 EXTENSION OF RANGE OF COMMODITIES INCLUDED IN CRD OPERATIONS

As another example of how the Grondona system might evolve as experience increased, Grondona himself suggested that a CRD might extend the range of commodities which it handled to include basic manufactured products which will not become obsolete. These might include basic steel or Aluminium strip of widely-used standard grades, basic chemical engineering inputs that are inexpensive to store, and rare metals which are traded in small quantities but are nevertheless of strategic importance for manufacturing certain high-tech products. Including the latter in a CRD's operations could contribute to geo-political stability by reducing threats of interruption of supplies.

13.3 SIMULATION OF CRD VARIANTS

In relation to the above discussion of extending CRDs' scope, a range of additional simulations covering these different commodities would be valuable for assessing costs and benefits. It will also be valuable to simulate different settings of CRDs handling gold and silver using past data covering periods of major price-swings, in order to evaluate the extent to which the CRD's operation might have required the monetary authorities to take offsetting actions. Repeated simulations using a variety of initial conditions and gearings different from the uniform rule used in the simulations in Chapter 10, so that the CRD accumulates and keeps useful quantities of reserves of all commodities, should help to determine initial conditions for different countries' CRDs that are as nearly optimal as possible.

13.4 POTENTIAL ADVANTAGE FOR EARLY ADOPTERS

The maximum benefits of implementing the Grondona system depend on the CRD acquiring reserves of a range of commodities – the more the better. The first few countries to establish a CRD will acquire reserves on the first downturn in commodity prices after implementation. However, countries adopting the system later may take longer to acquire reserves, and may require a second market downturn, which will also be lessened by the stabilizing influence of already established CRDs.

One possibility is that, in order to obtain reserves, later-implementing countries may choose to set their initial prices at relatively higher levels, since the system's influence in resisting rising prices does not activate until they acquire reserves. Such "competition" between newly established CRDs would have the benefit of further increasing the multiple CRDs' stabilizing influence on commodity prices, as well as on their mutual exchange-rates.

13.5 CURRENCY CRISIS COUNTER-MEASURE

The extreme volatility seen in international financial markets in recent years is a particular threat to the economic stability of smaller economies. There has been extensive analysis of the causes of currency crises, and a range of policy-measures have been developed to mitigate these risks. These include building up foreign-exchange reserves proportionate to a country's foreign-currency debts, making currency swap agreements with allied countries, use of "derivatives" such as currency futures, diversifying monetary reserves to include gold and other precious metals that are less vulnerable to manipulation, and others.

An additional factor that has to be considered is geopolitical risk. Although a country's government and corporations may be following normally adequate prudential policies, it may be targeted for destabilization for political reasons by the US government or its allies. As of 2021, this is being done openly against Russia, China, Iran, Syria, North Korea and Venezuela, among other countries, which are the target of publicly announced economic attack by the US government, apparently intended to achieve "regime change". Defence against such politically motivated economic pressure is more complex than defence against purely economic risks. That is, while the US government continues to use its dominant role in dollar-based economic activities to try to force other countries to follow its "orders" relating to a range of policies, relatively smaller countries in particular need to try to insulate themselves from such political pressures, in addition to the risks and problems caused by major market fluctuations.

A counter-measure that has been spreading in recent years is for countries to reduce the use of US dollars in their trade. This is typically implemented through bilateral agreements between pairs of countries to make arrangements to pay for mutual imports and exports in their own currencies. Before such agreements can be successful it is necessary to achieve an acceptable level of stability in the relative values of their respective currencies. However, due to the absence of any component of convertibility of currencies into real commodities today, the value of a country's currency is defined solely by activity in foreign-exchange markets. This dependence on foreign-exchange markets makes the currency of all but the largest countries subject to manipulation by large operators, whether commercial, financial or governmental.

As discussed above, the Grondona system offers a different approach, operating as an "automatic stabilizer" driven by market prices, which acts predictably, without discrimination, regardless of the causes of a crisis – whether economic or geopolitical – to reliably exert a stabilizing influence on the exchange-rate, as well as on various other economic parameters relevant to overcoming a currency crisis (Collins, 2020).

Unemployment insurance has been called a macro-economic "automatic stabilizer", since it automatically reduces the extent to which consumption falls as a result of rising unemployment. This is analogous to the stabilizers on a ship: whatever the cause of turbulence in the sea, whether storm, typhoon or other cause, they automatically reduce the extent to which the ship rolls from side-to-side. Likewise, unemployment insurance acts dependably, on a scale decided in advance by the government, to prevent the vicious circle by which recession worsens into depression, avoiding the risks of political misjudgment or cronyism, as well as being invulnerable to distortion or failure caused by speculative attack.

Although not widely discussed today, a system of currency convertibility based on primary commodities would likewise exert a range of such "automatic" macro-economic stabilizing effects, centring on international trade, for which it was advocated by both Keynes and Hayek, among other eminent economists (as discussed in Chapters 6 and 7). Because of the narrow range of the direct stabilizing influence of the operation of gold convertibility, the classical gold standard did not prevent recessions or deflation, although it was effective in preventing the loss of a currency's value through inflation over the long-term. By contrast, convertibility based on a range of industrial commodities has a wider range of economic stabilizing effects, notably including stabilizing the industries using the primary commodities which the system handles.

In the present day, when predatory hedge-funds managing tens of billions of dollars can exert severe pressure on smaller countries through manipulation of foreign-exchange and other markets, this dependable stabilizing influence of the Grondona system could be very valuable. In particular it could help to prevent the build-up of "one way" conditions in foreign-exchange markets in the grip of a panic, such as may be triggered by a news "shock", as happened against South-East Asian countries in the late 1990s. When traders are driven in a "herd" to sell a currency, a CRD standing ready to provide commodities in exchange for the currency on predictable terms could exert a valuable contrary influence.

Moreover, as discussed above, a group of countries could use the system's stabilizing effects to create an "oasis" of comparative stability, notably including improved stability of their mutual exchange-rates, instead of having to obey the dictates of neo-imperialist financial markets. While CRDs' stabilizing effect on commodity market prices is proportional to the total quantity of commodity reserves held by the CRDs, and so to the number of CRDs, their collective stabilizing effect on exchange-rates will benefit from the "network effect", and so will grow exponentially relative to the number of CRDs: with 6 CRDs the number of exchange-rate pairs experiencing mutual stabilization would be 15, but with 12 CRDs in operation the number of exchange-rate pairs will be 66. This mutually beneficial stabilizing influence on the exchange-rate pairs of each different "CRD country" with all the other "CRD countries" could be strengthened in various ways, such as through consultations concerning the terms of implementation of each country's CRD, or concerning optimal monetary policy response to CRDs' operations. Such a contribution to improving independent countries' ability to resist destabilizing financial influences will be a very welcome aspect of CRDs' operation.

SUMMARY

In view of the above possibilities for progressive improvement of a CRDs' influence, it is clear that implementation of a CRD will not be a one-off policy initiative with limited benefit. Instead, in addition to its immediate effects, it will start a process that could continue for many years through which a country can progressively enhance the stability of its currency and trade, and so its economic growth and overall political independence. It could also become the basis for collaboration with other countries in enhancing their mutual relations in the fields of trade, monetary policy and geopolitics.

This chapter has described some of the ways in which the Grondona system can be expected to evolve once implemented in one or more countries. Among many other possibilities, the inclusion of gold and silver, though on somewhat different terms from other industrially important commodities, is particularly interesting, since it could provide a valuable interim step towards their re-monetization. Other basic manufactured products, such as standard steel and aluminium strip could also be included. In addition, several countries might coordinate the terms of their CRDs' operations in order to enhance their influence in resisting destabilizing moves in foreign exchange markets, and thereby contributing to preserving their sovereignty.

REFERENCES

Collins, P. (2020). *Resisting Economic Crises with the Grondona System of Currency Convertibility*. https://www.scipod.global/resisting-economic-crises-with-the-grondona-system-of-currency-convertibility

Chapter 14
Frequently Asked Questions

ABSTRACT

This chapter comprises answers to a number of questions that are often asked about the Grondona system by people wishing to understand how it differs from other policy proposals. The questions covered include whether it is a commodity standard, whether it uses buffer-stocks, how it is possible for a single country to have a significant influence, how it can be better than an international system, whether the system could use a crypto-currency, why such government intervention in markets could be beneficial, and other questions. Although some of the content unavoidably repeats what is explained in other chapters, it is hoped that it will be helpful to readers to be able to focus on specific issues in this way.

INTRODUCTION

The Grondona system is not widely known, and most of those who do come across it mistake it as merely another variant on the well-known idea of buffer-stocks. However, the system's unique differences from all other superficially related proposals entail that the effects of the system's operation would be radically different, as described above in Chapter 8; demonstrated in the simulations shown in Chapters 9 and 10; and discussed further in Chapters 11, 12 and 13. This chapter is intended to make it easy for readers to find the answers to questions that typically arise about the Grondona system, due to its unfamiliarity, and to understand why it can succeed where other proposals have failed. These answers unavoidably repeat some of the contents

DOI: 10.4018/978-1-7998-8302-9.ch014

of other chapters, but it is hoped that they will enable readers to more easily understand the system's innovative details, of which the significance has not perhaps been made sufficiently clear in earlier chapters.

14.1 IS THE GRONDONA SYSTEM A "COMMODITY STANDARD"?

No. The Grondona system is not in itself a commodity standard. A commodity standard is a system that, like its most famous example, the gold standard, includes the control of monetary policy so as to stabilise the real value of the currency in terms of a selected commodity, which *ipso facto* keeps the price of the selected commodity between narrowly fixed limits. This requires monetary policy, including interest-rates, to be targeted to achieve this purpose, even over-riding other major policy objectives (such as encouraging economic growth or reducing unemployment) whenever necessary. This would be a major commitment for a government to implement, and a radical change of policy from today, which would in itself be extremely difficult to achieve.

By contrast, the Grondona system does not try to keep the market price of any commodity between fixed limits, and so does not need interest-rates or other policies to be changed. This makes it politically far more feasible than a classical "commodity standard", while obtaining many of the same benefits from partially stabilizing the real value of the currency in terms of a range of commodities, of which the extent can be increased progressively, if required. Consequently the Grondona system can be called a "conditional commodity standard", and it could be a valuable preparatory step towards a strict commodity standard for a government that wished to implement such a policy.

However, the potential for increasing the system's influence would make the implementation of a strict commodity standard less important. For many governments, the various stabilizing influences of a CRD would be sufficiently beneficial that they would not feel the need to take the further step to rigidify its influence by legislating that monetary policy must be adjusted so as to preserve the levels of reserves of selected commodities above zero – as was the case for the gold standard.

It is a measure of the lack of clarity in this field that, for example, the leading article in the British Guardian newspaper in 1958, which extolled Grondona's work, was confusingly titled "A Commodity Standard" (Guardian, 1958).

14.2 IS THE GRONDONA SYSTEM A "COMMODITY-RESERVE CURRENCY"?

No. Since the 1930s and 1940s there has been considerable discussion and analysis of the feasibility of a "commodity-reserve currency", as proposed by Benjamin Graham and others, of which the supply would be determined by the level of reserves of selected commodities held by a monopolistic, internationally funded and managed stock-holding organization (Graham, 1937). As discussed in Chapters 6 and 7 above, such a system would be politically very difficult to implement for several reasons. Not the least of these is that it would necessitate making an open-ended commitment to buy any quantity of reserves of the commodities involved that became available at its set "floor prices". Consequently discussions about how to implement such a system typically exclude any possibilities other than an international system funded by a number of major countries. However, this template would greatly limit the value of such an initiative, since it could stabilize only one of the currencies of the participating countries. It would also be geopolitically complex, with a single dominant currency, like the Bretton Woods system which was established at the height of the USA's relative economic dominance – even if the selected currency was a new international currency created for the purpose, or the IMF's currency, the Special Drawing Right (SDR). These weaknesses, discussed in more detail in Chapters 6, 7 and 8, explain the failure to implement such a plan to date, despite decades of efforts.

By contrast, the Grondona system's support for the price of each commodity involved is only conditional, adjusting reliably according to public, predetermined rules. The maximum commitment of an individual country implementing the system can thereby be much smaller than Graham's international system would need to be, but it is decided independently by each national government, of which the currency would be directly stabilized to the chosen extent. Moreover, as multiple countries established systems operating in their own currencies, which would require no international negotiations, the overall result would be that larger quantities of reserves than any single country could afford would be voluntarily held by different countries – thereby achieving a "multi-national" result that could not be achieved by any international system.

Milton Friedman was a famous opponent of Graham's "commodity-reserve currency", on the grounds that it would generally not be desirable for monetary policy to be dominated by the need to maintain reserves of certain commodities above zero, since there are other important policy objectives that legitimately influence monetary policy (Friedman, 1951). Graham countered by explaining that his system was not intended to dominate monetary policy, but that the expansion and contraction of the money supply which it caused would generally be desirable. Indeed, permitting the money supply to expand or contract to some extent in the direction of stabilizing the real value of the currency in terms of selected, essential, imported commodities is desirable in itself, and would give governments an additional means both of understanding current trends in the value of their currency, and of justifying sound monetary policies to the electorate. However, the particular means by which Graham proposed to achieve this result is very complex; it would distort commodity markets by giving enormous power to unelected officials; and it is politically very unwieldy, requiring an unrealistic extent of international cooperation by countries which would receive little or no direct benefit from the system.

14.3 WOULDN'T A CRD OPERATING ON THE SCALE WHICH GRONDONA SUGGESTED BE TOO SMALL TO HAVE ANY USEFUL STABILIZING INFLUENCE ON COMMODITY PRICES?

Even if a CRD was relatively small by comparison with world markets, it is likely that its various stabilizing influences, both direct and indirect, on the domestic economy of the country implementing it would be considered valuable. These would include reducing the volatility of prices of imported commodities, and introducing a counter-cyclical component into the growth-rate of the national money supply. Such an increase in the quantity of money leads to further growth in bank credit and economic activity, which could double or triple the scale of the direct change during the few years before the expansion is reversed as prices rose once more and the CRD's reserves were repurchased by market participants.

If a government which had implemented a CRD considered that its effects were too small, it would be straightforward to increase the scale of its operation. Doing this on the basis of direct experience of having a CRD operate the system initially on a small scale would minimise any risks: simulations such as those shown in Chapter 10 would enable the effects of a CRD operating on different scales to be evaluated in detail in advance.

If and when other countries implement the system by establishing their own CRDs, the collective stabilizing influence of multiple CRDs on commodity market prices will be proportionately greater. Several CRDs operating in different currencies, with physical reserves spread between different countries, would exert a wider range of stabilizing influences than a single, much larger, international system which could only operate in a single currency, and so would offer little direct benefit to most countries. Additional benefits of multiple smaller, national CRDs include partially stabilizing the real value of each of the CRDs' currencies, and stabilizing all the exchange-rate pairs between the countries establishing a CRD.

14.4 DOES A CRD USE A "COMMODITY BASKET"?

No. A CRD treats each of the commodities which it handles entirely separately. This avoids any possible problem whereby the operation of a "basket" of commodities could destabilize the market price of one or more commodities. This is because, if one component of a defined "commodity basket" became scarce, its price would rise, and traders would buy the basket in order to obtain the scarce commodity, and sell the other unwanted components, thereby driving their prices down. Any such distortion of commodity markets by linking different commodities' market prices is undesirable, due to making the economic meaning of actual market prices less clear. Hence a CRD decides and implements a price-schedule for each commodity separately.

14.5 WOULDN'T AN INTERNATIONAL SYSTEM BE BETTER THAN A CRD?

No. Although an international system could in principle operate on a larger scale than any single country could afford, and so larger than the scale which Grondona recommended for his system, any benefits from participating in an international system would be very indirect for all but at most one of the participating countries, since it could operate in only one currency. Hence the currencies of all the other countries would receive no direct stabilizing influence, unless an additional international agreement was achieved, like the 1944 Bretton Woods agreement to maintain fixed exchange-rates between forty-four countries, for which the IMF also needed to be established. The geopolitical situation today makes any such agreement vanishingly unlikely. In addition, an international proposal such as UNCTAD's proposed buffer-stock system with fixed "floor" and "ceiling" prices, would not be desirable from the economic point of view, since on occasions it would seriously distort market prices of some commodities, even if successful.

Grondona envisaged that many countries would each adopt his system using their own currency, thereby making it "multi-national". This would exert a direct stabilizing influence on the real value of each participating country's currency, and on the exchange-rate pairs between the currencies of all participating countries. It would also lead to greater stability of primary commodity prices due to the greater volume of counter-cyclical stockholding, and so to smoothing the trade cycle, as recommended by both Keynes and Hayek (Keynes, 1938; Hayek, 1943). Moreover, it would achieve all of these benefits without depending on international negotiations over different countries' shares of the cost of an international system, with all the scope for geopolitical manipulation, "horse-trading" and bullying which that would entail.

The predictable result of several countries implementing the Grondona system in the way best suited to their national needs would thereby achieve the stated goal of those trying to negotiate an agreement to establish an international system: multiple countries each voluntarily contributing to the cost of reducing both the extreme instability of primary commodity prices, and the cyclical instability of trade in primary commodities, as well as stabilizing their exchange-rates. Such a result is not actually achievable through international agreement, despite the verbal support of many governments over more than half-a-century for UNCTAD's proposed goal of international commodity agreements.

14.6 ISN'T IT A MAJOR WEAKNESS THAT A CRD DOES NOT GUARANTEE A MAXIMUM PRICE FOR ANY COMMODITY?

No. In making such a guarantee a government would take on an unlimited liability, which is extremely difficult to justify for policy-making, as well as threatening to seriously distort market prices. A CRD's guarantee to provide commodities in exchange for currency units on demand at specified prices would apply only as long as the system was holding reserves of those commodities, the exact levels of which would be publicly known at all times. Thus, on occasions, reserves of one or more commodities might fall to zero, making the system's guarantee of a minimal value of the currency in terms of those commodities temporarily ineffective. However, this would only occur after a period of rising prices and gradually falling reserves, giving the government, the general public and companies involved in that commodity industry clear warning of the trend, and also publicising the government's opportunity to prevent the reserves falling to zero, if considered desirable. In addition, even after reserves of some or all commodities fell to zero, the system would continue to provide support against those commodities' market prices falling sharply again, and reserves of the commodities would be likely to subsequently accumulate as market prices fell again, making the system's maximum prices effective once more.

Under inflationary conditions, as the quantity of a CRD's reserves fell progressively with successive Blocks being bought by market participants, the step-by-step fall in the real value of the currency would be apparent to the general public and commercial interests, and the government would feel the benefit of raising interest-rates to some extent. In addition, the public – who always prefer low interest-rates – would be able to see and understand the reason for raising them. This flexible system would be arguably more effective in enabling government to raise interest-rates when required to resist inflation than having a rise in interest-rates enforced by a guarantee to fix the maximum price of one or more selected commodities. Such a rigid commitment could seriously distort policy-making in the event of unusual market conditions for one or more commodities, which can arise for many different reasons.

14.7 ISN'T IT TOO EXPENSIVE FOR ANY SINGLE COUNTRY TO IMPLEMENT THE GRONDONA SYSTEM?

No. A government which decides to implement the Grondona system chooses the scale on which it will operate, and so will select a scale of operation which is not "too expensive". A system which aimed to keep the market price of one or more commodities between fixed limits would *ipso facto* face an unlimited liability: when prices were falling, the system would have to buy all surplus supplies – and when prices were rising, the system would have to own or obtain sufficient reserves to satisfy all demand at the fixed upper price. By contrast, there is no degree of price stabilization that must be reached in order for a CRD to be "worthwhile". Even if the CRD of a smaller country had no significant influence on the world market prices of the primary commodities which it handled, it would still exert several desirable influences: partially stabilizing input prices of its domestic industries that depend on imported commodities; adjusting the growth of the national money supply to some extent to counteract both deflationary and inflationary pressures; and improving the stability of the real value of its national currency. Moreover, because the prices which a CRD pays to purchase reserves adjust in proportion to their quantity, it can legitimately pay for purchases of reserves through expansion of the money supply, as occurred under the gold standard, enabling a larger financial commitment than if there was a need for offsetting taxation or government borrowing.

14.8 WOULDN'T IT BE BETTER FOR A CRD TO ACTIVELY INTERVENE IN MARKETS RATHER THAN TO ACT ONLY IN RESPONSE TO REQUESTS FROM TRADERS TO BUY OR SELL COMMODITIES?

No. Actively intervening in the market for any commodity would expose the CRD to the risk of making a mistake and thereby suffering a loss. It would also create uncertainty among market traders, as well as generating "insider information" which would create incentives for bribery and corruption.

By acting passively, essentially like banks which maintained convertibility under the historical gold standard, a CRD would not try to alter market prices of commodities, but its "automatic" operation would slow down large price movements, either upwards or downwards, to a certain extent. By being predictable, a CRD's passive counter-cyclical operation would provide a reliable link between the monetary world and the real economy, and its conditionality would make it compatible with the country's existing monetary system.

14.9 DOES THE GRONDONA SYSTEM USE "BUFFER-STOCKS"?

No. Grondona repeatedly stressed that his system did not use "buffer-stocks", because these words have a particular meaning. As used in relation to the commodity reserve currency proposal and in international discussions related to UNCTAD's program to stabilize primary commodity prices, the word "buffer-stock" means a stockholding system of which the manager actively buys and sells commodities in order to keep their market prices between fixed "floor" and "ceiling" prices. By contrast the Grondona system is passive, responding automatically to requests to purchase or sell commodities that meet its published requirements at predetermined prices. Hence it would be as misleading to call the Grondona system a buffer-stock system as to call the gold standard a buffer-stock system, although it did indeed stabilize the price of gold.

It is worth noting that, unlike the Grondona system, but like buffer-stock systems, the gold standard also involved an open-ended liability. Guaranteeing to maintain fixed upper and lower prices for gold, or for other commodities, constitutes an open-ended liability, which no single government nowadays would choose to take on, and which would also distort market prices, which is economically undesirable. By contrast, the Grondona system implements a "price-schedule" for each commodity, whereby the CRD will buy or sell, on demand, but only up to a predetermined quantity of reserves at any single price. This limits the CRD's maximum possible liability to an amount which policy-makers decide in advance to be acceptable. The Grondona system thereby avoids all the geo-political and diplomatic problems of international negotiations that have prevented an international system of buffer-stocks from being implemented even after more than half-a-century of negotiations.

14.10 WOULD IT BE POSSIBLE FOR A PRIVATE COMPANY TO IMPLEMENT THE GRONDONA SYSTEM – PERHAPS FOR A CRYPTO-CURRENCY?

Yes, although it would be on a considerably different basis from that which Grondona proposed for governments using their national currency. It is necessary to recognise that stabilizing the real value of a currency is a legitimate and fundamentally different objective from earning a profit from trading commodities. In order for a CRD to earn sufficient profits to cover the costs of stockholding, it would need to sell reserves reasonably frequently – but this is unpredictable. If commodity prices became much more stable than they are today, perhaps due to successful implementation of the Grondona system by several different countries, a CRD might come to make hardly any sales, and so it might operate at a loss, through not covering its operating costs, for years on end. This cost would be acceptable for many governments in exchange for stabilizing the real value of their currency, but would be a significant, open-ended cost for a company.

The creators of some crypto-currencies have reputedly earned many billions of dollars of profit, mainly through the rise in price of their "crypto" as its users grow in number. It is possible that, as managers of such a successful crypto-currency, they would find the cost of subsidizing a CRD acceptable due to the expected benefits from its stabilizing influence on their crypto's real value. However, such benefits would depend on permitting the CRD to operate independently as an "automatic stabilizer" according to its fixed rules – not to be operated in order to try to earn a profit.

In view of these facts, it would be necessary for a crypto-currency's managers to recognise that stabilizing their crypto's real value with a CRD is a cost, not a profit-centre, as governments in the past recognised that the cost of maintaining their currency on a gold standard was necessary and acceptable in order to obtain the benefits of preventing inflation and facilitating international trade.

Among the nearly 10,000 crypto-currencies apparently being used today, there are a number of "stablecoins", of which the value is kept as stable as possible in terms either of an existing currency, or of some real asset such as gold or other precious metals, essentially by guaranteeing their convertibility. A crypto-currency which was flexibly convertible into a wide range of industrial commodities via a CRD would thereby achieve a degree of stability that some market participants might find preferable to one that was more strictly stabilized in terms of a single commodity such as a precious metal. A growing number of years of successful operation of a CRD would provide cumulative evidence of reliability. If a CRD used such a "stablecoin", it might thereby compete with national currencies as a "world currency". How far privately controlled currencies will come to compete with existing currencies is a major topic of discussion today, as discussed in Chapter 5 above. Continuing technological change is inevitable, and affects the monetary world as well as industry. The items used for money as a unit of account, a measure of value and store of value have evolved from seashells and other durable objects to bullion, convertible paper, *fiat* paper, bank transactions, and now Internet-based blockchain data, as discussed by (Bordo, 2021). Central banks are planning their response to the invention of the Internet and Blockchain, and may collaborate with private banks or private companies issuing crypto-currencies in order to achieve maximum benefits. Leading crypto-currencies are already more convenient, reliable and fast for international transactions than the existing SWIFT system for inter-bank payments, at least for retail payments, and the technology is still advancing rapidly, so that it is not possible to rule out the possibility of a privately-operated CRD.

However, an important proviso is that the details of establishing a CRD for a private currency would involve different considerations than a national system. For example, Grondona's suggested guidelines on the scale of operation and siting of warehouses are based on historical national import data. These would not exist for a new crypto-currency, and so different considerations would be involved in deciding the scale on which to implement a CRD, including the existing supply of the crypto-currency in question; existing rules controlling the growth of its supply; convenience for trade in the siting of warehouses, and other factors.

There would also be a need to decide whether and how to permit increases in the supply of the currency in purchasing reserves. Due to their novelty, there is still great uncertainty about the correct market value of many crypto-currencies, of which the prices are consequently very volatile. Three key questions about any crypto-currency that are vital for judging its real value are: Where does the supply come from? How may it increase? Who controls it? (. . . and can they be trusted?)

In the case of the most famous crypto-currency, Bitcoin, the supply is said to be strictly limited, and for this reason its price has risen several thousand percent. However, having a market value that is rising is far from optimal for a currency that is meant to be widely useful. For example, a CRD using a currency of which the market price was continually rising would be continually requested to purchase more reserves of commodities. But just as unvarying values are optimal for engineering units, so a constant real value is optimal for a currency.

Stabilizing the real value of a currency is a service that depends on the establishment of a CRD which will reliably follow its rules of operation for decades. However, crypto-currencies are still a new phenomenon, so it is not yet clear how truly reliable they will be over the longer term. Another problem is lack of transparency about the ownership of crypto-currencies. For example, there are known to be still anonymous holders of tens of billions of dollars worth of Bitcoins – notably the unknown founder or founders who reportedly own about 1 million bitcoins, valued at tens of billions of US dollars at the time of writing – of which the possible release is seen as posing a significant risk of destabilizing or diluting the market price of Bitcoins. It would clearly be possible for the founders to use some of these large holdings to establish a Bitcoin-based CRD in such a way as to significantly stabilise the real value of circulating Bitcoins. However, this would reduce the popularity of Bitcoin as a form of savings, which is motivated by its large rise in value enriching its holders. Moreover, in order to achieve this beneficial influence, more transparency would be necessary in order for Bitcoin to be acceptable to large-scale sellers of commodities to be held in the CRD's reserves.

Perhaps most importantly, a CRD which operated in terms of a crypto-currency might be uniquely effective in defining its real value in the event of national *fiat* currencies declining to zero. At times of relative economic stability it is difficult to imagine the phenomenon of the value of a national currency falling to zero. Nevertheless, this has happened to *fiat* currencies repeatedly throughout history. Of course, the survival of a CRD-backed currency would depend on the CRD remaining in operation. It is possible to envisage scenarios in which a number of currencies, both national and crypto, which were convertible into real commodities, would preserve their value as "islands of stability" through a period of severe monetary turbulence during which the value of a number of major *fiat* currencies eventually declined to zero. In view of the susceptibility of financial markets to waves of optimism or pessimism causing rapid movements in prices, rapid increase in the popularity of a CRD-backed currency could lead to its rise in value and thereby to a large increase in its reserves of commodities, causing difficulties for their storage, as discussed in Chapter 11 above.

14.11 WOULDN'T RESERVES OF SOME COMMODITIES HELD BY A CRD DETERIORATE, LEADING TO LOSSES?

Grondona specified that a CRD should handle only durable, essential and basic imported commodities. Consequently the primary commodities to be handled by CRDs comprise three groups: metals, which do not deteriorate; fibres, which deteriorate only very slowly; and foodstuffs which can be safely stored for a few years. Hence the only foodstuffs considered could be held for several years without deterioration. Modern warehousing techniques enable stocks of commodities to be monitored closely, and "rotated" as necessary at low cost – that is, selected quantities of older reserves are sold, and the same quantity of newer supplies are bought at the same time, thereby avoiding deterioration. Hence, in the absence of incompetence or actual fraud, deterioration is not a problem.

14.12 WON'T SPECULATORS OR VESTED INTERESTS TRY TO PREVENT IMPLEMENTATION OF THE GRONDONA SYSTEM?

With the growth of financial derivatives markets over recent decades, there are unlimited opportunities for speculation, even on a scale as large as billions of US dollars. Consequently there is no need for commodity prices to be unstable in order for speculators such as "hedge funds" to have opportunities for high risk – high reward speculation. Nevertheless, there may be vested interests who wish to keep economic conditions unstable, such as lobbyists for financial companies and global corporations which benefit relative to smaller companies and countries from market instability, who might therefore use their influence to try to prevent governments from implementing the system.

It should be remembered that innovations are famously disruptive, and so they are resisted by those whose career or business would be upset by their acceptance. Consequently, throughout history many successful innovators have necessarily been outside the "mainstream" – and those in positions of economic or political influence have often used their position to delay or even suppress valuable innovations. Fortunately, this damaging influence of powerful vested interests has not yet been able to entirely prevent innovation, which is the source of economic growth, and continues to greatly improve living standards worldwide.

Although at its best, economists' work is scientific, anything relating to policy-making is much like the field of history, in which fame and fortune go to "court historians", rather than to those who take a scientific approach to revealing the truth about past events. Likewise, the people who make policy frequently choose economic advisers who will provide convincing-sounding justifications for the policies that they have decided to implement, for whatever hidden reason. Sadly, there are plenty of economists who are prepared to provide this service in exchange for the fame and fortune similar to that which court historians receive (as discussed further in Chapter 16.3). Notably, many economists who work as economic policy-advisers are "internationalists" – or nowadays "globalists" – and provide cover for politicians who favour international institutions such as the EU or UN over national interests. Such people continue to support the UNCTAD plan for international commodity agreements, even though it is clear that this would mean that no progress will be made.

14.13 IS THE GRONDONA SYSTEM A NEW MONETARY SYSTEM?

No. The Grondona system does not create a new currency, nor does it determine or require new monetary policies. Grondona did not set out to create a new monetary system, but simply to improve existing monetary systems by reducing the instability in the real value of their currencies. Consequently his system has no direct implications for discussions about the proper roles of public banks, private banks and central banks, which are very important for the future of society and economic growth.

Nor did Grondona intend to create a new basis for the world economic and monetary system. However, in view of the fundamental problems facing the world economy today, with the end of US dollar dominance approaching but no single successor currency apparent, a stable multi-polar world economy would now be a very desirable outcome for most countries. But in order for such a system to be successful there is a need for greater financial stability and less volatility of exchange-rates.

Consequently, in this context, it is very significant that the Grondona system would operate so as to stabilize the real value of the currencies used by different national CRDs, and in addition contribute to stabilizing the exchange-rates between them. It would thereby reduce the vulnerability of foreign-exchange markets to manipulation and/or destabilization, and make them more resilient to shocks. In the absence of any promising proposal for a widely acceptable new international system, the Grondona system could therefore greatly contribute to the creation of a more stable foundation for a multi-polar world economy. In this it is perhaps especially attractive for smaller economies, of which the currencies are more vulnerable to destabilization or manipulation than those of larger economies, and which would lose their independence if pressured to participate in a single global monetary system.

Thus it is not too much to say that Grondona's system could indeed provide a new, more stable basis for the existing system of multiple national currencies. This puts it at centre-stage in the discussion of the pros and cons of globalization and/or decentralisation. One of the main arguments by advocates of globalization, most notably lobbyists for global corporations and the politicians to whose election campaigns they contribute, is that it will be more stable than a world of independent competing countries. However, like the argument for establishing a single, monopolistic system of buffer-stocks to stabilize commodity prices worldwide, there is no evidence for supposing that such a system would or could operate fairly and transparently in the interests of all the different peoples involved. While it may be that the world economy will continue to evolve towards ever greater integration, it would certainly be premature to try to enforce a single global money system today, although in the interest of global corporations and their investors, at the cost of citizens and taxpayers worldwide.

14.14 IS GRONDONA'S IDEA OF A CRD REALLY SO SIGNIFICANT? (IT SEEMS RATHER SIMILAR TO THE OLD IDEA OF BUFFER-STOCKS)

In every field, major innovations occur from time to time which enable progress that was previously impossible. It is famous that, once made, articulated and widely understood, many innovations such as scientific breakthroughs, come to seem "obvious". It is the very nature of innovation that even such ideas were not obvious before they were discovered and clarified, and so it needed a rare person with rare insight to recognise them for the first time. Grondona himself continually stressed that his system is extremely simple, and the differences from related ideas are quite small – as illustrated in Figure 1 in Chapter 8. But these differences have enormously far-reaching implications, which most economists and commentators have not been prepared to take the effort to study, preferring instead to dismiss the idea as "just another buffer-stock system". Those who took such trouble, however, have praised the system extravagantly, calling it "epoch-making", "a modern equivalent of the gold standard" and other similarly unique praise, some of which is quoted in Chapter 16 below.

If Grondona's contribution was so trivial, some other economist – from as far back as the 19th century, and including Keynes and Hayek – would have been able to come up with the same or a better idea. Or else they would have been able to show that it is flawed, so that under certain circumstances it would fail to operate as planned. Grondona's particular range of experience, from farming to journalism, soldiering, government administration, business consulting and public relations, gave him a unique ability to think more clearly than other people about what was and what was not needed to solve the problem in question. To take four examples:

1. A fixed commodity price-range – as included in buffer-stock schemes – is not needed: indeed, market prices must be able to move as far as necessary to match supply and demand, which can vary widely for many reasons beyond human control.
2. Likewise, a guaranteed maximum price is not needed – contrary to "conventional wisdom" in the field. More specifically, by handling many commodities, no one commodity's reserves falling to zero is sufficiently harmful to require government to accept an unlimited liability, as would be necessary in order to be able to defend a fixed maximum price for any commodity. The steady fall in reserves of a commodity that would precede their falling to zero would serve most of the purpose of a rigid guarantee, alerting the general public as well as the government to the declining value of the currency.
3. On the contrary, a fixed rule ensuring automatic adjustment of each commodity's price-range in response to market price pressure is needed: the conflicting interests of producers and users of commodities are a major reason preventing them agreeing on buffer-stock systems at UNCTAD, in which periodic price changes would need to be negotiated, rather than occurring impersonally as a result of market forces, as occurs under the Grondona system.
4. Likewise, lack of any scope for discretion in the operation of a CRD, as the guarantee of convertibility of currency into gold under the classical gold standard was unconditional, is essential to guarantee the system's reliability, and maximise public confidence, as well as to minimise the risk of errors or corruption.

Avoiding being distracted by innumerable details, including numerous elite experts' mistaken opinions; seeing through the "conventional wisdom" to understand the truly essential issues; and thereby being able to solve a major problem outstanding since the nineteenth century, is what, in other fields, is typically recognized as genius.

14.15 SURELY MOST COUNTRIES ARE TOO SMALL TO ESTABLISH A CRD THAT WOULD BE LARGE ENOUGH TO HAVE A USEFUL IMPACT?

Being too small to have much direct effect on world commodity market prices is very different from being too small to have a useful stabilizing effect on the domestic currency and international trade of a relatively small country. One of Grondona's important insights was that it is not necessary to achieve "complete" currency convertibility, as under the gold standard, in order to exert a valuable stabilizing influence on various facets of the economic system.

Because of the Grondona system's flexibility it can be implemented initially on a scale that poses no risks for economic or monetary policy. Once in operation, the government will be able to evaluate its costs and benefits, and increase its scale if considered beneficial. It is an important additional strength of the system that implementation by additional countries will add to the system's collective stabilizing influence on market prices, which will thereby also further stabilize commodity import prices of the first country. It will also reduce volatility of the currency's exchange-rates with all other countries that implement the system. Multi-national implementation involves different countries independently establishing CRDs – but their operations will automatically be complementary and synergistic. Consequently, establishing a CRD could be an attractive policy option even for many countries with economies considerably smaller than the major OECD members.

14.16 ISN'T IT MORE EFFICIENT TO LEAVE COMMODITY STOCKHOLDING TO THE PRIVATE SECTOR?

There are indeed many companies that perform stockholding and warehousing services for commodities as well as other products. However, they need to earn profits in order to operate. This is a different objective from stabilizing the real value of a currency, which is a legitimate objective of government policy-making.

Capitalist "fundamentalists" like to claim, and/or to imagine, that all services can be supplied better by private companies than by government. But there is clear evidence that this is not true for all services. For example, control of the US monetary system by the privately-owned Federal Reserve System since 1913 has not led to stable currency, but to the opposite. Starting with the US dollar on the gold standard, this was ended in 1971, since when cumulative inflation has reduced the dollar's value by 98%, while the distribution of wealth in the USA in the 21st century has reached a historically extreme level of inequality. Another example is the American medical system, which is largely controlled by privately-owned insurance companies, and is several times more expensive for its users than systems in other OECD countries in which the government plays a major role in providing basic health services. Moreover, Americans' health in general is the worst among the rich countries, according to the US government's own 2013 "Woolf Report". Hence there is no *a priori* reason for believing that private stockholding companies must be able to stabilize the value of the currencies in which they operate better than a government organisation.

Stabilizing the real value of a currency is economically very desirable, and so governments which fail to supply a currency of which they preserve the value can be fairly criticized as failing in their responsibility. The maintenance of the gold standard by central banks was a service that private gold merchants did not provide. Likewise, reducing the volatility of the real value of the currencies in which they trade is not achieved by the private stock-holding companies that operate world-wide today. Keynes discussed these issues with Benjamin Graham (Woods, 2021), and economic analysis since then has helped to clarify under what conditions profit-seeking stockholding tends to stabilize prices and under what conditions and why it destabilizes them, demonstrating the need for government to play a role.

14.17 WHEN WOULD BE THE BEST TIME TO ESTABLISH A CRD?

The timing of the start of a CRD's operation relative to each commodity's price-cycle will determine how long it takes for a CRD to accumulate reserves of the commodities it handles. In some cases, such as when market prices are rising strongly, it might take several years before a CRD accumulated substantial quantities of reserves of some commodities, so the optimal timing would be when prices are near the peak of the current price cycle. As they fall back CRDs will accumulate reserves, while preventing commodity prices falling so low that producers get into difficulties and world trade suffers once again. However, market prices cannot be reliably predicted, and so it is unlikely that CRDs will be established with optimal timing. Provided that they are implemented as Grondona designed, with automatically adjusting price-schedules, less than optimal timing of their start will not prevent them operating as planned, though their full influence may take a few years to develop.

14.18 SURELY IMPLEMENTING THE GRONDONA SYSTEM WOULD BE GOVERNMENT INTERFERENCE IN MARKETS AND DISTORTION OF PRICES?

No. Defining the value of a currency in real terms is a traditional duty of governments, so maintaining a currency on the gold standard was a legitimate government role – although this could be said to have "distorted" the price of gold by keeping it within very narrow limits. By comparison, although the Grondona system handles a wider range of commodities, it does not prevent the price of any commodity from moving to any extent, but reduces their volatility by resisting price-movements to a certain extent. By contrast, establishing international buffer-stocks, which are intended to keep the prices of many different commodities between relatively narrow, fixed limits, would indeed greatly distort markets, hindering their role in balancing supply and demand. This is a major reason why UNCTAD's plan for international commodity agreements has not been implemented.

14.19 IS IT A FAIR ANALOGY TO DESCRIBE THE GRONDONA SYSTEM AS BEING LIKE A MECHANICAL REGULATOR?

Yes. Mechanical dampers, regulators and shock-absorbers are widely used to resist excessively wide or excessively fast movement of parts of a machine, to a predetermined extent, in order to prevent oscillations which would hinder the machine's operation, or even damage it – but without preventing the parts from moving as required. Likewise, the Grondona system would slow or resist large or sudden movements in commodity market prices, but without preventing them from moving as far as required to enable demand to match supply.

If the needle of a mechanical thermometer is "under-damped" it oscillates, thereby making it difficult to read the temperature accurately. If it is excessively damped, the needle cannot move sufficiently when the temperature changes. But when optimally damped, the needle moves as required to show the temperature accurately, without oscillating. For example, while such a needle moving in air might be under-damped, it would likely be over-damped if moving in treacle, but optimally damped if moving in alcohol. Although mechanical regulators are typically much smaller than the machines they regulate, they prevent the machine from misfunctioning or destroying itself through violent vibrations.

Using this analogy, commodity prices today are clearly under-damped, to an extent that their oscillations can hinder the efficient operation of markets, even causing cyclical fluctuations in world trade – which is the reason why so many economists, including Keynes and Hayek, have discussed the benefits of reducing their volatility. However, what is needed to solve this problem is not a monopolistic international organization that tries to control world commodity prices on a centralized basis, but a simple mechanism to damp unstable prices appropriately. From this viewpoint, the Grondona system is precisely such a mechanism, modeled on that used to maintain convertibility of currencies on a gold standard, but ingeniously designed to permit much greater flexibility in commodity prices, while similarly avoiding any scope for administrative discretion or political interference.

Once government policy-makers implement the Grondona system, it will then operate automatically to reduce the volatility of commodity prices in their national currency, as well as simultaneously stabilizing the real value of the currency in terms of the same commodities. The title of one of Grondona's last booklets reflects this well: "A Built-in Basic-Economy Stabilizer" (Grondona, 1972). Once implemented, it seems likely that many people will be surprised and puzzled that it took so many decades for such an obviously beneficial mechanism to be used to damp excessive market volatility, with a wide range of indirect benefits.

SUMMARY

Wider understanding, by as many people as possible, of the problems caused by the continuing extreme volatility of primary commodity prices, and of the potential benefits of reducing them, is very desirable in order to lead to action to solve this problem. As part of this, wider awareness of Grondona's ingenious system to simply reduce volatility in commodity prices is essential.

This chapter lists a number of questions that people typically ask when studying the Grondona system, and explains the answers.

REFERENCES

Friedman, M. (1951). Commodity-Reserve Currency. *Journal of Political Economy*, *59*(3), 203–232. doi:10.1086/257077

Graham, B. (1937). *Storage and Stability*. McGraw-Hill.

Grondona, L. (1972). A Built-in Basic-Economy Stabiliser. Economic Research Council (ERC).

Guardian. (1958, Jan. 16). A Commodity Standard. *The Guardian.*

Hayek, F. (1943). A Commodity Reserve Currency. *The Economic Journal, 53*(210/211), 176-186.

Keynes, J. (1938). The Policy of Government Storage of Foodstuffs and Raw Materials. *Economic Journal (London)*, *48*(191), 449–460. doi:10.2307/2225437

Woods, J. (2021). Benjamin Graham on Buffer Stocks. *Journal of the History of Economic Thought*. osf.io/preprints/socarxiv

Chapter 15
Summary:
Implementing Real Convertibility of Existing National Currencies Is a Realistic Alternative to a "Great Reset"

ABSTRACT

As the controversy over the "Great Reset" being advocated by supporters of globalization continues, those who consider the prospect of a centralized monetary system controlled by unelected and largely unknown people to be profoundly undesirable will be greatly strengthened in their resistance if they can agree on a preferable alternative. What is needed most of all is a means of reducing the vulnerability of smaller countries to destabilization by large financial corporations and government organisations. This book advocates close consideration of the politically and economically simple initiative to implement the Grondona system, which enables individual countries to improve the working of existing monetary policy arrangements incrementally, notably by stabilizing the real value of their national currency in terms of a range of industrial commodities. Eminent economists have argued in favour of this policy for more than a century, but without offering a satisfactory means of implementing it.

DOI: 10.4018/978-1-7998-8302-9.ch015

INTRODUCTION

As discussed in earlier chapters, the idea of stabilizing the real value of a currency by making it convertible into a range of primary commodities other than gold and silver is not new: it has a history of well over a century, having been discussed by 19th century western economists. Moreover, a significant number of well-regarded western economists, including Fisher, Graham, Hart, Tinbergen, Kaldor, as well as the two "giants" of 20th century academic economics, Keynes and Hayek, have all strongly endorsed the idea – and a number of economists continue to vigorously promote it today. However, although not a few of these advocates worked hard over many years trying to design a practical means of implementing the idea, none of their efforts were successful. Above all, the various proposals did not offer sufficient benefits to outweigh the major costs and uncertainties that would be involved in creating the new international institution that they recommended was needed. Despite this, many people in the political world continue to press for an international solution, or more often nowadays a "global" solution, although as explained above, this is not attainable today due to its serious flaws, unless such a plan was enforced by a hegemonic power.

The author hopes that he has convinced readers that, in contrast to those efforts, the Grondona system offers a genuinely practical means whereby many different countries can independently stabilize the real value of their national currency in terms of primary commodities, to the extent that they choose, without the need for a new international institution, nor any international negotiations, agreements or regulations at all. This is especially desirable today in view of the currently heightened economic uncertainty and geo-political difficulties as the world economy faces a new era, no longer centered on the US dollar, but of which many details still remain to be decided.

Grondona did not develop his system in order to provide a new basis for the world economy: for most of the time when he was writing, the Bretton Woods system still apparently provided a stable foundation for the world economy – although the Soviet Union and the countries which it dominated were not participants. However, the fundamental problem now facing governments around the world has been triggered and aggravated by the absence of any remaining element of real convertibility of the US dollar or other major currencies. The end of gold convertibility in 1971 ended the era of near-hegemony of the US dollar, which changed from being "as good as gold" to being merely *fiat* currency subject to endless depreciation. With no successor currency in sight today, the logical solution is a "multi-polar" system with no single dominant currency, which is in effect gradually coming to reality. However, for such a system to be stable and long-lasting, there needs to be less volatility in financial markets, and less vulnerability of foreign-exchange markets to shocks and/or manipulation by large operators.

It is precisely such improved multi-polar economic stability that the Grondona system is uniquely able to provide. Although Grondona advocated that it should be pioneered by a major commodity-importing country such as the UK, the OECD countries' governments today are politically dominated by "globalists", and so are not likely to take such an initiative. So it is a great strength of his system that it also empowers governments of smaller economies, which have less international influence, to implement it. In addition, the synergistic benefits of mutual exchange-rate stabilization which the system offers to implementing countries would help to strengthen the collective defence of a group of implementing countries against stronger economic actors, both governments and giant corporations.

The main contribution of the present book is to have explained this, and to have provided evidence to justify further attention to the Grondona system, in the form of simulations of how it could have operated in five different countries, Japan having a major economy, the other four having much smaller economies. These simulations have shown how the direct stabilizing effects of the system's operation are exerted on the country's commodity trade, by adding substantial, strictly counter-cyclical stock-holding capacity to existing market operations, enhanced by counter-cyclical variation in the national money supply. Such a stabilizing influence on commodity prices and trade flows is fundamentally desirable, particularly for smaller countries and businesses, for which market price volatility is costly and destabilizing.

While exerting a continuous, direct damping influence on commodity market price volatility, the system's counter-cyclical variation of the implementing country's money supply would in turn have an indirect stabilizing influence on a range of other economic parameters, including the real value of the currency, the balance of payments, exchange-rate, interest-rates and inflation. In this way the stabilizing influence of the Grondona system could help to preserve the economic independence of smaller countries, enabling them to resist pressure to prematurely join a centralized global system which would, at best, be insufficiently responsive to their needs.

15.1 A "RESET" THAT WORKS FOR EVERYONE

Returning to the question raised in Chapter 1 about what is to follow the US dollar-dominated economic system, the opportunity for a single country to achieve global hegemony has surely passed – at least in the absence of a major war. Instead, a multi-polar world economy would seem to be a logical, natural evolution. However, for such a system to be sufficiently flexible to encourage economic growth, but not vulnerable to destabilization – remembering that major corporations today have huge funds available for manipulating markets and lobbying politicians to implement their plans – is a challenging requirement.

Although many details of "The Great Reset" being planned and advocated by the World Economic Forum (WEF) and their allied politicians and globalist organizations, are not yet clear, it is known to involve a global digital currency, which it is claimed would improve world economic stability. Such a system could well increase profits of giant corporations, but the dangers of such a scheme, whether managed by government or by global corporations, far outweigh any possible benefits to the general public. At the present stage of database technology, a global digital currency linked to a database containing everyone's personal details could absolutely not be trusted to preserve privacy – and the end of privacy would be essentially the end of civilization, and so of human progress, far outweighing any other putative benefits of such a system.

An argument used by globalists to encourage smaller countries' governments to adopt such common global policies is that their currencies are unavoidably vulnerable to exchange-rate volatility. However, the cost of joining an international currency, even without the loss of privacy involved in a central bank digital currency, is already seen in the smaller countries which are "victims" of the Euro, suffering from high unemployment and loss of their population, and particularly their youth, as economic migrants to the richer countries.

The famous phrase "*Noblesse oblige*" is a useful reminder of the nature of genuine elites. In certain fortunate countries, at certain fortunate periods of history, the leaders of society have been patriotically motivated to help create successful societies – peaceful, just, stable and productive. The historically great contributions to their countries of such figures as the Medici family in Renaissance Italy, Peter the Great of Russia, or the Founding Fathers of the USA continue to be recognized for centuries.

These great people were quite different from today's "feral elites", such as those behind the WEF, who manipulate governments behind the scenes in ways to enrich themselves ever further, while aggravating economic inequality. Like "rack-renters" who enrich themselves from the poorest tenants by charging brutal rents for overcrowded apartments, the plans of the WEF would further impoverish the already weakest in society worldwide. Their megalomaniac plans are a strong argument for the need for more effective anti-monopoly regulations to prevent anti-social individuals from gaining such inordinate "power of the purse" over supposedly democratic politicians.

15.2 WHICH COUNTRY WILL INITIATE THE GRONDONA SYSTEM?

By contrast to the WEF's planned "great reset", a system which enables each country's currency to be progressively stabilized with respect to other currencies through the actions of national CRDs, is a natural, incremental step towards greater stability of the world economy. As such it would clearly be far preferable to the imposition of a global currency, and would not abandon existing civilized society to control by over-reaching governments and corporations which dishonestly claim that there is no alternative to their globalist plans. By enabling individual countries to stabilize the real value of their currency to a certain extent, which can be increased as the government chooses, the Grondona system offers a unique escape route from the dilemma facing governments today of jumping out of the "frying pan" of exchange-rate volatility into the "fire" of a global currency.

So, as a final consideration, which countries might take the initiative to implement the system? Unfortunately it would seem unrealistic to expect a move in this direction from the OECD countries, which appear to be still tied to the US dollar system and the dream of globalization. Nevertheless, the Euro, Yen, Sterling and other currencies of commodity-importing countries could all benefit from establishing CRDs to stabilize their real value. Indeed, during the 1950s Grondona envisaged his system to be optimal for the UK and other OECD countries, which are major importers of raw materials.

However, decades later many smaller economies which used to depend on exporting raw materials, such as the countries discussed in Chapter 12 as members of D-8, ASEAN, Mercosur and the African Union, are now themselves industrialising, and so have become importers of many primary commodities. They have therefore now become candidates for implementing the Grondona system themselves. Moreover, as smaller economies with currencies lower in the "currency hierarchy", they are susceptible to volatility in foreign-exchange markets, and so would benefit particularly from stabilizing the value of their currencies in terms of real commodities.

A CRD of even a relatively small country would play at least three roles of value to policy-makers. First, the CRD's continuous, underlying, counter-cyclical stabilizing influence on the real value of the currency and various aspects of the economy could be expected to grow over the years following its implementation, as its role became familiar to market participants. Gradual recognition of the CRD's function as a "modern equivalent of the gold standard" would make a sudden major loss of confidence, such as could precipitate a currency crisis, progressively less likely as its successful operation continued.

Second, movements in the CRD's reserves will provide a clear and undeniable, objective public measure of changes in the real value of the currency in terms of the commodities handled by the CRD, trends therein, and the effect of government policies. This will be of great help to governments in resisting pressure to distort monetary policy by expanding (or contracting) the money supply excessively, for whatever reason. It will also be valuable for members of the general public, politicians, economists and others trying to judge or improve government policy. For example, inflationary policies would lead to steady reduction in the CRD's reserves of all commodities. *A fortiori*, permitting the reserves of many or all commodities to fall to zero, which would temporarily end the CRD's role of preserving the minimum real value of the currency, would be widely seen as putting the currency and the economy at risk, thereby strengthening the case for tightening monetary policy appropriately.

Third, a CRD's successful initiation of conditional currency convertibility will serve as a demonstration to other countries of the feasibility and potential benefits of following suit. Growing experience of the synergistic stabilizing influence of several different countries' CRDs, including stabilizing their mutual exchange-rates, could in turn lead to wider resumption of real convertibility in this way. In addition, as their operations continued, each CRD's stabilizing influence could be strengthened and extended to wider scale by tightening its "gearing", including additional commodities such as gold and silver, and in other ways.

Because of these multiple benefits, even relatively small countries could achieve significant benefits by establishing a CRD, and particularly if a group of countries, such as those discussed in Chapter 12, established CRDs together, as a joint initiative.

Sir Roy Harrod ended his preface to Grondona's last book with the following sentence: "It has been said that the implementing of his system would mark the beginning of an era as surely as did the initiation of the gold standard, but without its fatal weaknesses. I believe that statement to be well warranted" (Harrod, 1975). It is hard to imagine a stronger endorsement than this.

A great strength of the 19th century gold standard was that it enabled countries to implement the system in terms of their own currency following a common framework with other countries. Nevertheless, due to the rigid guarantee involved, and the overall lack of gold reserves, gold standard countries were not entirely independent, and had to cooperate unofficially by lending gold reserves to each other and in other ways, in order to preserve the system.

By contrast, the maximum possible liability borne by a CRD is limited to what the government of the implementing country chooses, making it truly independent. And by making the prices at which commodities and currency can be exchanged adjust according to openly published "price-schedules", the system's operation is made "automatic", and so predictable by both governments and by market participants. By avoiding any role for discretionary decisions, which are essentially unpredictable, and potentially mistaken or corruptible, the operation of the Grondona system is made transparent and dependable like the gold standard – and possible to simulate reliably.

Simulating how a national CRD might operate, using trade and exchange-rate data, is a reliable means by which governments can evaluate the benefits, costs and risks of implementing the system on different terms, before they "take the plunge". It is greatly to be hoped that governments of one or more candidate countries will investigate the feasibility of implementing the Grondona system in detail in this way in the near future, and decide to implement it – thereby establishing the "*effective monetary constitution*" which Buchanan argued will "*work miracles*" for economic growth and society, as quoted at the head of Chapter 6.

SUMMARY

The idea of making a currency convertible into a range of commodities other than gold and silver is an old one, but the approach that has been followed by those trying to devise a realistic means of implementing it, has been to propose a major new international institution which would assume monopoly control of world commodity markets. In addition to the fact that such a system would inevitably greatly distort markets at times, this prospect has never become popular, despite the considerable support for the overall objective of stabilizing commodity prices, which are notoriously unstable.

By contrast, implementation of the Grondona system can enable a country to independently improve the stability of the real value of its currency, without any need for negotiations with other countries, while also helping to stabilize the prices that domestic industries pay for their imported raw materials. This is a much more attractive policy than allowing themselves to be bullied into joining a new global monetary system, over which they would have no control whatever. Many countries with economies smaller than most OECD countries are nowadays industrializing, and so are candidates to implement the Grondona system. It is much to be hoped that some of these countries will study the feasibility of initiating the system by simulating its operation, and that one or more will decide to implement it.

REFERENCES

Grondona, L. (1975). *Economic Stability is Attainable*. Hutchinson-Benham.

Harrod, R. (1975). *Preface. In L. Grondona (Ed.), Economic Stability is Attainable*. Hutchinson-Benham.

Chapter 16
Past Response to Grondona System

ABSTRACT

The Grondona system was sufficiently well-known during the 1950s to be the subject of debate in the British Parliament in 1958, when it was vigorously praised by supporters, as well as in the press. Examples of this support are given in this chapter, which show how those who took the time to study the Grondona system recognized its unique strengths and strongly recommended its adoption by government. Unfortunately, when the British government finally set up a committee in 1976 to consider the problem of commodity price instability, it was chaired by a long-term advocate of the international buffer-stock system advocated by UNCTAD. As Grondona predicted, the result was that the committee's report contained no substantive criticism of his system but merely reiterated the government's existing policy of continuing participation in UNCTAD negotiations – to no effect nearly half a century later.

INTRODUCTION

Grondona's work is not widely known today. However, when first published, his system for stabilizing commodity prices (and so also the real values of currencies) received a wide range of very positive commentary and support, including being the subject of a debate in the British parliament. The contemporary comments quoted below show detailed understanding of the unique strengths of Grondona's system. Grondona's last book, "Economic

DOI: 10.4018/978-1-7998-8302-9.ch016

Stability is Attainable", published in 1975 (Grondona, 1975), also received strong praise, of which some excerpts are quoted in section 16.2 below. However, implementation of the Grondona system was not recommended by a House of Lords select committee which reported in 1977, although its report contained no substantive criticism of the system, as discussed in section 16.3.

16.1 SUPPORT FOR GRONDONA SYSTEM IN 1958

The following are some representative comments from some of the many highly supportive reviews of Grondona's book "Utilizing World Abundance" published in 1958, as well as by some of the members of the British parliament from all political parties who spoke in favour of implementing Grondona's proposal.

Financial Times

The simplicity of the system outlined by Mr Grondona is one of its major attractions. The objective of his proposals would be to help stabilize both commodity prices and the value of the national currency, so mitigating the sharp inflationary and deflationary movements which hinder economic growth. In principle, the system described in his book seems capable of achieving such an objective. It would encourage world trade and prosperity by linking currency values to commodities; it would help to stimulate investment in primary producing countries, and to increase production of raw materials at stable prices ... Mr Grondona's constructive proposals should receive widespread discussion and investigation. (Financial Times, 1958)

The Times of London

Of all the proposals for increasing the stability of commodity prices Mr Grondona's is much the most realistic and comprehensive, and goes furthest in making practical allowances for the difficulties ... it seems that on a sufficient scale the activities of valorisation would in their turn go far to determine the values of currencies. (Times, 1958)

Manchester Guardian Leading Article

Most schemes for commodity price stability suffer two weaknesses: they rely too much on altruism, and they call for more international co-operation than is readily forthcoming. On the face of it, the system outlined by Mr St. Clare Grondona in his book published today should overcome these difficulties. It is thought out in ingenious detail; and it could be a step towards a sensible commodity standard. (Guardian, 1958)

The Tribune

This devastatingly simple scheme to bring stability to prices by stabilizing those of basic commodities is so attractive ... and the benefits from its operation could be so great that it ought to be taken off the drawing board and sent to the workshop – in this case the Commons. (Tribune, 1958)

Federation of British Industries Review (FBIR)

Mr. St.Clare Grondona's scheme for effecting reasonable price stability bears scrutiny better than any other known to the reviewer. It is comprehensive and yet effectively simple... . The automatic functioning ... devised to keep commodity price fluctuations down to moderate proportions ... is the fundamental distinction between Mr Grondona's scheme and most of the failures of the past, and is its great strength. The acumen with which he has worked out his design give it high claims to be allowed the test of experience ... This book deserves close consideration by those who shape the nation's economic policies. (Shenfield, 1958)

The Manager

'Epoch-making' is a word too often and too lightly used. But to apply it to Utilizing World Abundance is to restore it to its original, its literal meaning. It can be only a question of time before man's reason and self-interest overcome his inertia and Mr. St.Clare Grondona's proposals are accepted. When they are they will define the beginning of an era as surely as did the introduction of the gold standard (but without its fatal weakness) ... That Mr Grondona's scheme is not international, but either national or multi-national,

is its greatest merit. No international agreement has to be reached, no other country's good faith relied on (Manager, 1958)

Several members of the British parliament also spoke in favour of Grondona's proposal in a debate on February 12, 1958, of which the following two excerpts are representative.

Patrick Maitland

Does not the government realise that some of us have raised this in the House over and over again and have never had a single answer ... I press the government for a proper statement about their views on the Grondona system ... we have not had a proper, lucid and thorough exposition of the government's view of the Grondona plan. (Grondona, 1962)

Mr A.E. Oram

It has been praised by a great diversity of critics of considerable authority. No review that I have seen, and no comment made in this House, has faulted his proposals in any major sense. Since these are so revolutionary and yet in essence so simple; and since the outcome of their implementation would be so beneficial both to this country and to the world, the government are duty-bound to have them thoroughly examined. It is not too much to say that this question of fluctuations of world prices is of major significance in the world's fortunes at the present time. It seems to me that, at a very high level and with a very great sense of urgency, we should be tackling it in a spirit of international cooperation. (Grondona, 1962)

A number of notable economists also praised the system, as published in 1958.

Graham Hutton

Mr Grondona's system is more practical and timely now than ever before... It is economically sound, practicable and desirable; it is basically different from any superficially-similar projects hitherto propagated or tried; ... and could gradually provide a firmer foundation for our national economy. (Hutton, 1957)

Roy Harrod

The author deals with matters that are of urgent importance and proposes treatment on a scale worthy of the problems ... His proposals are clear-cut and precise... His advocacy of what is indeed an orderly advance is lucid ... I strongly support his basic principles. (Harrod, 1957)

16.2 SUPPORT FOR GRONDONA SYSTEM IN 1975

In 1975 Grondona published his last book, "Economic Stability is Attainable" (Grondona, 1975), which once again received strong praise from commentators who understood the unique strengths of his system.

The Times of London

Economics editor, Peter Jay, devoted an editorial to Grondona's book under the title "Snatching Stability from the Jaws of Chaos".

It is an unmitigated pleasure to welcome a thoroughly coherent, fully worked out and long matured set of strategic proposals which could at one and the same time restore the initiative to Britain and set our own and the world's economy back on the path to stability and openness. Mr Grondona has been perfecting and adapting his scheme for stabilising world commodity prices – and so currencies, whose values are ultimately related to commodity prices – for nearly 50 years; and along the way he has collected endorsements and commendation from almost every authority except the one needed to put his scheme into practice, namely the government of a major commodity-importing country. (Jay, 1975)

International Currency Review

Independent financial and political publisher Christopher Story (1938 – 2010), legendary for his uncompromising criticism of inflationary policies of *fiat* currencies, published strong support for the Grondona system:

For nearly fifty years Mr Grondona has been refining his proposals for commodity stabilization: in the process he has won bouquets from a wide range of eminent economists and politicians – yet no government has been far-sighted enough to implement what are essentially simple and practical ideas... . The merits of the scheme are several: first, being nationally based, it would avoid problems of major international co-ordination; secondly, it would not try to buck market forces, yet it would help to dampen the amplitude of commodity price fluctuations; and thirdly, in doing this, it would also restore stability to currency values. As producers sought to obtain the best price obtainable in the consuming countries, they would tend to establish a uniform set of commodity prices among all the consuming countries. The effect would be the same for currency values. (Story, 1975)

Sir Roy Harrod

It has been said that the implementing of his system would mark the beginning of an era as surely as did the initiation of the gold standard, but without its fatal weaknesses. I believe that statement to be well warranted. (Harrod, 1975)

As of 1975 the abandonment of the US dollar's link to gold was still recent, and was leading to unprecedentedly rapid inflation. In this situation it would have been very beneficial for the UK to establish a CRD, thereby helping to stabilize the real value of sterling. However, the only UK government report on the Grondona system failed to investigate it in any detail, as discussed next.

16.3 PAST MISREPRESENTATION OF THE GRONDONA SYSTEM

Although the Grondona system was the subject of a debate in the British parliament in 1958, the government took no action, and made no statement giving a reason for not investigating it. In 1976, partly in response to the recommendation by leading British economist Sir Roy Harrod (1900 - 1978) in his lengthy preface to Grondona's last book, "Economic Stability is Attainable", a House of Lords select committee on commodity prices was set up to advise government policy-makers on this topic. As seen in the supportive comments above, such a formal investigation had been called for by supporters of Grondona's work over several decades.

Unfortunately the person selected to chair the committee was Lord Roberthall (1901-1988), an Australian who, as Robert Hall, had earlier worked as economic adviser to the British government. Grondona had known

Bob Hall for many years, being a fellow Australian working in London, and Grondona knew that he did not understand his system. Roberthall too had written a short preface to Grondona's last book supporting Harrod's call for a government enquiry, but he described himself as having been in favour of international buffer-stocks as a means of commodity price stabilization for many years. Consequently, as soon as he was named as the committee chairman, it was clear to Grondona that his report would be unlikely to do any more than restate existing British government policy to participate in UNCTAD negotiations to establish buffer-stocks (of which the many problems are discussed in earlier chapters). However, even Grondona was surprised at how little consideration Roberthall's report gave to his proposal (Roberthall, 1977) – far from the "close scrutiny" which Harrod urged (Harrod, 1975).

Grondona submitted documents, and was invited to speak to the committee, and to answer questions. The comments that he received revealed that, indeed, Roberthall did not understand how multi-national implementation of his system would, without any need for international negotiations, greatly increase the stabilizing effects of the system initially set up by one country, and spread its influence worldwide. In response to this, Grondona had one of the authors prepare the illustration in Figure 1 in Chapter 12 (which is discussed in the text that follows it). This shows clearly, although in slightly simplified form, the inherently complementary and synergistic effects of three CRDs operating simultaneously, and so how multi-national implementation would enable many different countries to partially stabilize commodity prices directly in terms of their own currencies – an outcome which an international buffer-stock system such as UNCTAD's plan could not achieve. However, Roberthall omitted this important illustration from the select committee's report without explanation.

Even worse, the committee's final report contained no "scrutiny", no analysis of the strengths and weaknesses of Grondona's proposal, nor any comparison with the UNCTAD plan, as might have been expected, but instead dismissed it in just a few lines. That Roberthall and his committee members did not understand Grondona's proposal is shown by the report's comment that it would be "*well beyond the resources* (of the UK to achieve) *the stabilizing effect which he seeks*". This comment is curiously vague – and essentially meaningless, since the scale on which any country's CRD is established would be decided in advance by the government to be within its resources. Roberthall and his committee members seem to have assumed that Grondona' proposal was merely for national "buffer-stocks" like those advocated by UNCTAD, and that his real intention was to try to stabilize prices between fixed limits – which is utterly different from Grondona's repeatedly stated intention, for which he was well-known!

As the only substantive alternative to the official *status quo* policy of participating in UNCTAD's fruitless negotiations, Grondona's system deserved more professional consideration. A serious assessment would have at least included consideration of the potential costs, risks and benefits of implementing a British CRD exactly as Grondona advocated, as well as on different scales, and comparing these with other policy proposals. Although personal computers were not yet available in 1976, a rough simulation could have been commissioned from independent researchers. Based on this the committee's report might have included a recommendation to UNCTAD to consider this multi-national approach to stabilizing commodity prices, since the effects of multi-national adoption of the Grondona system would be far superior to what UNCTAD could achieve via international agreement.

As an economic adviser to the committee, Roberthall chose Professor Alasdair Macbean, an academic who had published research to the effect that there was little evidence that stabilizing commodity prices would be economically beneficial for commodity-exporting developing countries. As readers will appreciate, unless a person makes the effort to understand the Grondona system's critical differences from other proposals – and the far-reaching implications of these differences – they will not be able to understand why it has received such strong praise from those who have made the effort to understand it. In order for Roberthall and Macbean to take such a dismissive stance, without offering even a cursory analysis of Grondona's actual proposal, they had to believe that every one of the succession of economists, politicians and journalists who had praised Grondona's work over several decades were all mistaken – and indeed so stupid that they failed to see the trivial flaw that Roberthall and Macbean were clever enough to understand at a glance, and which invalidated Grondona's and his supporters' decades of advocacy.

In addition, Roberthall's report made no reference to the issue of currency convertibility based on commodities. Although the select committee was not specifically asked to consider this issue, in view of its inextricable and widely-understood connection with commodity price stabilization – and *a fortiori* in view of the support of both Keynes and Hayek, the long-standing leaders of British economics, for this very policy – it was surely the role of the economic adviser to the committee to give advice on this aspect of the subject. To fail to even mention this possibility, and to have acquiesced in the dismissive and misinformed comment that establishing the Grondona system would be "*well beyond the resources*" of the UK, is not the behaviour of an independent professional. Acting as a rubber-stamp for a political "whitewash" is a frequent role for "expert advisers" in the political world – but it is no less shameful for that. Perhaps even more shameful for a professional is to fail to even recognise the value of important new ideas in their own field of supposed expertise.

A career as a university researcher, whether in economics or in any other field, offers various opportunities. Major breakthroughs occur rather rarely, but the possibility of making an important contribution to knowledge, with the public recognition and personal satisfaction it brings, is a significant incentive for many researchers. The prospect of contributing to such an advance requires researchers to continually use their expertise to judge ideas that they come across, wherever they may arise. A justly famous example of this was that of Cambridge mathematicians Godfrey Hardy (1877 – 1947) and John Littlewood (1885 – 1977), who recognized the genius of the poor and unknown Indian mathematician Srinivasa Ramanujan, (1887 – 1920), who sent Hardy several pages of hand-written notes by post from India. Going through the notes together, Hardy and Littlewood recognized Ramanujan's genius and invited him to Cambridge, where he worked for several years. To this day, the Ramanujan Journal publishes mathematical research inspired by his unique work.

The converse is that there is surely no greater failure for a researcher than to be unable to even recognise the value of a major breakthrough in the very field of their supposed expertise – as if Hardy and Littlewood had failed to recognise the genius in Ramanujan's letter!

In this context, for Macbean to have acquiesced in Roberthall's ignorant dismissal of Grondona's system as "*well beyond the resources*" of the UK is surely as great a failure as any in economics. It is comparable to the widespread failure of academic economists to understand that, after President Nixon ended gold convertibility of the US dollar in 1971, it would rapidly lose value relative to gold, which they liked to deride as a "barbarous relic". They thereby revealed the strange divorce from reality, and the deep ignorance about how the real world of business actually operates, found in many academic economists.

There is a long history of a principled dissenter in a committee insisting on publishing a "Minority Report" or a dissenting Appendix, thereby showing that the committee's conclusion is not unanimous, and that there is a significant alternative viewpoint. This requires intellectual ability, integrity and courage, since the powers directing a committee may not take kindly to having their preferred narrative undermined in this way. A justly famous example of this is the world-wide acclaim which American physicist Professor Richard Feynman received for derailing the attempts of the chairman of the committee investigating the disastrous failure of the space shuttle "Challenger" to deflect responsibility away from NASA. Feynman exposed the dysfunctionality of the safety management system within NASA, leading to public pressure being imposed to improve it.

Missing the chance to make a historic contribution to economic policy-making, supported though not implemented by both Keynes and Hayek, for which he could have received considerable "reflected glory", is perhaps the ultimate failure of a researcher – to not even understand a breakthrough in their own field! For an honest intellectual, the exposure of such a profound failure eclipses any other achievement they may have had.

The extreme difference between the balance of benefits, risks and costs of the impractical international system advocated by UNCTAD, Roberthall and Macbean, in contrast to Grondona's multi-national system, was discussed in Chapters 8 and 12 above. These differences entail that the political requirement for an "international" solution to the problem *ipso facto* makes it impossible to solve. Roberthall's report shows no understanding of this. Recommending that the British government continue to participate in international negotiations within UNCTAD was just a restatement of the existing policy which he had already been supporting for years. But it was already clear in 1976 that negotiations at UNCTAD could not result in the establishment of successful international commodity agreements. This is because, as discussed above, the benefits would be few – most notably only one currency could be stabilized; the costs and risks for participating governments would be substantial; and the distortion of markets unacceptable. But this did not deter "internationalists" like Roberthall and Macbean from continuing to advocate an unrealistic international solution. This is similar to "globalists" today, who are not deterred by the unpopularity of their plans, or the lack of benefits they offer to the general public, as they work behind the scenes to persuade governments to implement policies that favour global corporations over the general public.

As head of the committee, Roberthall's correct role should have been, together with his economic adviser, to consider the potential benefits of implementing Grondona's system as proposed, and to estimate to what extent these might outweigh the costs and risks of doing so. Performing such a "Cost-Benefit Analysis" is the basic form of assessment of all policy-proposals. However, as devotees of the "*idee fixe*" that the only possible solution must be via international commodity agreements, Roberthall and Macbean clearly had no interest in exploring a better alternative which would eliminate the need for a major new UN institution, and they made no attempt to do so. That is, Roberthall's report contains no objective analysis and no scientific or scholarly criticism of the Grondona system. If it was presented as an essay by an economics student, it would receive a mark of zero, since it contains no substantive argumentation. So Roberthall's report is not even a "hatchet job" – it is a "Nothing to see here, move along please" report. As such, it follows in a long line of select committee reports of which the objective is political, and which are used to close down discussion rather than to solve a problem.

If international commodity agreements to establish "buffer-stocks" were feasible, it seems fair to conclude that 45 more years of efforts since the select committee's report would have succeeded at least once: but they have not, despite being the subject of UNCTAD's continuing efforts, paid for by taxpayers. Moreover, the inextricable connection with currency convertibility, which is surely the most fundamental issue in the entire field of economic and monetary policy, requires that this aspect should also have been included in the comparison between the Grondona system and the UNCTAD plan. While every country implementing the Grondona system reaps the benefits of direct convertibility, the UNCTAD plan could not achieve this – except indirectly via detailed international agreements between the participating countries in order to link their currencies to the buffer-stock's operating currency. The Bretton Woods system of US dollar convertibility was feasible only because of the USA's dominance – and even so it collapsed within less than 30 years. It was and is clearly unrealistic to expect a similar agreement to be achieved through UNCTAD. Consequently Roberthall's and Macbean's recommendation was in fact a complete failure, and a predictable one.

When people with public responsibility make a statement that is untrue, the question immediately arises whether they are "mad or bad?" That is, do they not know that they are mistaken? – in which case they are incompetent. Or do they know that what they are saying is false? – in which case they are dishonest. In either case, whether incompetent or dishonest, the people making the false statement should not have the role of advising government.

Fifty years since the end of the Bretton Woods system, many pessimistic commentators are predicting monetary chaos due to the rapid inflation of the money supply in the USA, UK and elsewhere. In the continuing absence of any contrary evidence, it seems clear that the British economy would benefit greatly from implementing the Grondona system, now as then. International trade having been a major component of the economy for centuries, many British businesses have major trade links to the world, and London and Edinburgh are important international financial centres. In addition, since leaving the

EU, Sterling has become a vital component of the country's independence. The benefits to other countries of holding Sterling would be greatly improved if its real value was stabilised as the Grondona system could achieve.

However, having resisted implementing the system for more than 60 years so far, without any explanation based on analysis of its likely costs and benefits, there is no reason to expect the UK government to take any steps toward this in the foreseeable future. Consequently, other countries need to take the initiative. Importantly, the automatic adjustments made by a CRD in its buying and selling prices enable even a country with a much smaller economy than Britain to safely set up a CRD on a scale appropriate for its domestic industry, even if its effects on international commodity markets are small. Such a CRD could be enlarged or improved later, and/or could be followed by other countries establishing CRDs operating in their respective currencies: either of these outcomes would be beneficial in further stabilizing both primary commodity prices and foreign-exchange markets.

In this way, a decentralized approach based on CRDs established by multiple countries' governments, and activated by market forces operating within the framework devised by Grondona, can be judged to be politically realistic, effective and economical, as his numerous supporters long understood. This is in sharp contrast to Roberthall's and Macbean's mistaken support for a centralized system that would try to override market forces – and is proven to be politically unrealistic by more than half a century of failed efforts. UNCTAD's failure is the failure of other huge, excessively centralized systems such as the US federal government and the EU, which nevertheless continue to extend their interventions ever further into their citizens' lives.

Good government recognizes the strengths and weaknesses of both government and markets. The Grondona system gives markets their rightful role in solving the problem of how to reintroduce real currency convertibility. Roberthall and Macbean, wedded to the idea of a massive international bureaucracy to manage world commodity trade, were unable to recognise how unrealistic and economically undesirable this is. As OECD countries continue their dangerous flirtation with unrealistic and dangerous "global" solutions, it is to be hoped that other countries will lead the way out of this trap, and defend themselves by establishing CRDs to stabilize and preserve the real value of their national currencies.

SUMMARY

This chapter includes excerpts from several of the eulogistic reviews of the Grondona system written in the British press in the 1950s and 1970s, epitomized by the judgements that its implementation would be "epoch-making" and " a modern equivalent of the gold standard". Some short excerpts of speeches made in the British parliament in 1958 are also quoted. However, the British government took no action, and made no statement on its evaluation of the proposal.

It seemed that the government might make a statement about it in 1976, after the publication of Grondona's last book, when a House of Lords Select Committee was established to consider commodity prices. Unfortunately, the chairman and economic adviser made no attempt to analyse the system's likely benefits and costs, and the committee's report failed to recognize Grondona's unique contribution to solving a problem that has baffled economic policy-makers for more than a century. Instead, it merely recommended that the government continue to participate in discussions on an international system of buffer-stocks under the auspices of UNCTAD – a policy which has achieved nothing after more than four decades.

REFERENCES

Financial Times. (1958). *Review of Grondona, L. (1958). Utilising World Abundance*. George Allen & Unwin, London.

Grondona, L. (1958). *Utilising World Abundance*. George Allen & Unwin.

Grondona, L. (1962). *A Firm Foundation for Economy*. Anthony Blond.

Grondona, L. (1975). *Economic Stability is Attainable*. Hutchinson-Benham.

Guardian. (1958, Jan. 16). A Commodity Standard. *The Guardian*.

Harrod, R. (1975). *Preface. In L. Grondona (Ed.), Economic Stability is Attainable*. Hutchinson-Benham.

Jay, P. (1975, Apr. 3). Snatching Stability Out of the Jaws of Chaos. *The Times*.

Roberthall. (1977). *Report of House of Lords Select Committee on Commodity Prices*. UK Government Printing Office.

Shenfield, A. (1958). *Federation of British Industries Review*. Academic Press.

Story, C. (1975). Commodities and Currencies. *International Currency Review, 7*(3).

Times. (1958). Review of Grondona, L. (1958). Utilising World Abundance. George Allen & Unwin, London. *The Times.*

Tribune. (1958, Jan. 24). Editorial. *The Tribune.*

About the Author

Patrick Collins graduated in economics from Cambridge University in 1976, and worked as part-time assistant to Leo St.Clare Grondona while working for his MSc and PhD at Imperial College Management School. He devised a means to simulate how Grondona's system of conditional currency convertibility based on commodities would operate, and performed a first simulation for the case of Japan when working there in 1996. He has presented papers on various aspects of the Grondona system at conferences of the Public Choice Society, Japanese Monetary Society, Japanese Economic Policy Association and RIFCON (Riba-Free Conference) in Kuala Lumpur. He also collaborated in the development of a computer model of the Grondona system which has been used to simulate its operation in Indonesia, Malaysia, Turkey and Pakistan. Having taught economics for 19 years in the Department of Environmental Science at Azabu University in Japan, he became Emeritus Professor on his retirement in 2018. He continues to advocate the implementation of the Grondona system as the ideal foundation for the coming multi-polar world economic system that is necessitated by the decline of the US dollar-based system.

Index

A

Ahmed, Jamil 43, 118-119, 123
Artificial Intelligence (AI) 55, 66, 69
automatic stabilizer 167, 194, 206

B

Bank for International Settlements (BIS) 52, 70
Bank of England 14-15, 18, 22, 25, 28, 32-35, 52, 98-99
banks x, xiv, xv, xvii, 2, 6-7, 10-12, 15-17, 19-24, 26, 29-33, 35, 37, 39, 47, 52-53, 56-57, 59, 66-67, 69-72, 76-77, 98-99, 109, 145, 185, 204, 207, 210, 214
Belloc, Hilaire x, xviii, 26, 34
Bibow, Joerg 109-110, 123
Bitcoin 55, 57, 59-61, 73, 207-208
Block of reserves 128-129, 176
Blockchain 55, 57-59, 66, 69, 71-73, 207
Bordo, Michael D. 69, 73, 207
Bretton Woods vii, ix, xii, xiii, xiv, 1-2, 5, 13, 44, 48, 51, 78, 81, 90, 93-94, 101, 114, 163, 172, 199, 201, 219, 236
Brown, Ellen 29-30, 34, 43
Buchanan, James 27-28, 34, 74, 83, 224
buffer-stock 88, 90, 97, 99, 101, 112-114, 123, 164, 173, 202, 205, 211-212, 226, 232, 236

C

central bank ix, xv, 22, 25-26, 28-29, 32, 47, 52-53, 66-67, 69-70, 73, 99, 109-110, 159, 162, 165, 191, 221
Central Bank Digital Currency (CBDC) 47, 67, 69-70
China 5, 7, 23, 29, 51, 62, 70, 193
Christianity 36-39
Cobbett, William 25, 34
Collins, Patrick 102, 104, 122-123, 129, 132, 167, 169, 177, 180, 185, 187-188, 194, 196
Commodities Reserve Department (CRD) 96, 101-111, 113, 118-120, 122, 126-129, 131-137, 139-141, 143-165, 167-169, 171, 173-174, 176-185, 187, 189-192, 195, 198, 200-208, 211-214, 223-224, 231-233, 237
commodity convertibility 79, 93
Commodity Reserve Currency xviii, 84, 87, 89, 113, 115, 123, 164, 170, 205, 217
commodity standard xii, 197-198, 217, 228, 238
convertibility viii, ix, xii, xiv, xv, xvi, xvii, xviii, 2-5, 9, 11-12, 14, 16, 41-42, 44, 51, 53-54, 58, 72, 74-80, 82-83, 86-87, 91-98, 101-102, 105-106, 108-109, 117, 120, 122-123, 132, 153, 160-161, 163-164, 169, 171-173, 179, 182, 187, 190-191, 194, 196, 204, 206, 212-213, 216, 218-219, 223, 233-234, 236-237
counter-cyclical xv, xvi, 79-80, 89, 106, 108-111, 118, 120, 122-123, 131-132, 148, 153, 156-161, 163, 167, 169, 173, 191, 200, 202, 204, 220, 223
crypto-currency 62-63, 66, 197, 205-208
currency convertibility xii, xiv, xv, 58, 74-75, 79-80, 82-83, 86-87, 93-98,

101-102, 105-106, 108-109, 117, 120, 122-123, 132, 164, 169, 173, 179, 187, 194, 196, 213, 223, 233, 236-237
currency crisis 183, 189, 193-194, 223

D

debt-based money 19, 21-24, 26, 29-31, 33, 42-43, 45, 57
Decentralized Finance 55
DeFi 47, 55, 60, 66
deflation 19, 22, 46, 53, 61, 75, 77, 81, 107, 163, 170, 194
derivatives 4, 37, 41, 193, 209
digital currency 67, 70, 73, 175, 221
Dodd, David L. 79, 84

E

economic growth ix, xii, xv, 4, 13, 27, 38-39, 43-44, 48, 53-54, 60-61, 69, 79-82, 153, 161, 163, 183, 187, 195, 198, 209-210, 221, 224, 227
economic policy viii, xiii, 27, 79, 81, 107, 110, 115, 167, 169, 188
economics xii, xiii, xv, 16, 21-22, 27-29, 31-33, 35-43, 46, 54, 58, 73-74, 79-81, 83-87, 95, 117-118, 124, 132, 170, 183, 219, 230, 233-234, 236
exchange-rate 2-3, 48, 51, 69, 90, 95, 110-111, 114, 120, 128, 132-133, 135, 139, 157, 160-163, 166, 175, 178-180, 182, 184-185, 194-195, 201-202, 220-222, 224

F

Federal Reserve ix, 14-15, 22-23, 26, 28, 30, 34-35, 43-44, 69-70, 213
fiat xiv, xv, xvii, 1, 8, 12-13, 17, 19-20, 36-37, 41-42, 44-45, 48, 53, 60, 70, 72-73, 75-77, 119-121, 158, 183, 207-208, 220, 230
Fisher, Irving 79, 83, 219
fractional reserve banking 20-21, 39
Friedman, Milton 199-200, 217

G

Garavini, Giuliano 4, 8
globalist xvii, 49-50, 102, 221-222
gold convertibility viii, ix, xv, 3-5, 41-42, 44, 53, 72, 77, 79, 82-83, 153, 161, 190-191, 194, 219, 234
gold merchants 10, 20, 214
gold standard vii, viii, ix, xii, xiii, xiv, xvi, 2, 8, 11, 14-15, 42, 51-54, 76, 78-79, 82-83, 94, 98-103, 105, 108, 116, 121-122, 133, 153, 159, 162-163, 165, 168, 176, 194, 198, 204-206, 211-216, 223-224, 228, 231, 238
Goodson, Stephen 32, 34
Graham, Benjamin 73, 80, 84-85, 87-89, 91-92, 95, 113-116, 123-125, 164, 169-170, 199-200, 214, 217, 219, 229
Grant, Victoria 31, 34
Great Reset x, xi, 19, 50, 175, 218, 221-222
Greater Reset 50, 73
Grondona system xii, xiii, xv, xvi, xvii, xviii, 43, 88, 96, 98, 100-102, 107-108, 110-113, 117-118, 120-123, 126, 128, 131-134, 136, 156-157, 159-160, 162-163, 165, 168, 171-173, 176-177, 179, 183-190, 192, 194-199, 202-203, 205-206, 209-210, 212-213, 215-220, 222, 224-227, 229-231, 233, 236-238
Grondona, Leo St. Clare vii, xii, xiii, xiv, xv, xvi, xvii, xviii, 43, 88, 96-98, 100-103, 105-124, 126-128, 131-136, 138-139, 142, 147, 152-153, 156-160, 162-165, 168, 171-173, 175-177, 179, 183-190, 192, 194-203, 205-213, 215-220, 222, 224-239

H

Harrod, Roy xiv, 114, 116, 224-225, 230-232, 238
Hart, Albert Gailord 79, 84, 89, 164, 170, 219
Hassan, Tarige Abdulrahim 5, 8
Hayek, Friedrich xiii, xv, xviii, 22, 58, 73, 79-85, 87-89, 115, 164, 170, 194, 202, 211, 216-217, 219, 233, 235

Hosein, Sheik Imran 31, 36, 42-43, 46
Hutton, Graham 229

I

Indonesia xvi, 122, 133-134, 138-142, 145-147, 149, 157, 164, 179, 184-185
inflation viii, ix, 1-7, 9, 11, 14, 19, 22, 44-45, 61, 67, 73, 75-77, 80-82, 84, 106, 124, 127, 136, 138, 142, 152-153, 161-164, 169, 194, 203, 206, 214, 220, 231, 236
International Monetary Fund (IMF) 2, 70, 90, 93-95, 163, 172, 175, 199, 201
Internet xiv, xv, 7, 23, 29-30, 32, 47, 55-59, 61-63, 65-66, 69, 72, 75, 91, 207
Islam 36-39, 42, 46, 54
Islamic economics xv, 36, 38-41, 43, 54, 118, 183

J

Japan xvi, 3, 29, 122, 126, 128, 131-132, 185, 188, 220
Jay, Peter 230, 238
Jefferson, Thomas xiv, 19, 22-24, 30
Jevons, Stanley 79, 84

K

Kaldor, Nicholas 79, 84, 87, 89, 95, 115-117, 124, 164, 170, 219
Keynes, John xiii, xiv, xv, xviii, 5, 14-15, 17, 22, 27, 76, 79, 81-85, 87-89, 91, 95, 114-116, 124, 164, 170, 194, 202, 211, 214, 216-217, 219, 233, 235

L

Lietaer, Bernard 79, 84, 114, 124
Luke, Jon 79, 84

M

Magna Carta 21, 32-33, 35
Malaysia xvi, 43, 46, 54, 63, 73, 122, 133-134, 147, 149, 157, 184-185
market expectations 166, 169
Marshall, Alfred 79, 84
Martens, Pam 15, 17, 35, 37, 46
McLeay, Michael 35
Meera, Akameel 41, 43, 46, 54, 73, 123
Mill, John Stuart 12, 17, 77-78, 84, 92, 163
monetary policy vii, 16, 53, 77, 85, 87, 94-95, 109, 114, 121, 124, 157, 161-162, 169-170, 172, 182, 190-191, 195, 198-200, 213, 218, 223, 236
monetary unit xii, 45, 58, 72, 74, 76, 83, 104
Mullins, Eustace 26, 35
multi-national implementation 171, 174, 188, 213, 232

N

negative interest-rates 23, 69, 81
network effect 55, 179, 184, 195
Nguyen, D.T. 112-113, 124

O

Organisation of petroleum exporting countries (OPEC) 4-5, 8

P

Pakistan xvi, 32, 41, 122, 133-134, 152-157, 179, 184
paper money 9, 11-14, 17, 20-21, 28, 31, 37, 56, 74, 76
Peneder, Michael 58, 69, 73
petro-dollar 1, 5, 7
Pettifor, Ann 42, 46, 163, 170
Pittaluga, Giovanni Battista 13, 17
Prates, Daniela Magalhaes 109, 111, 124
Price Stabilizing Corporation (PSC) 101
price-schedule 96, 100-101, 103-105, 108, 122, 133-135, 139-140, 142, 162, 201, 205
Public Choice Economics 16, 27, 74

R

Radia, Amar 35
recession 4, 8, 22, 27, 73, 84, 124, 161, 168, 194

regulatory capture 116
Riba 32, 35-37, 39, 41-44, 46, 119, 183-184
Ricardo, David 9, 11, 18, 25, 35
Rickards, James 54, 73
RIFCON 31, 43
Roberthall 231-238
Roberts, Paul Craig 27, 35
Rubinstein, Paul 5, 8

S

Schiller, Robert J. 8
Seghezza, Elena 13, 17
seigniorage 10-11, 13, 21
Shariah-compliant 37, 118-119, 121, 185
Shenfield, Arthur Asher 228, 238
silver convertibility xvi, 190
Smith, Adam xi, 11, 28
Stiglitz, Joseph 163, 170
Still, Bill 30, 43
Story, Christopher ix, 1, 11, 230-231, 239

T

Tanous, Peter J. 5, 8
Tapscott, Alex 57, 73
Thomas, Ryland xiv, 19, 22, 24, 30, 35
Tinbergen, Jan 79, 84, 164, 170, 219
Totten, Bill 32, 35
Turkey xvi, 122, 133-134, 149, 157, 179, 184

U

USA viii, ix, xiii, xiv, 2-3, 5-8, 13, 23-24, 26-29, 39, 48, 51, 57, 81, 182, 186, 199, 214, 221, 236
Usmani, Taqi 32, 35, 41, 46
Ussher, Leanne 79, 84-85, 89, 95, 114-117, 123-124, 164, 170, 173
usury 38, 40, 119

W

Wagner, Richard E. 27, 34
Wapshott, Nicholas 80, 82, 85
Werner, Richard 29, 32, 35
Woods, John 79

Z

Zarlenga, Stephen 28, 35
zero interest-rates 6, 81
Zucman, Gabriel 23, 35

www.ingramcontent.com/pod-product-compliance
Lightning Source LLC
LaVergne TN
LVHW081324300926
849161LV00008B/1870
* 9 7 8 1 7 9 9 8 8 3 0 2 9 *